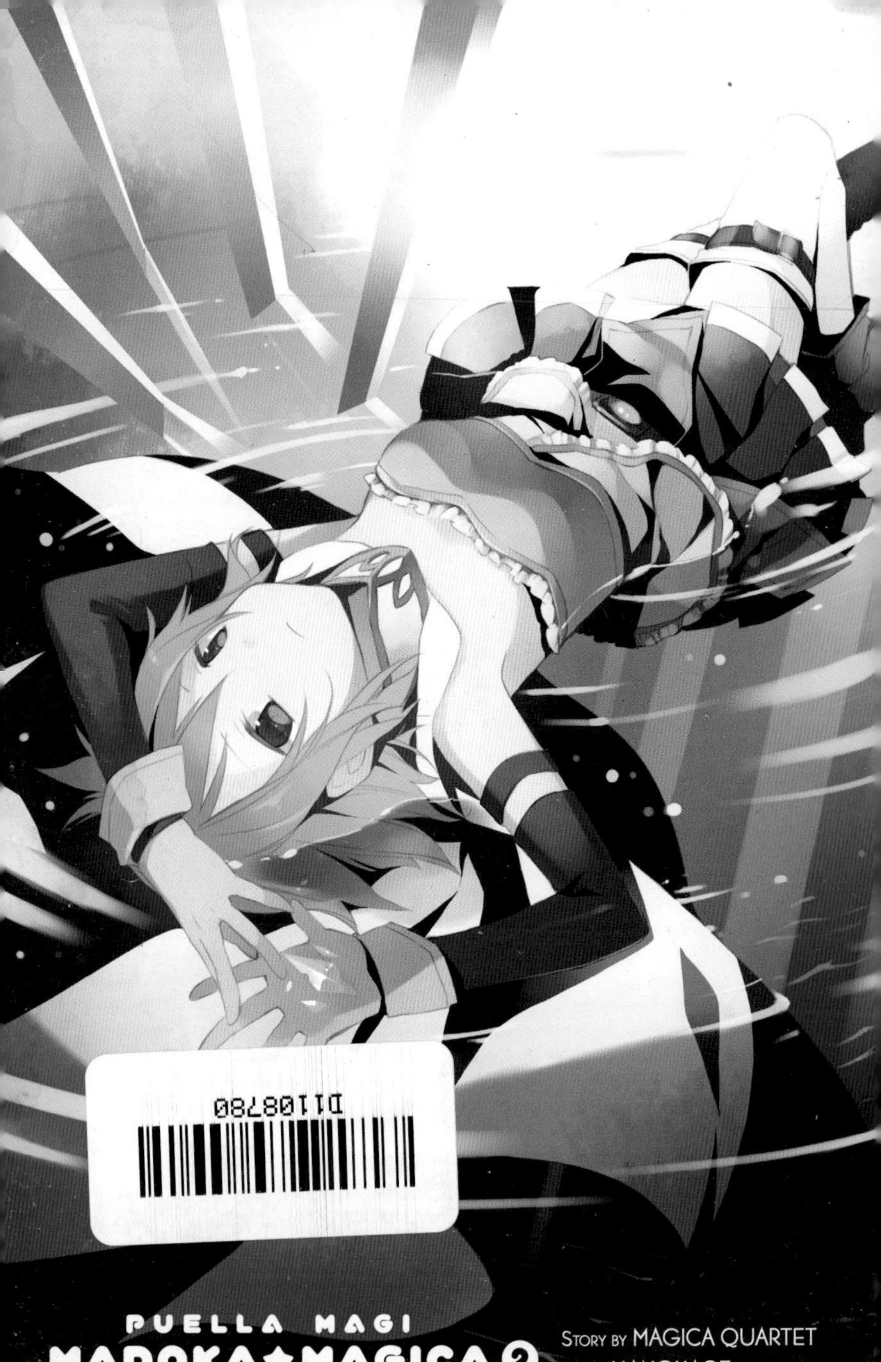

PUELLA MAGI
MADOKA★MAGICA 2

STORY BY MAGICA QUARTET
ART BY HANOKAGE

PUELLA MAGI
MADOKA ☆ MAGICA
VOLUME TWO

*She will not know yet if this encounter is a mere coincidence or a necessity.
Which would be an encounter that would change her destiny.*

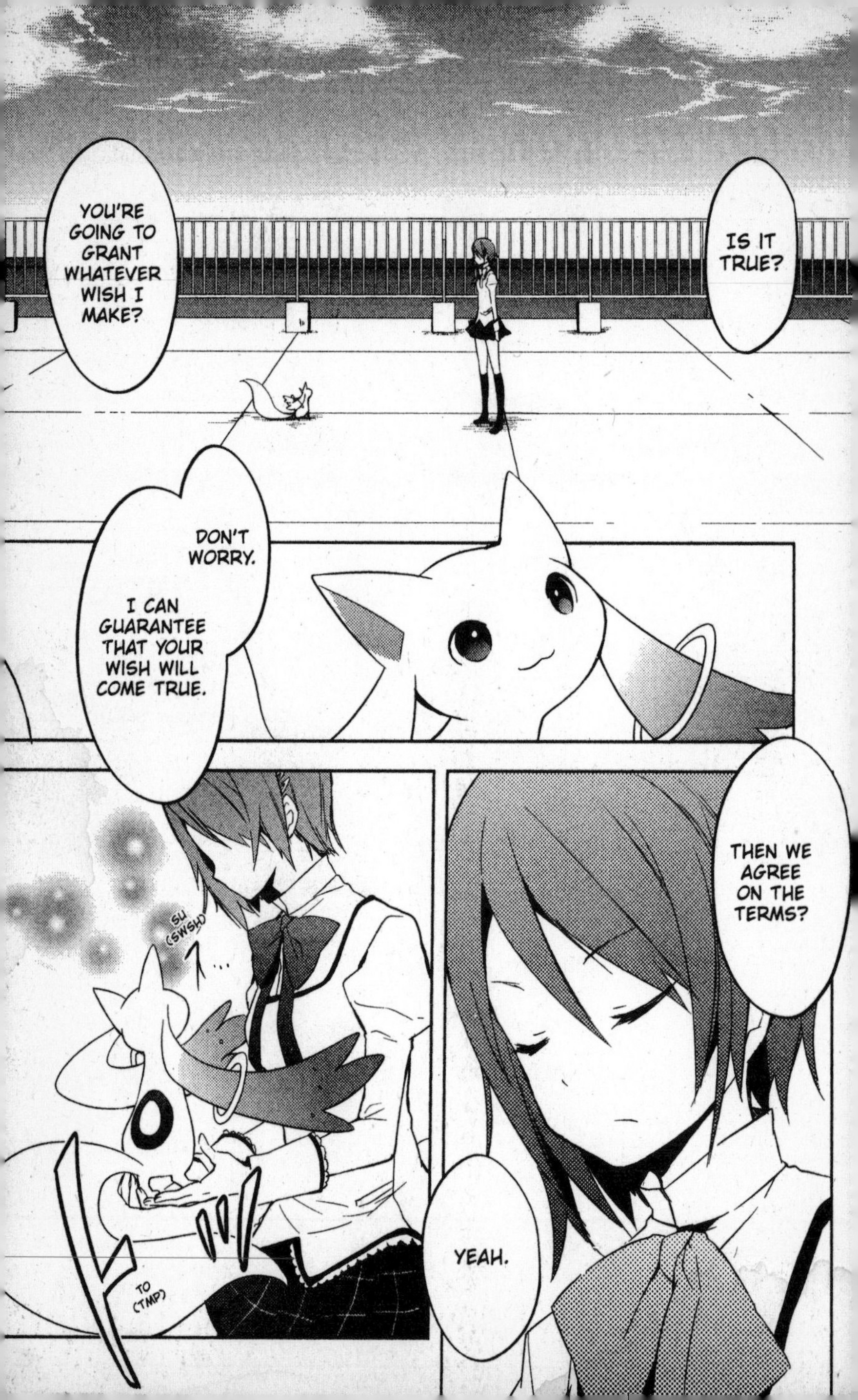
IS IT TRUE?
YOU'RE GOING TO GRANT WHATEVER WISH I MAKE?
DON'T WORRY.
I CAN GUARANTEE THAT YOUR WISH WILL COME TRUE.
THEN WE AGREE ON THE TERMS?
YEAH.
SU (SWSH)
...
TO (TMP)

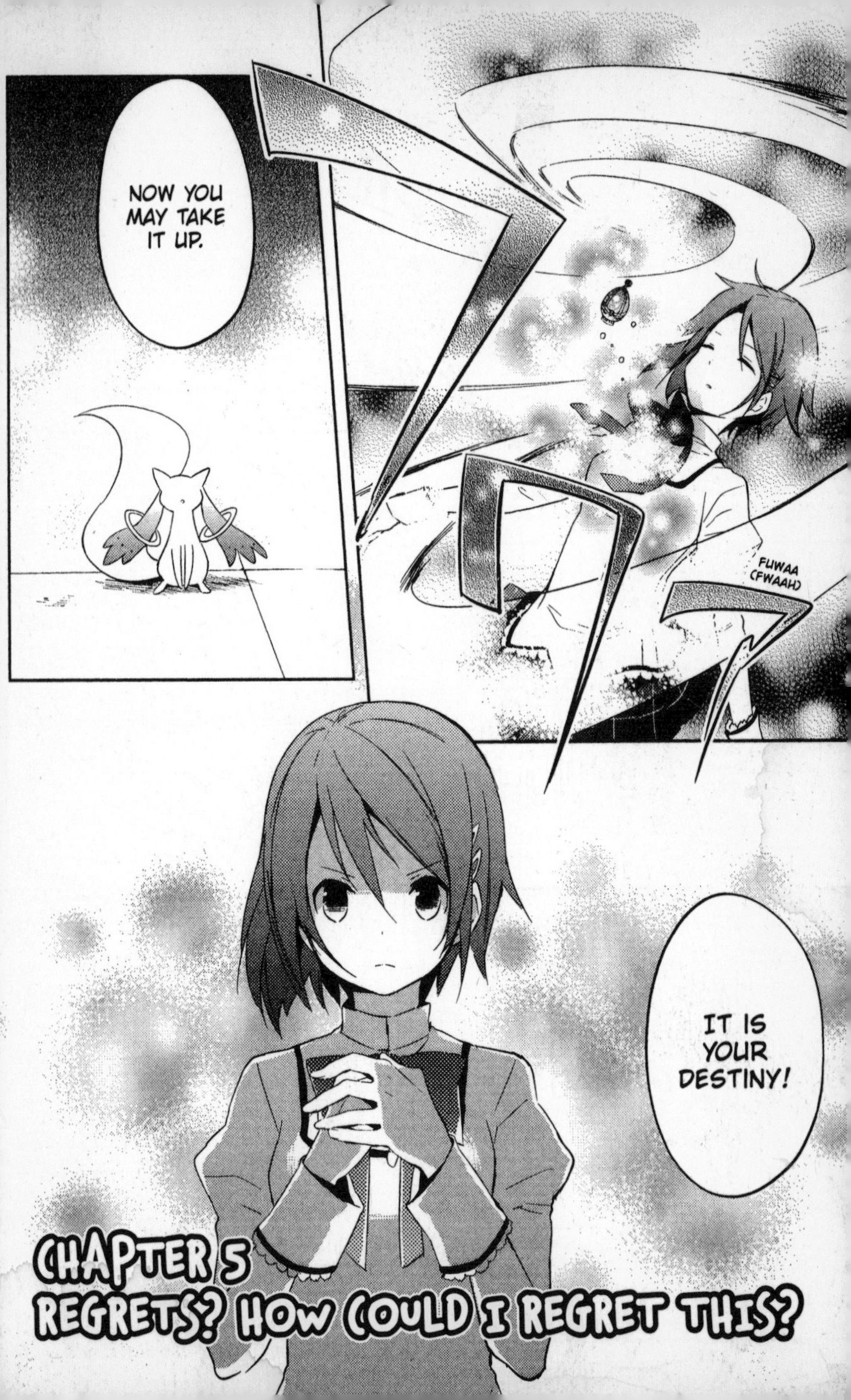
FUWAA (FWAAH)
NOW YOU MAY TAKE IT UP.
IT IS YOUR DESTINY!
CHAPTER 5
REGRETS? HOW COULD I REGRET THIS?

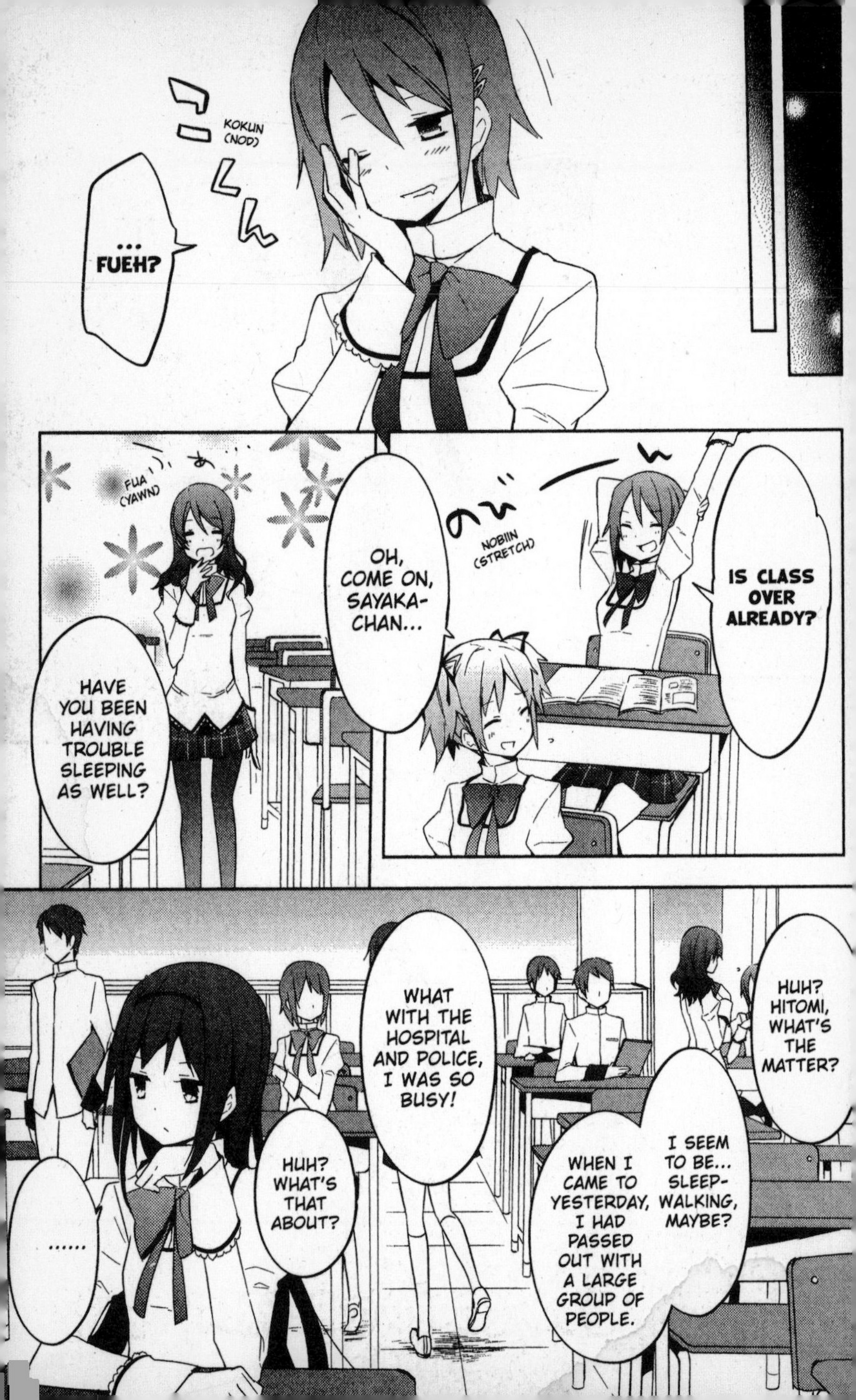
KOKUN (NOD)
...FUEH?
IS CLASS OVER ALREADY?
NOBIIN (STRETCH)
OH, COME ON, SAYAKA-CHAN...
FUA (YAWN)
HAVE YOU BEEN HAVING TROUBLE SLEEPING AS WELL?
HUH? HITOMI, WHAT'S THE MATTER?
WHAT WITH THE HOSPITAL AND POLICE, I WAS SO BUSY!
I SEEM TO BE... SLEEP-WALKING, MAYBE?
WHEN I CAME TO YESTERDAY, I HAD PASSED OUT WITH A LARGE GROUP OF PEOPLE.
HUH? WHAT'S THAT ABOUT?
......

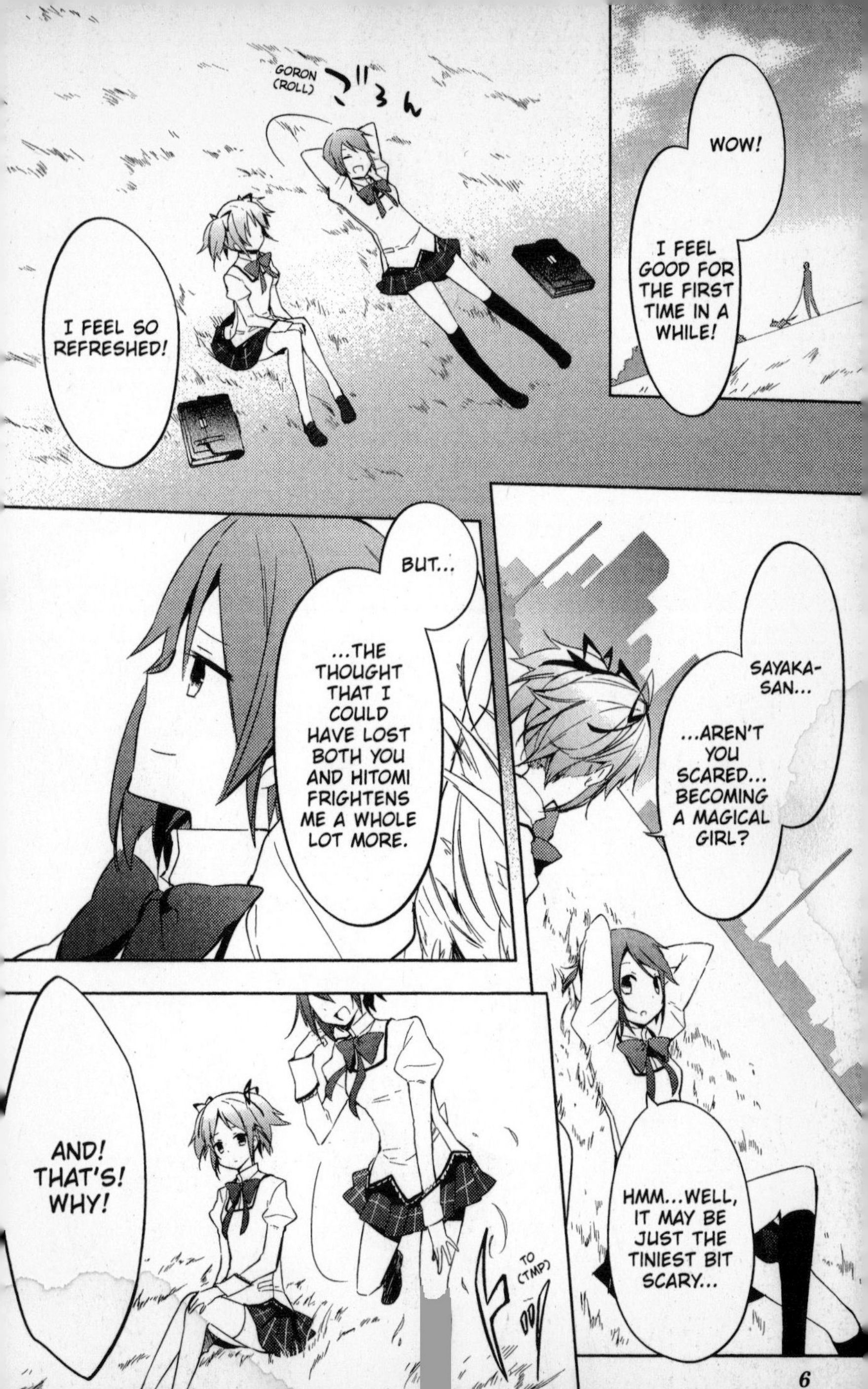
WOW!
I FEEL GOOD FOR THE FIRST TIME IN A WHILE!
GORON (ROLL)
ごろん
I FEEL SO REFRESHED!
SAYAKA-SAN...
...AREN'T YOU SCARED... BECOMING A MAGICAL GIRL?
HMM...WELL, IT MAY BE JUST THE TINIEST BIT SCARY...
BUT...
...THE THOUGHT THAT I COULD HAVE LOST BOTH YOU AND HITOMI FRIGHTENS ME A WHOLE LOT MORE.
TO (TMP)
AND! THAT'S! WHY!

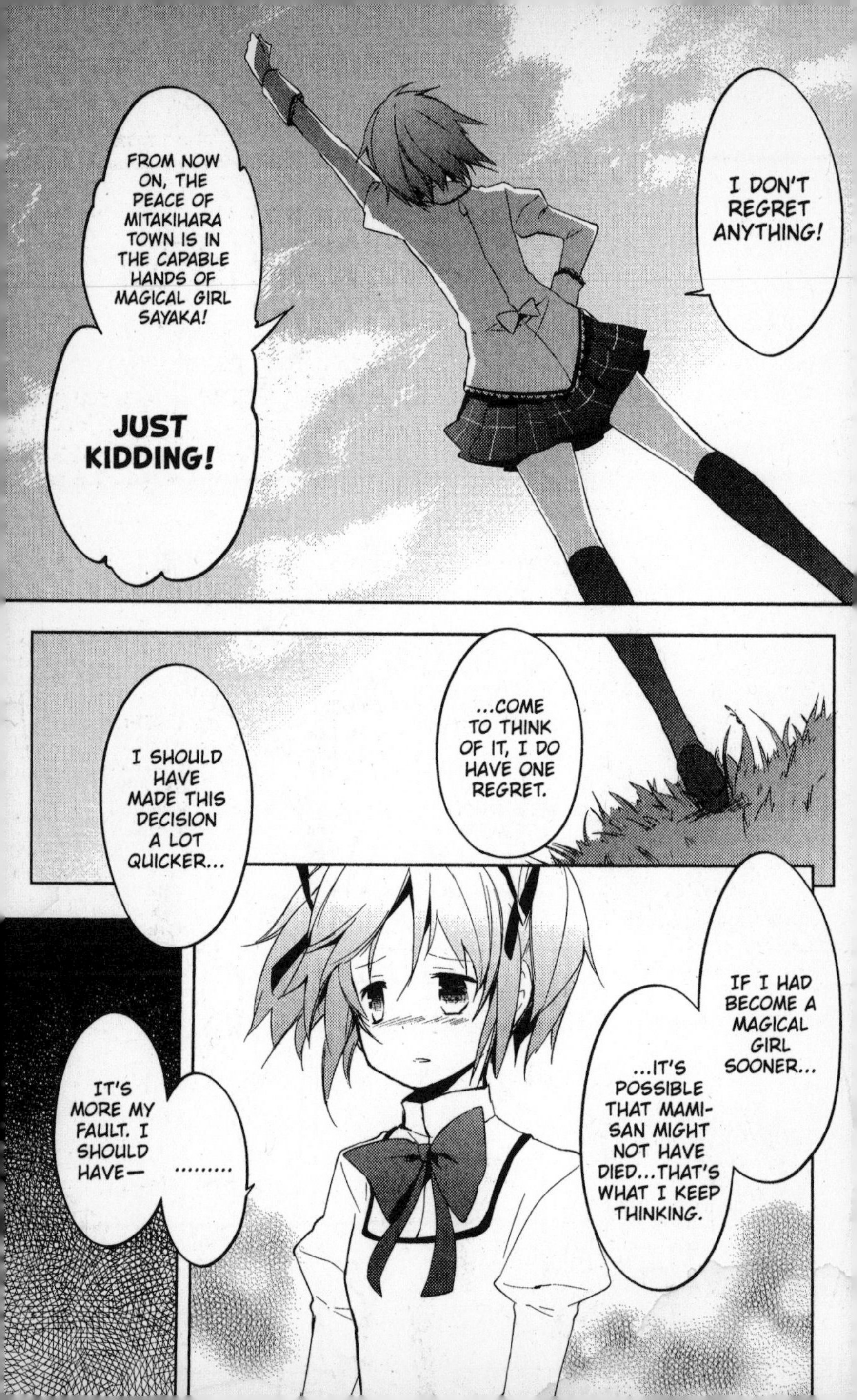
I DON'T REGRET ANYTHING!
FROM NOW ON, THE PEACE OF MITAKIHARA TOWN IS IN THE CAPABLE HANDS OF MAGICAL GIRL SAYAKA!
JUST KIDDING!
...COME TO THINK OF IT, I DO HAVE ONE REGRET.
I SHOULD HAVE MADE THIS DECISION A LOT QUICKER...
IF I HAD BECOME A MAGICAL GIRL SOONER...
...IT'S POSSIBLE THAT MAMI-SAN MIGHT NOT HAVE DIED...THAT'S WHAT I KEEP THINKING.
....
IT'S MORE MY FAULT. I SHOULD HAVE—

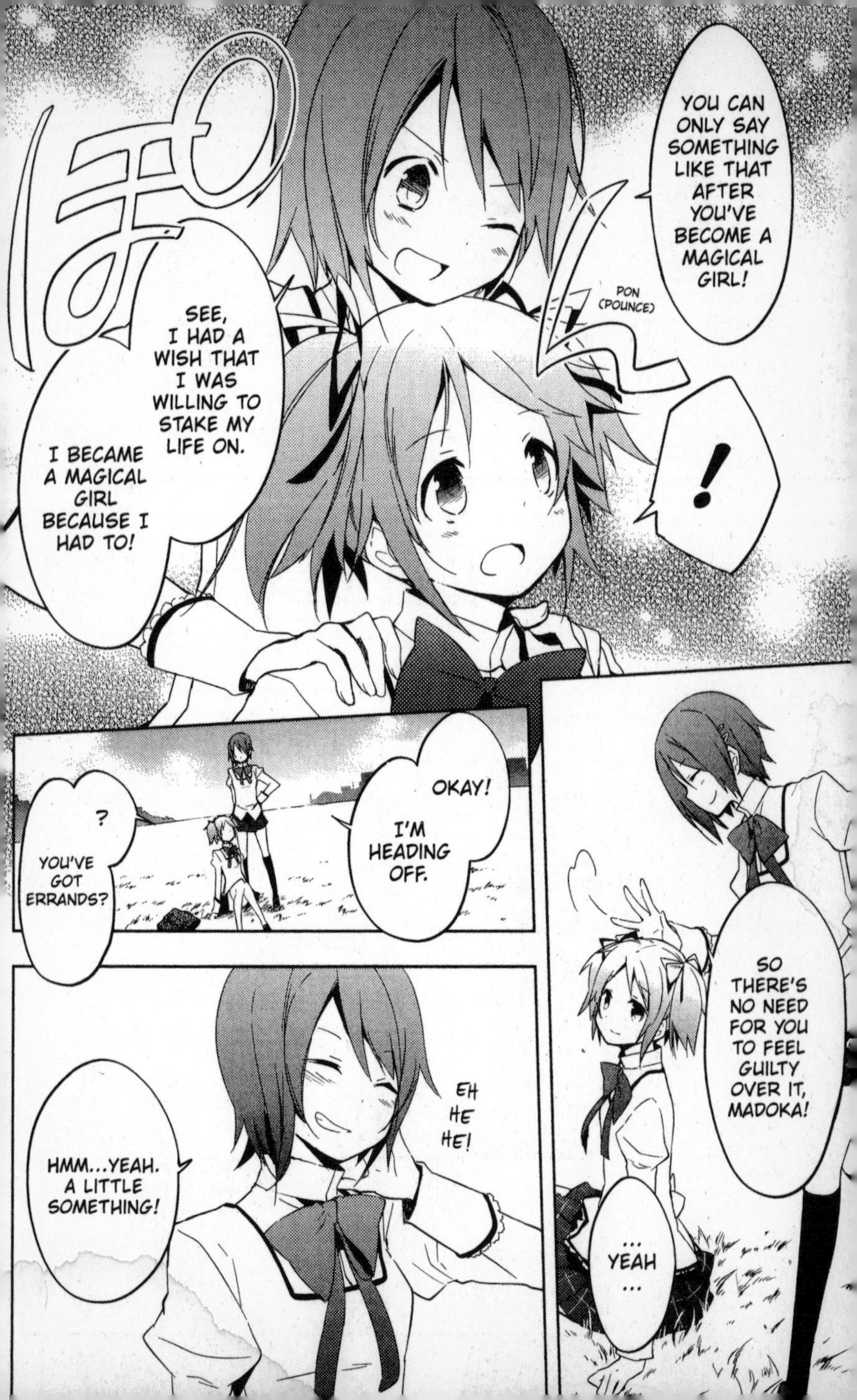
YOU CAN ONLY SAY SOMETHING LIKE THAT AFTER YOU'VE BECOME A MAGICAL GIRL!
PON (POUNCE)
!
SEE, I HAD A WISH THAT I WAS WILLING TO STAKE MY LIFE ON.
I BECAME A MAGICAL GIRL BECAUSE I HAD TO!
SO THERE'S NO NEED FOR YOU TO FEEL GUILTY OVER IT, MADOKA!
... YEAH ...
OKAY!
I'M HEADING OFF.
?
YOU'VE GOT ERRANDS?
EH HE HE!
HMM...YEAH. A LITTLE SOMETHING!

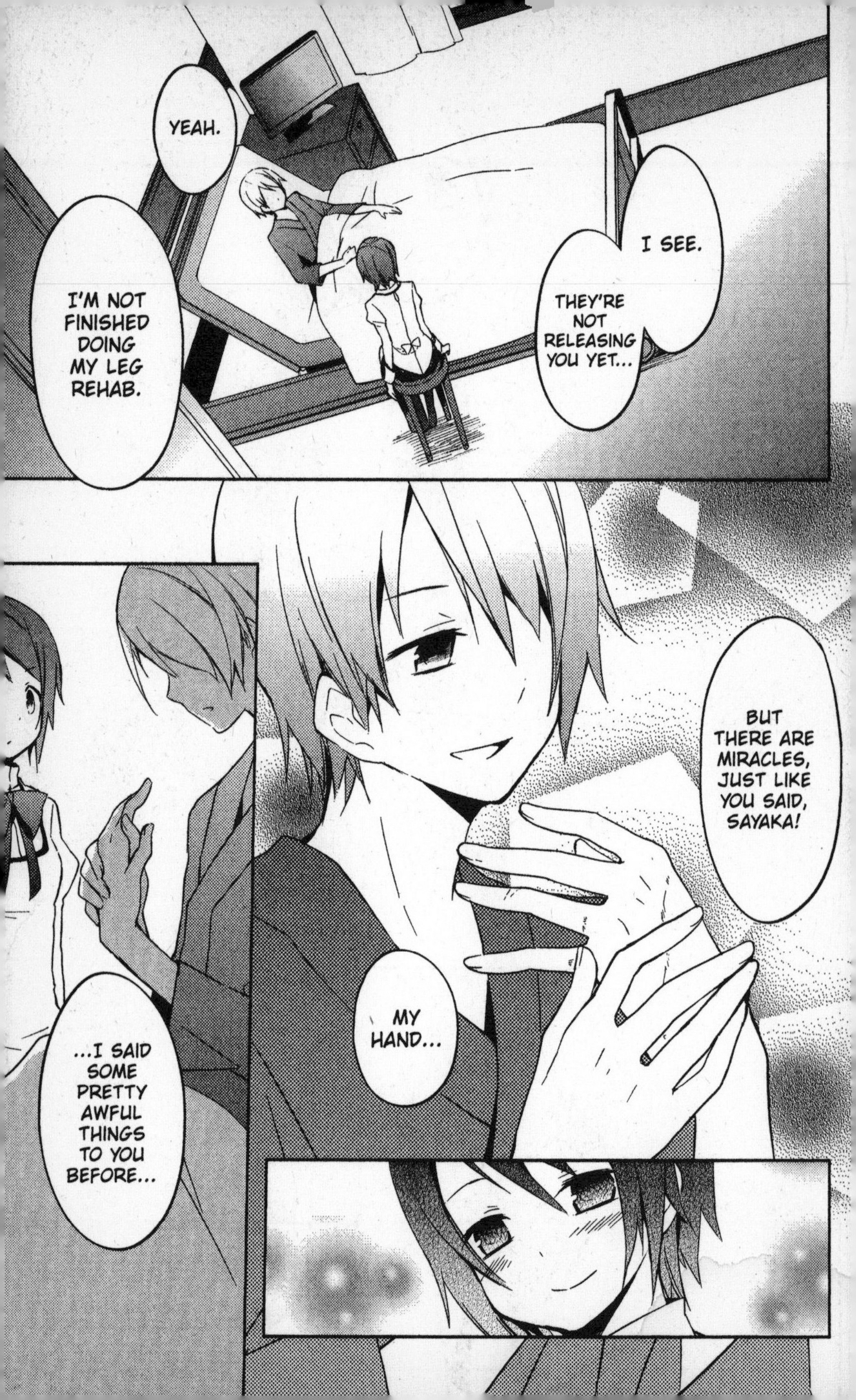
I SEE.
THEY'RE NOT RELEASING YOU YET...
YEAH.
I'M NOT FINISHED DOING MY LEG REHAB.
BUT THERE ARE MIRACLES, JUST LIKE YOU SAID, SAYAKA!
MY HAND...
...I SAID SOME PRETTY AWFUL THINGS TO YOU BEFORE...

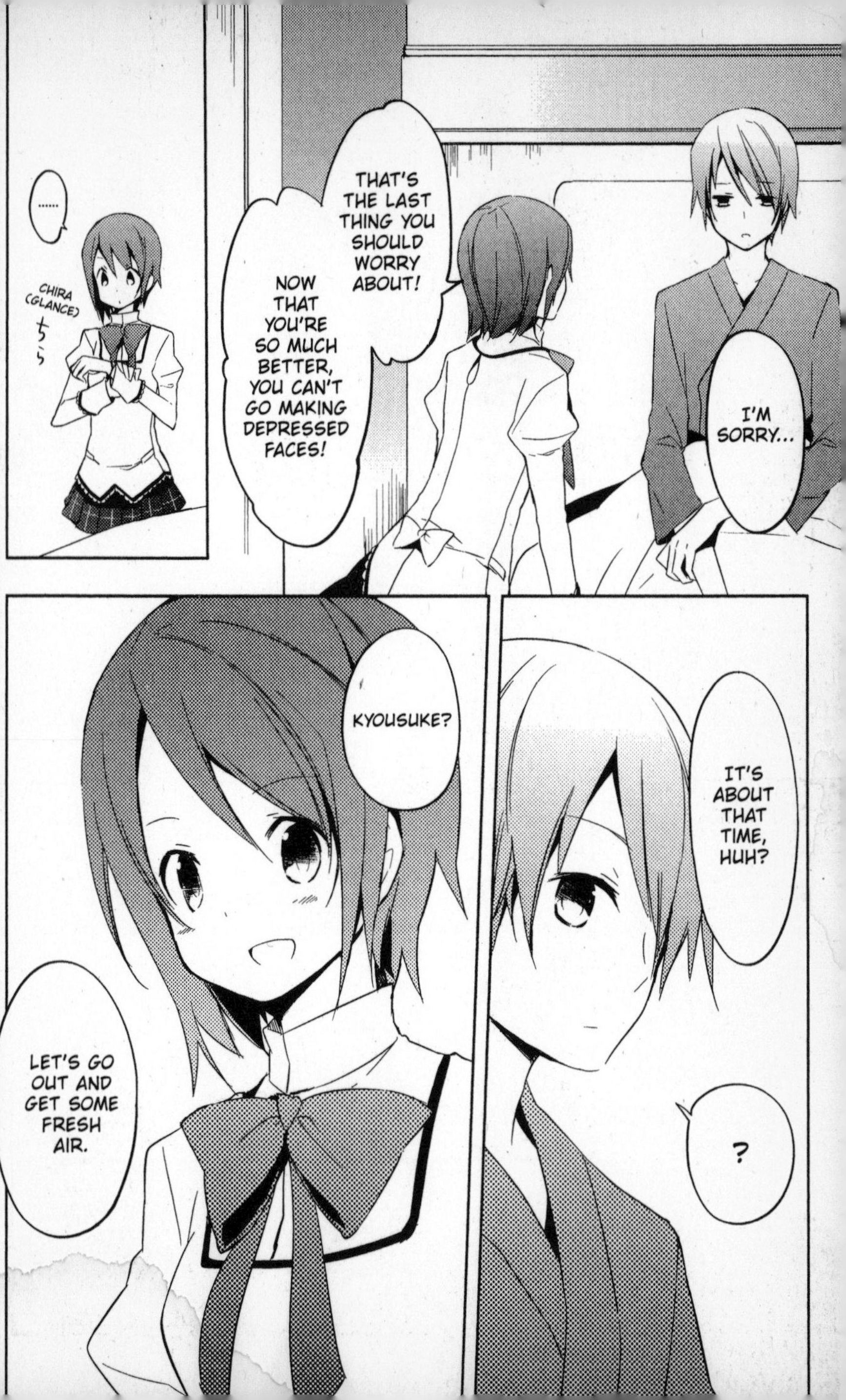
I'M SORRY...
THAT'S THE LAST THING YOU SHOULD WORRY ABOUT!
NOW THAT YOU'RE SO MUCH BETTER, YOU CAN'T GO MAKING DEPRESSED FACES!
......
CHIRA (GLANCE) ちら
IT'S ABOUT THAT TIME, HUH?
?
KYOUSUKE?
LET'S GO OUT AND GET SOME FRESH AIR.

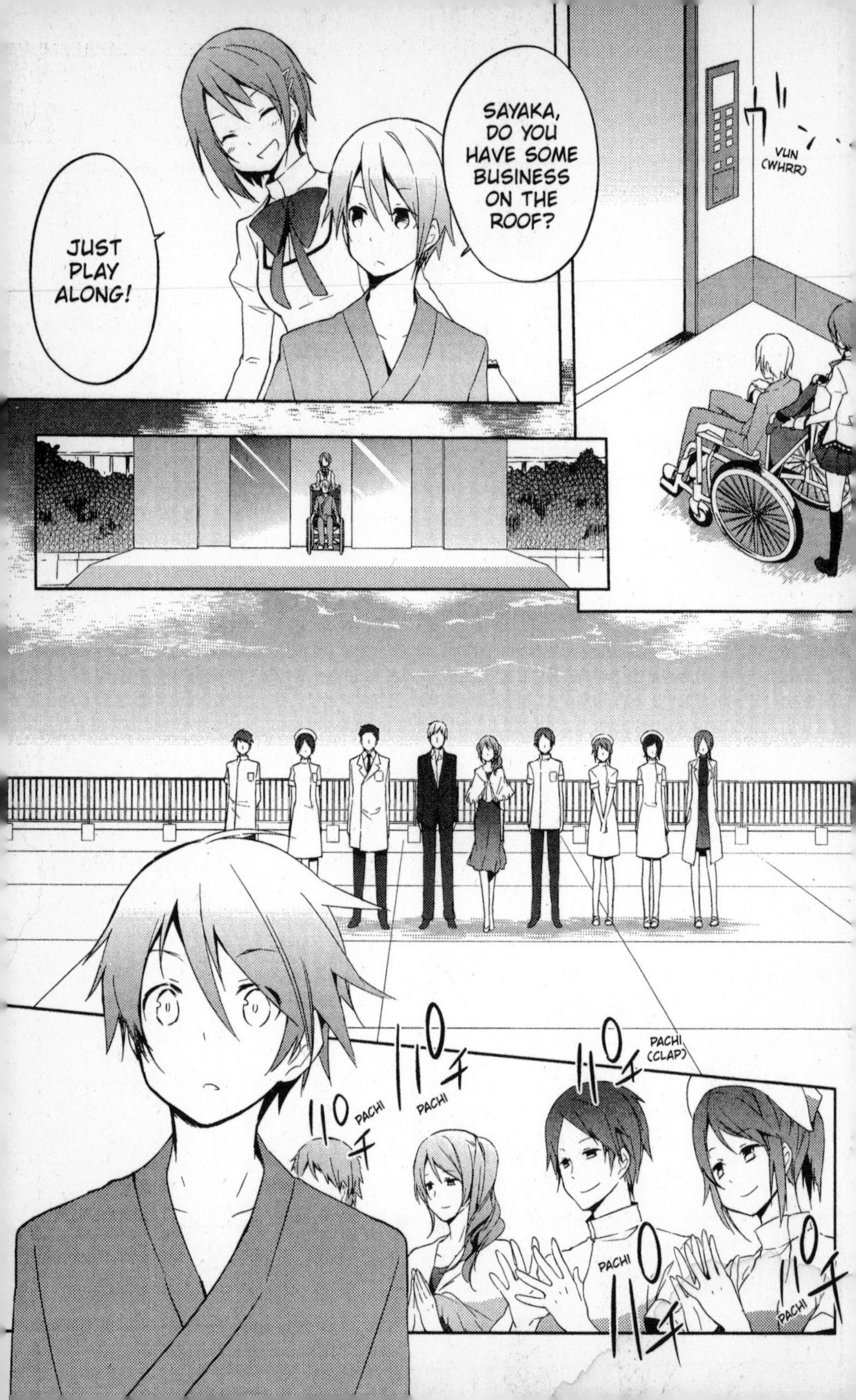
VUN (WHRR)
SAYAKA, DO YOU HAVE SOME BUSINESS ON THE ROOF?
JUST PLAY ALONG!
PACHI (CLAP)
PACHI
PACHI
PACHI
PACHI

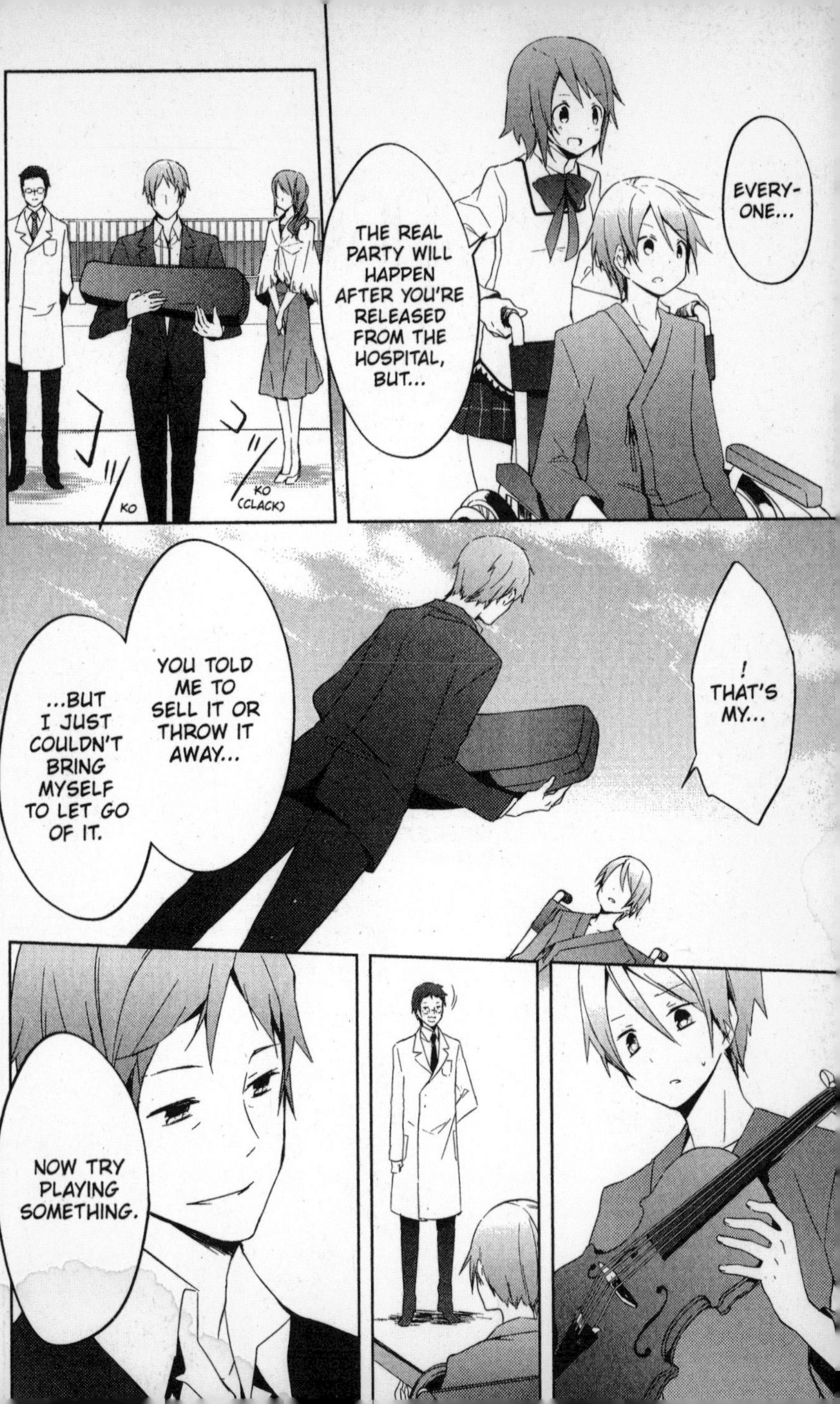
EVERY-ONE...
THE REAL PARTY WILL HAPPEN AFTER YOU'RE RELEASED FROM THE HOSPITAL, BUT...
KO (CLACK)
KO
! THAT'S MY...
YOU TOLD ME TO SELL IT OR THROW IT AWAY...
...BUT I JUST COULDN'T BRING MYSELF TO LET GO OF IT.
NOW TRY PLAYING SOMETHING.

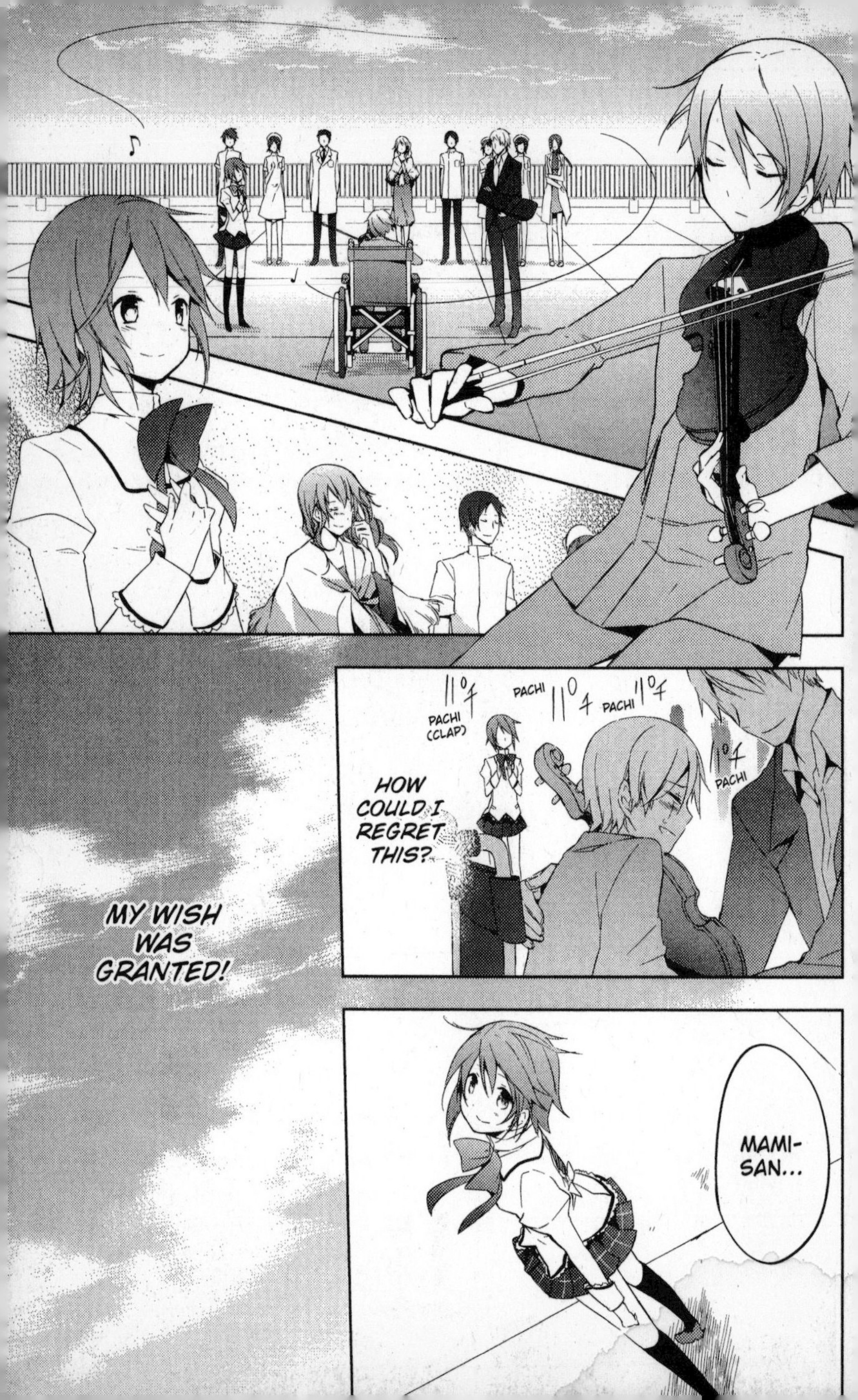
PACHI
PACHI
PACHI
PACHI (CLAP)
HOW COULD I REGRET THIS?
MAMI-SAN...
MY WISH WAS GRANTED!

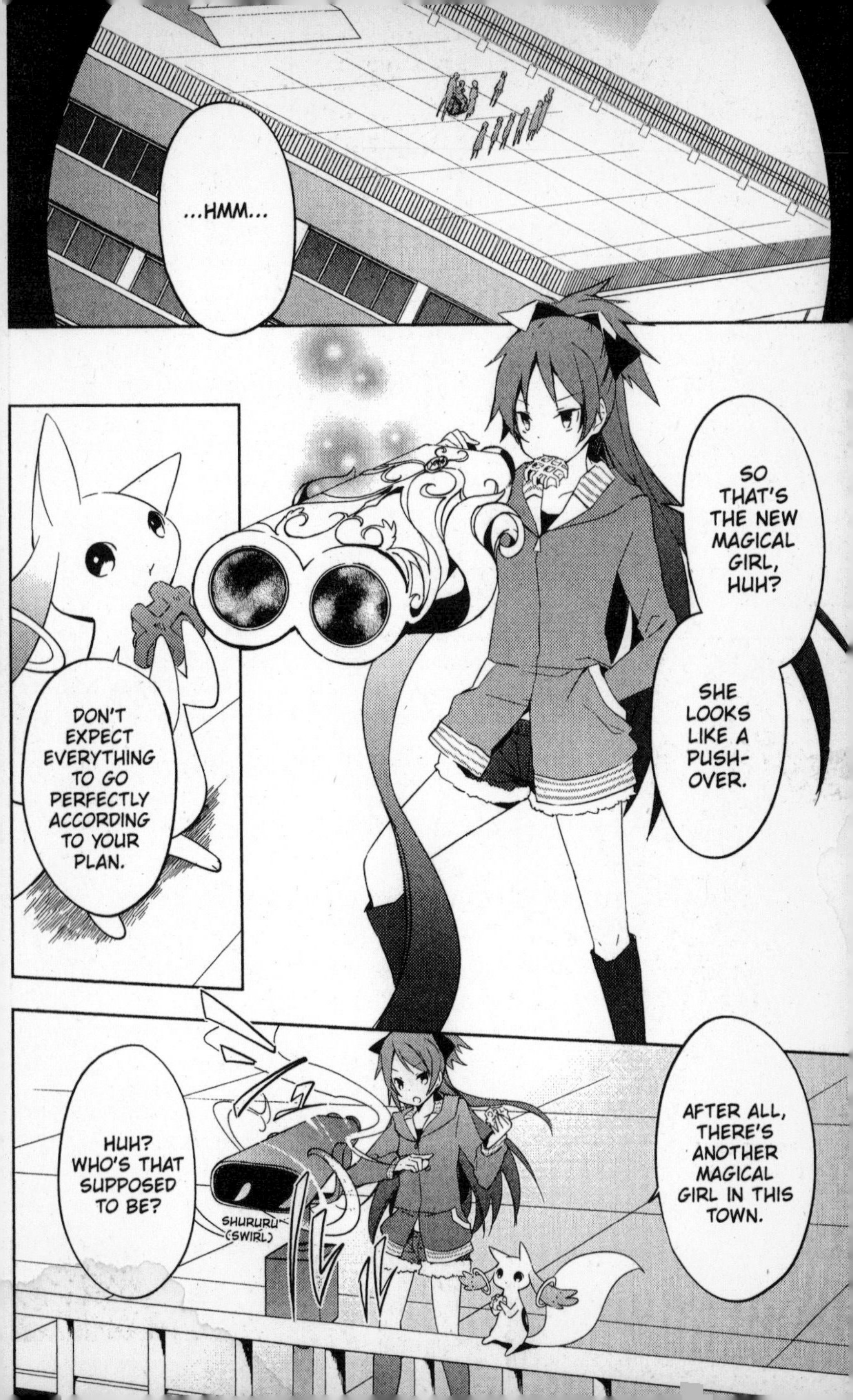
...HMM...
SO THAT'S THE NEW MAGICAL GIRL, HUH?
SHE LOOKS LIKE A PUSH-OVER.
DON'T EXPECT EVERYTHING TO GO PERFECTLY ACCORDING TO YOUR PLAN.
AFTER ALL, THERE'S ANOTHER MAGICAL GIRL IN THIS TOWN.
HUH? WHO'S THAT SUPPOSED TO BE?
SHURURU (SWIRL)

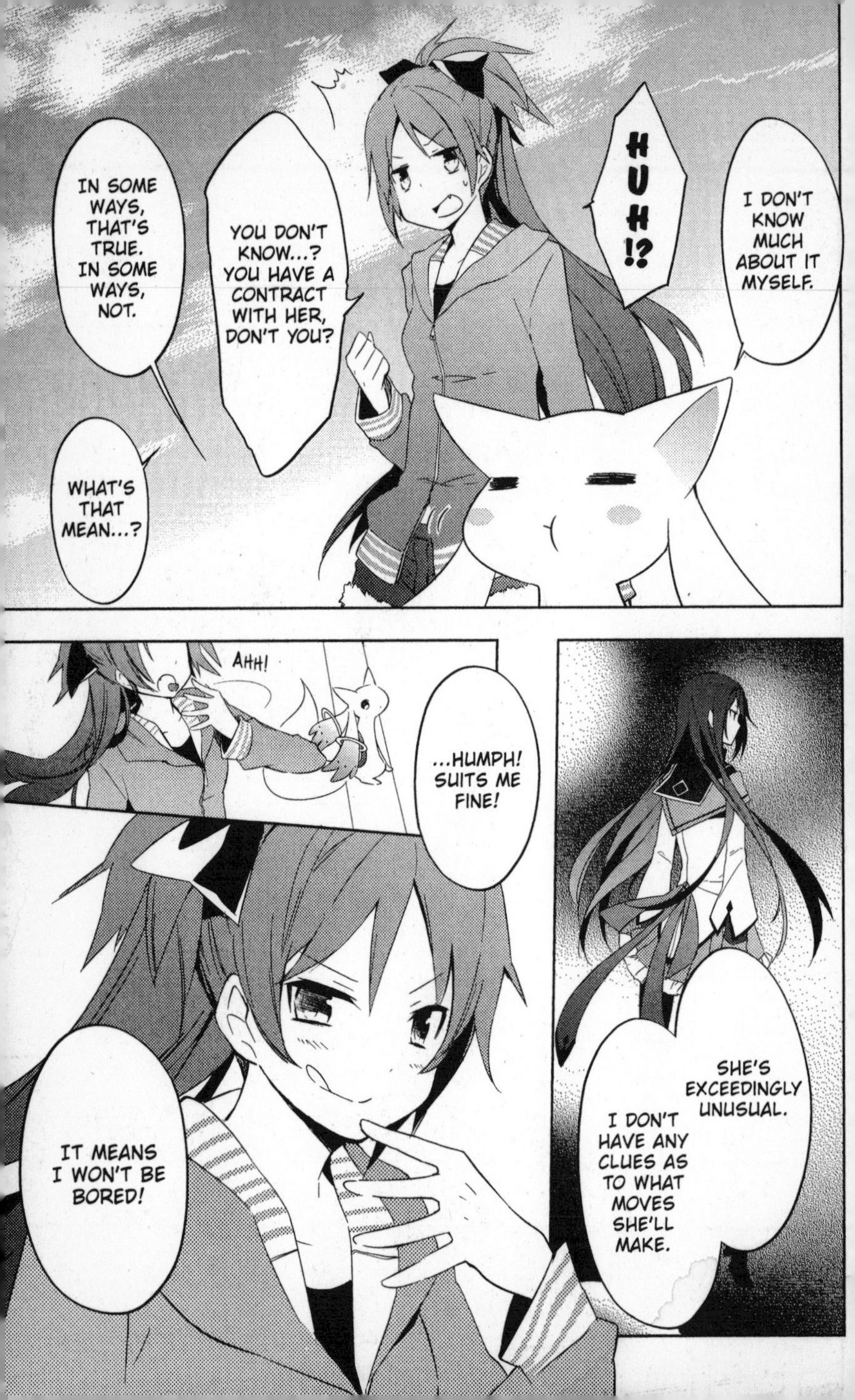
I DON'T KNOW MUCH ABOUT IT MYSELF.
HUH!?
YOU DON'T KNOW...? YOU HAVE A CONTRACT WITH HER, DON'T YOU?
IN SOME WAYS, THAT'S TRUE. IN SOME WAYS, NOT.
WHAT'S THAT MEAN...?
SHE'S EXCEEDINGLY UNUSUAL.
I DON'T HAVE ANY CLUES AS TO WHAT MOVES SHE'LL MAKE.
AHH!
...HUMPH! SUITS ME FINE!
IT MEANS I WON'T BE BORED!

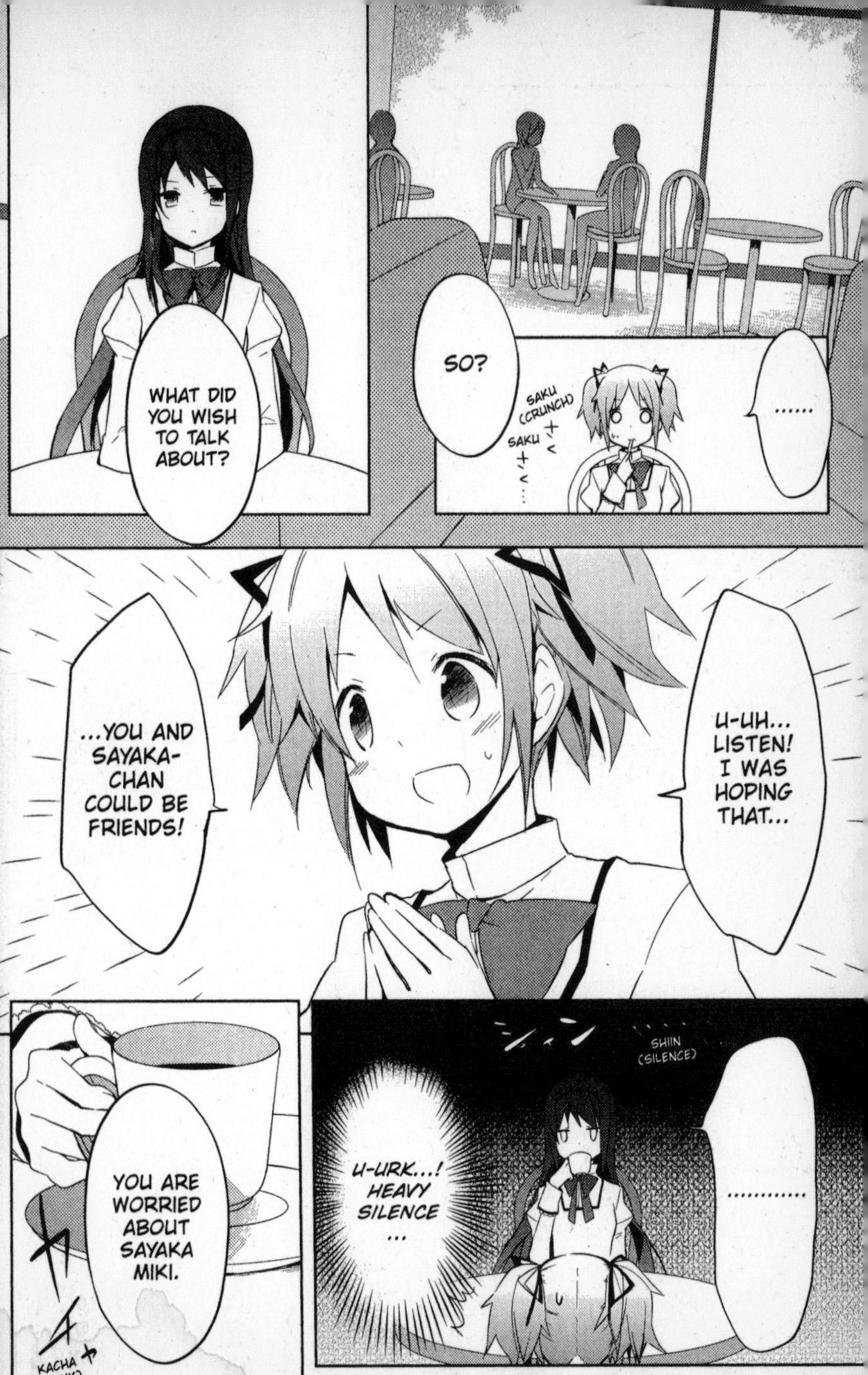
......
SAKU (CRUNCH) SAKU
SO?
WHAT DID YOU WISH TO TALK ABOUT?
U-UH... LISTEN! I WAS HOPING THAT...
...YOU AND SAYAKA-CHAN COULD BE FRIENDS!
....
SHIIN (SILENCE)
U-URK...! HEAVY SILENCE ...
YOU ARE WORRIED ABOUT SAYAKA MIKI.
KACHA (CLINK)

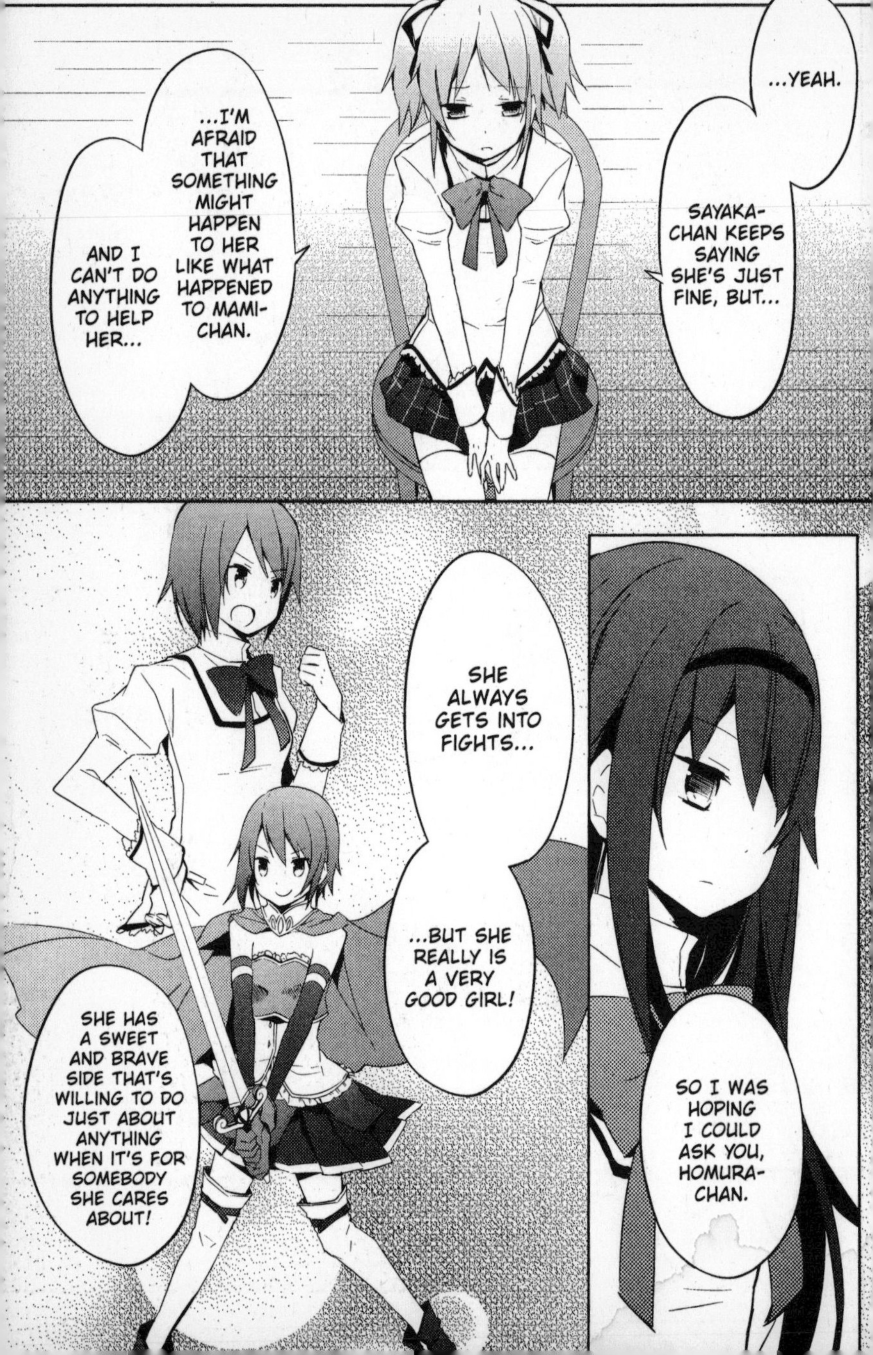
...YEAH.
SAYAKA-CHAN KEEPS SAYING SHE'S JUST FINE, BUT...
...I'M AFRAID THAT SOMETHING MIGHT HAPPEN TO HER LIKE WHAT HAPPENED TO MAMI-CHAN.
AND I CAN'T DO ANYTHING TO HELP HER...
SO I WAS HOPING I COULD ASK YOU, HOMURA-CHAN.
SHE ALWAYS GETS INTO FIGHTS...
...BUT SHE REALLY IS A VERY GOOD GIRL!
SHE HAS A SWEET AND BRAVE SIDE THAT'S WILLING TO DO JUST ABOUT ANYTHING WHEN IT'S FOR SOMEBODY SHE CARES ABOUT!

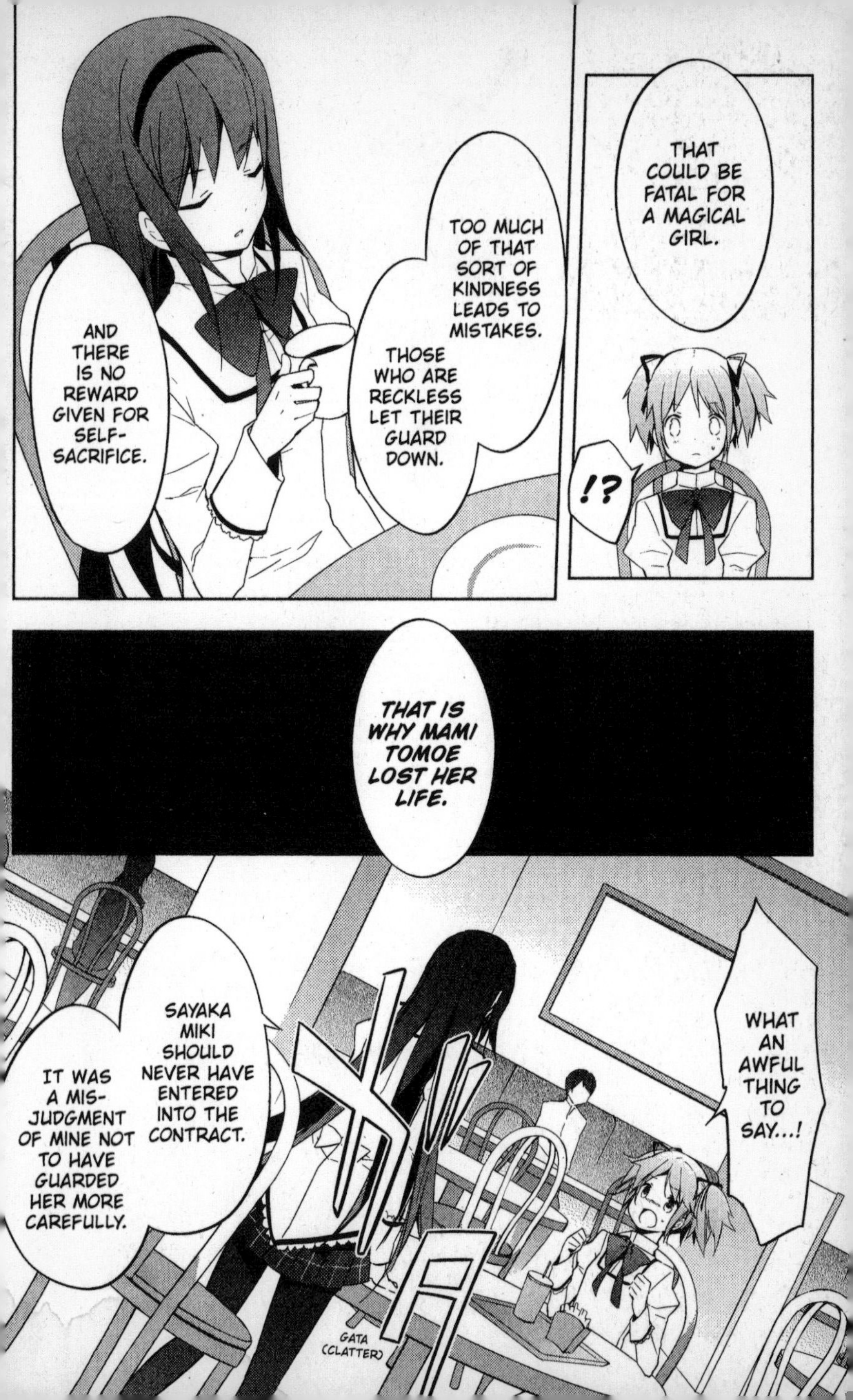
THAT COULD BE FATAL FOR A MAGICAL GIRL.
!?
TOO MUCH OF THAT SORT OF KINDNESS LEADS TO MISTAKES.
THOSE WHO ARE RECKLESS LET THEIR GUARD DOWN.
AND THERE IS NO REWARD GIVEN FOR SELF-SACRIFICE.
THAT IS WHY MAMI TOMOE LOST HER LIFE.
WHAT AN AWFUL THING TO SAY...!
SAYAKA MIKI SHOULD NEVER HAVE ENTERED INTO THE CONTRACT.
IT WAS A MIS-JUDGMENT OF MINE NOT TO HAVE GUARDED HER MORE CAREFULLY.
GATA (CLATTER)

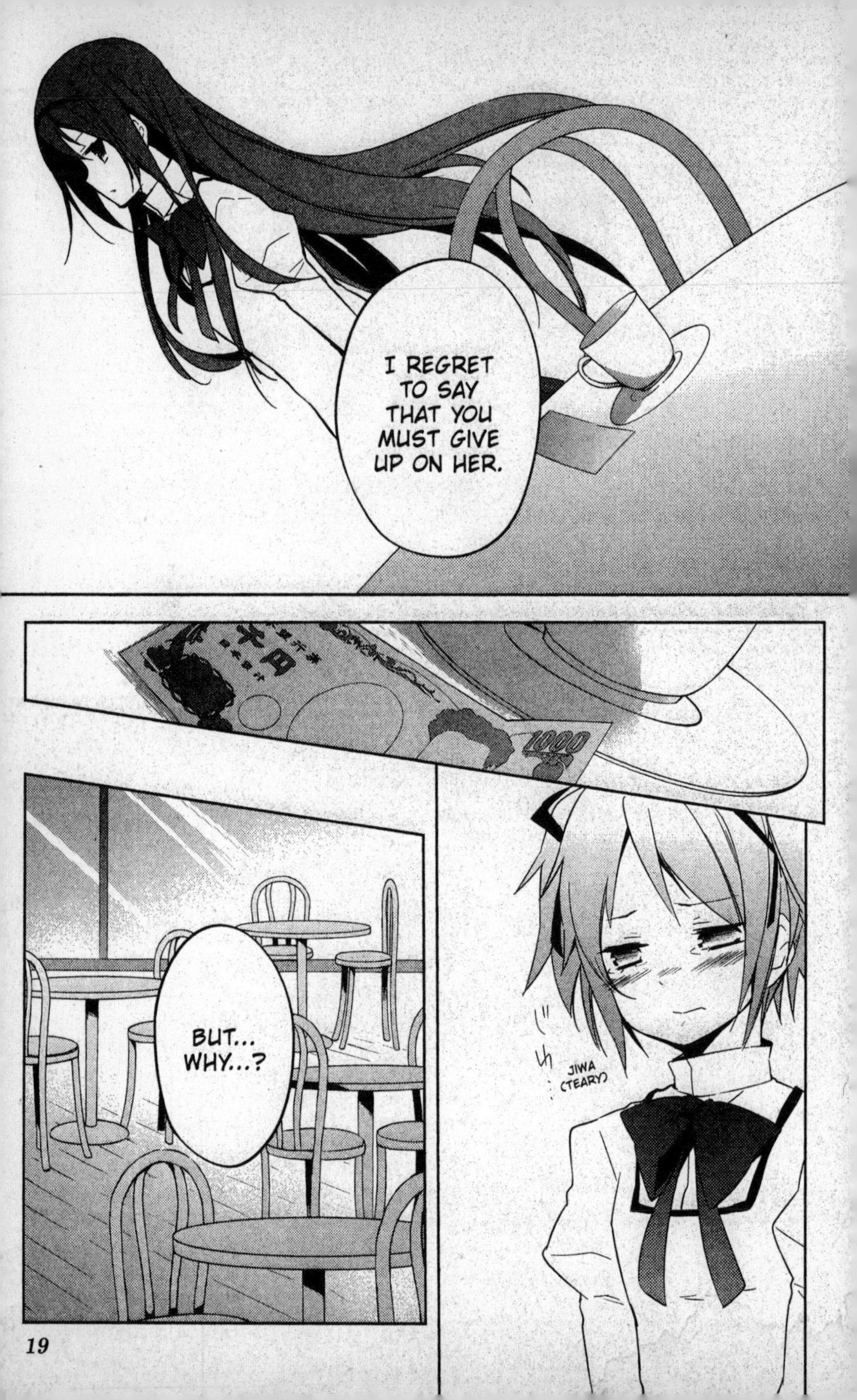
I REGRET TO SAY THAT YOU MUST GIVE UP ON HER.
じわ
JIWA (TEARY)
BUT... WHY...?

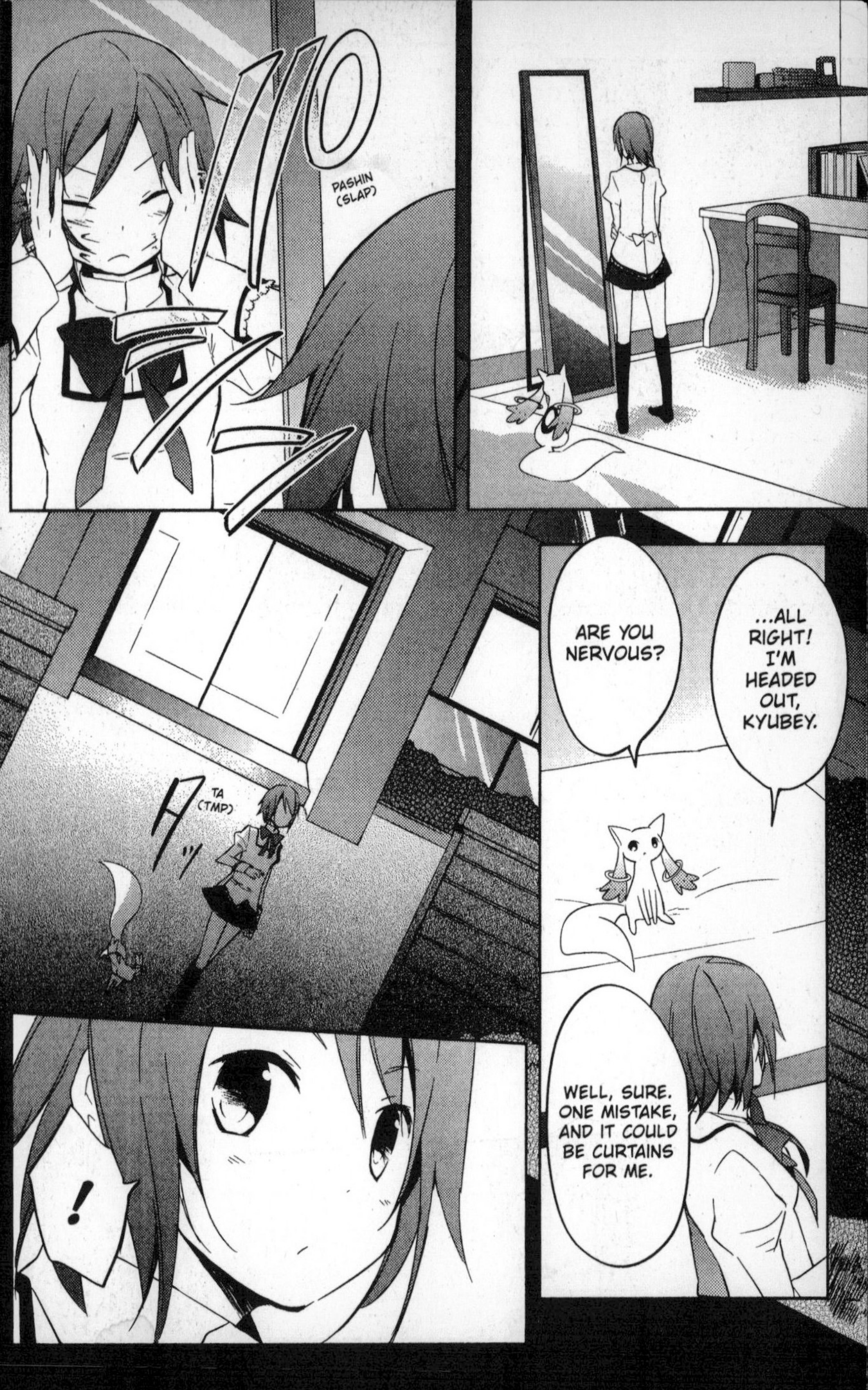
PASHIN (SLAP)
...ALL RIGHT! I'M HEADED OUT, KYUBEY.
ARE YOU NERVOUS?
WELL, SURE. ONE MISTAKE, AND IT COULD BE CURTAINS FOR ME.
TA (TMP)
!

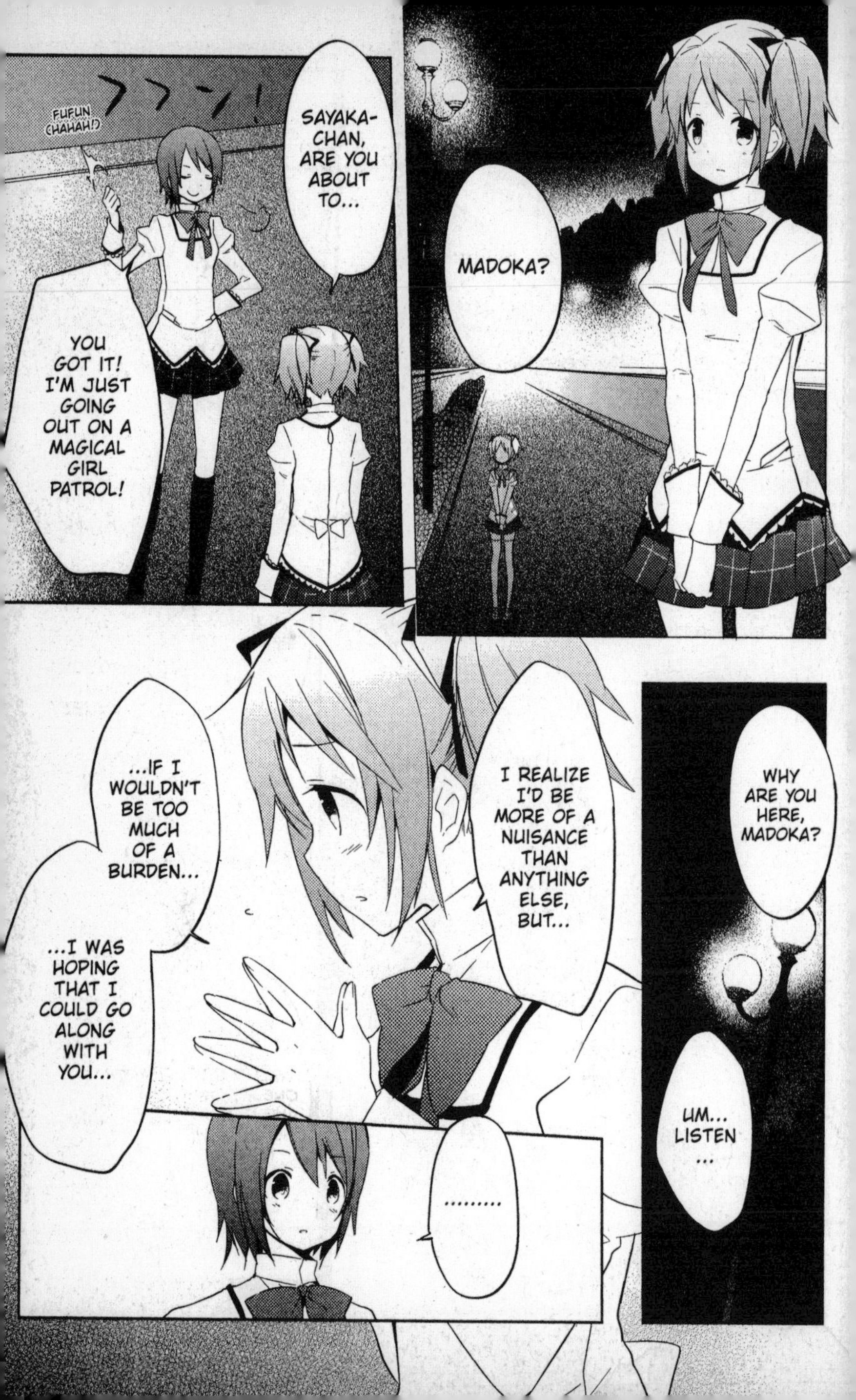
MADOKA?
SAYAKA-CHAN, ARE YOU ABOUT TO...
FUFUN CHAHAH!?
YOU GOT IT! I'M JUST GOING OUT ON A MAGICAL GIRL PATROL!
WHY ARE YOU HERE, MADOKA?
UM... LISTEN ...
I REALIZE I'D BE MORE OF A NUISANCE THAN ANYTHING ELSE, BUT...
...IF I WOULDN'T BE TOO MUCH OF A BURDEN...
...I WAS HOPING THAT I COULD GO ALONG WITH YOU...
....

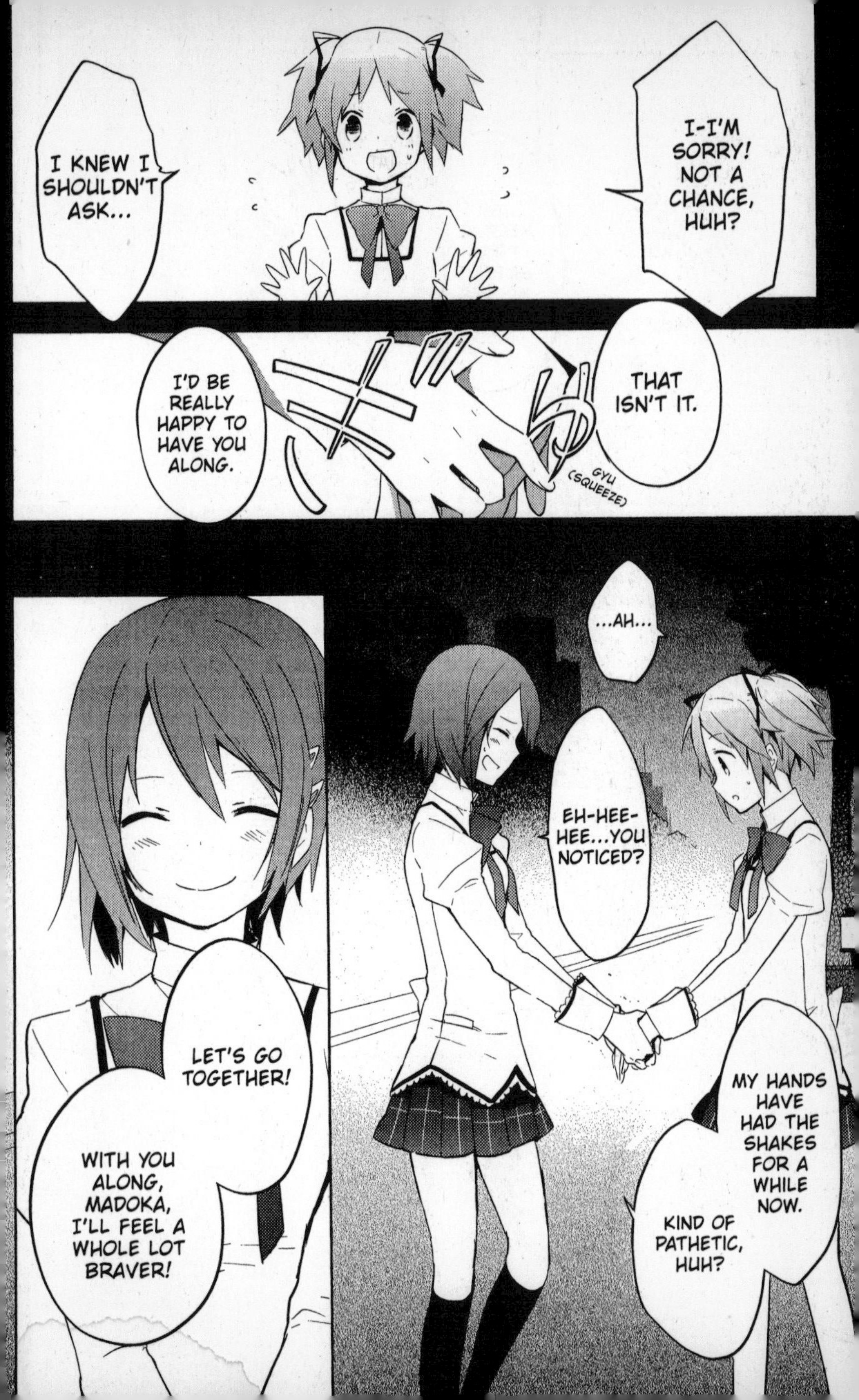
I-I'M SORRY! NOT A CHANCE, HUH?
I KNEW I SHOULDN'T ASK...
THAT ISN'T IT.
GYU (SQUEEZE)
I'D BE REALLY HAPPY TO HAVE YOU ALONG.
...AH...
EH-HEE-HEE...YOU NOTICED?
MY HANDS HAVE HAD THE SHAKES FOR A WHILE NOW.
KIND OF PATHETIC, HUH?
LET'S GO TOGETHER!
WITH YOU ALONG, MADOKA, I'LL FEEL A WHOLE LOT BRAVER!

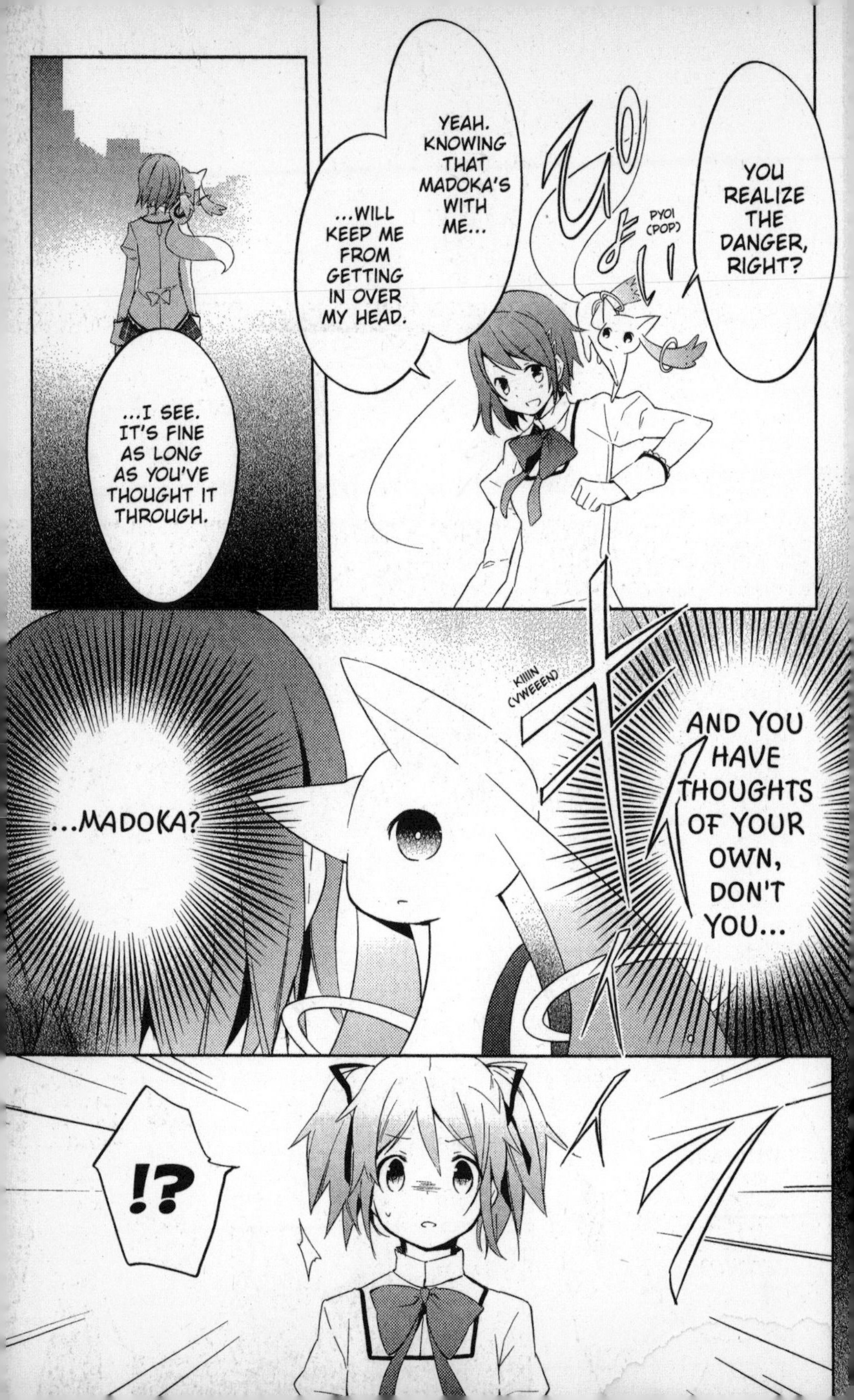
YOU REALIZE THE DANGER, RIGHT?
PYOI (POP)
YEAH. KNOWING THAT MADOKA'S WITH ME...
...WILL KEEP ME FROM GETTING IN OVER MY HEAD.
...I SEE. IT'S FINE AS LONG AS YOU'VE THOUGHT IT THROUGH.
AND YOU HAVE THOUGHTS OF YOUR OWN, DON'T YOU...
KIIIIN (VWEEEN)
...MADOKA?
!?

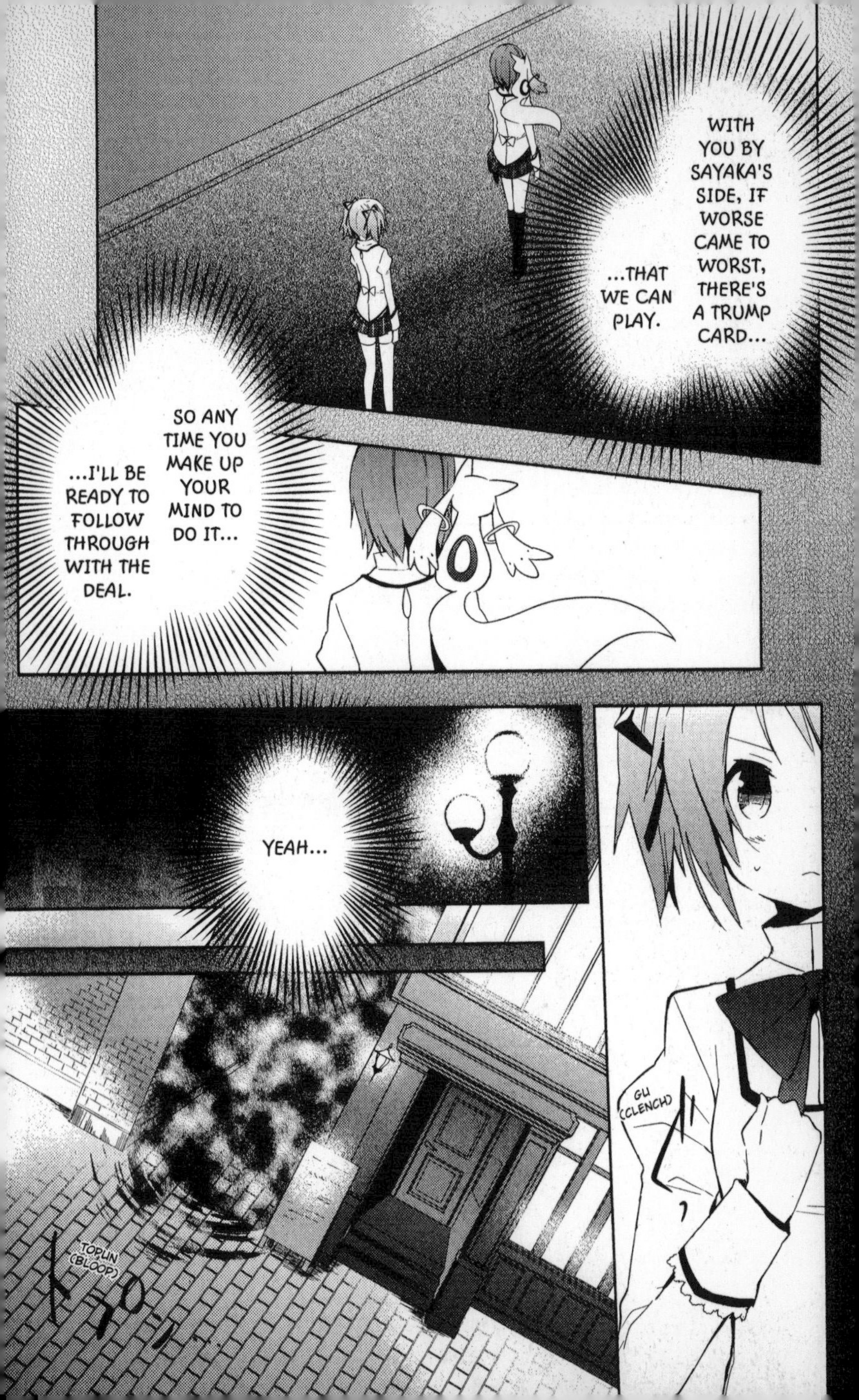
WITH YOU BY SAYAKA'S SIDE, IF WORSE CAME TO WORST, THERE'S A TRUMP CARD...
...THAT WE CAN PLAY.
SO ANY TIME YOU MAKE UP YOUR MIND TO DO IT...
...I'LL BE READY TO FOLLOW THROUGH WITH THE DEAL.
GU (CLENCH)
YEAH...
TOPUN (BLOOP)

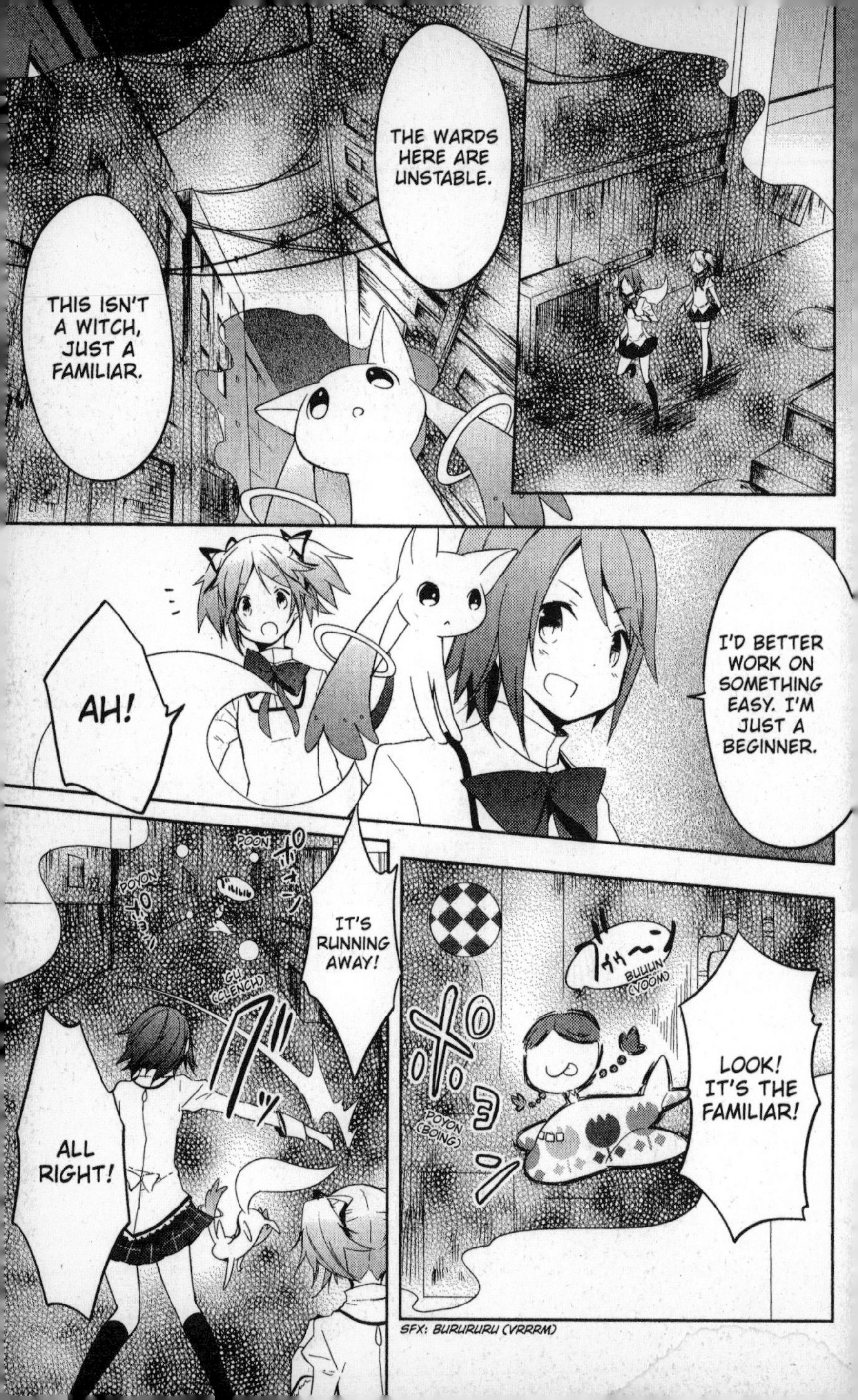
THE WARDS HERE ARE UNSTABLE.
THIS ISN'T A WITCH, JUST A FAMILIAR.
I'D BETTER WORK ON SOMETHING EASY. I'M JUST A BEGINNER.
AH!
LOOK! IT'S THE FAMILIAR!
BUUUN (VOOM)
POYON (BOING)
SFX: BURURURU (VRRRM)
POON
POYON
IT'S RUNNING AWAY!
GU (CLENCH)
ALL RIGHT!

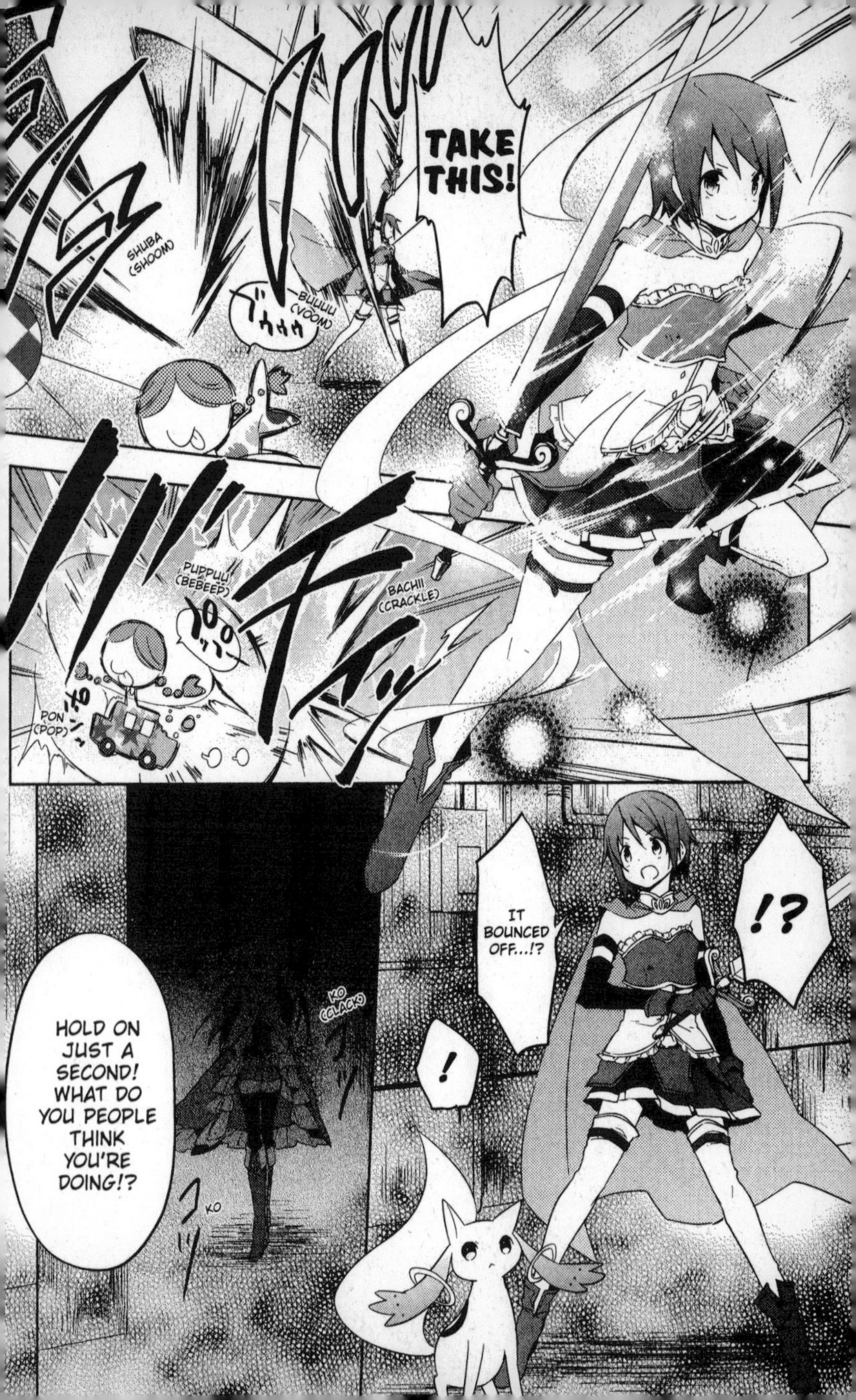
TAKE THIS!
BUUUU (VOOM)
SHUBA (SHOOM)
BACHII (CRACKLE)
PUPPUU (BEBEEP)
PON (POP)
!?
IT BOUNCED OFF...!?
!
KO (CLACK)
HOLD ON JUST A SECOND! WHAT DO YOU PEOPLE THINK YOU'RE DOING!?
KO

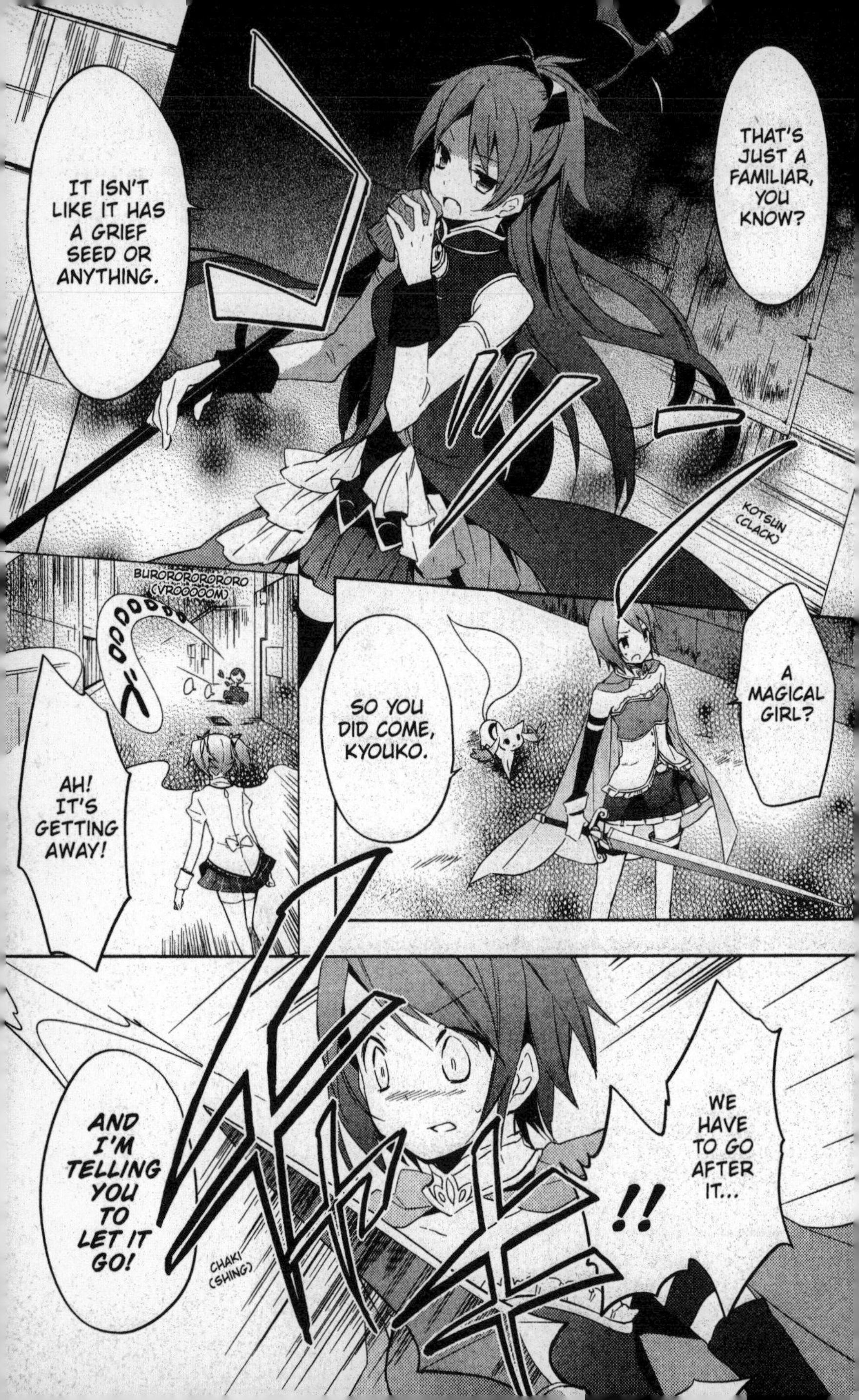
THAT'S JUST A FAMILIAR, YOU KNOW?
IT ISN'T LIKE IT HAS A GRIEF SEED OR ANYTHING.
KOTSUN (CLACK)
A MAGICAL GIRL?
SO YOU DID COME, KYOUKO.
BURORORORORORO (VROOOOOM)
AH! IT'S GETTING AWAY!
WE HAVE TO GO AFTER IT...
!!
AND I'M TELLING YOU TO LET IT GO!
CHAKI (SHING)

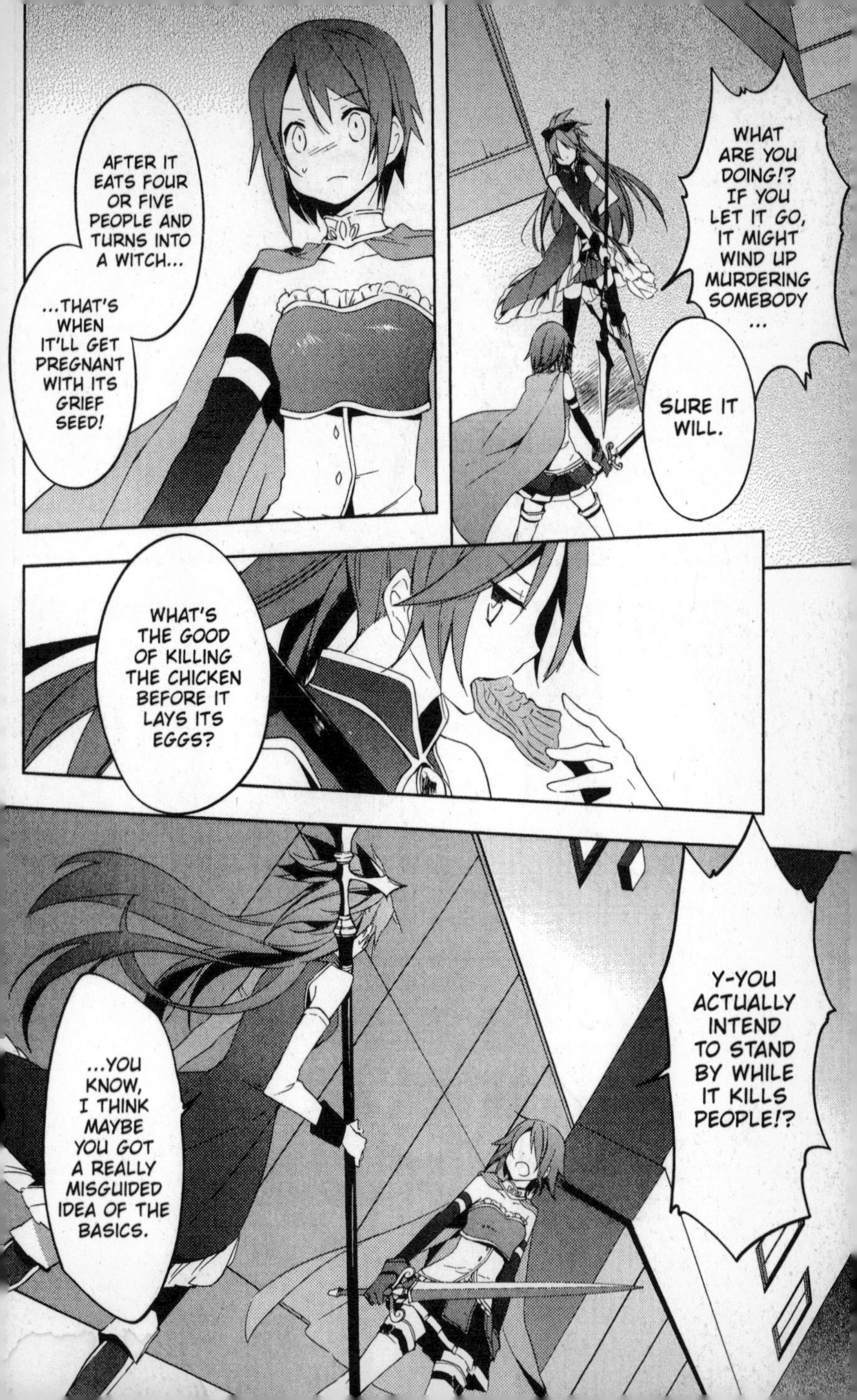
WHAT ARE YOU DOING!? IF YOU LET IT GO, IT MIGHT WIND UP MURDERING SOMEBODY ...
SURE IT WILL.
AFTER IT EATS FOUR OR FIVE PEOPLE AND TURNS INTO A WITCH...
...THAT'S WHEN IT'LL GET PREGNANT WITH ITS GRIEF SEED!
WHAT'S THE GOOD OF KILLING THE CHICKEN BEFORE IT LAYS ITS EGGS?
Y-YOU ACTUALLY INTEND TO STAND BY WHILE IT KILLS PEOPLE!?
...YOU KNOW, I THINK MAYBE YOU GOT A REALLY MISGUIDED IDEA OF THE BASICS.

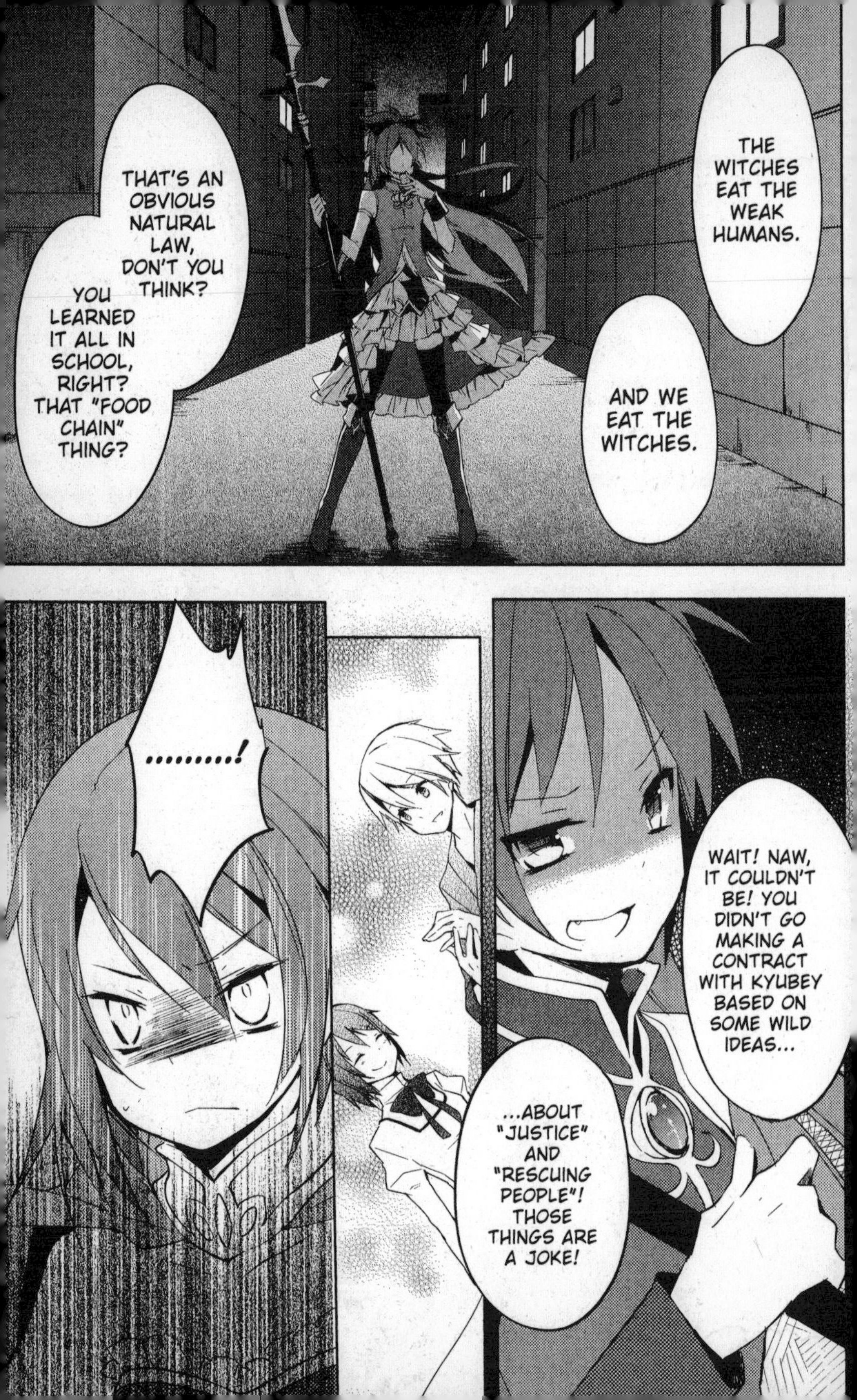
THE WITCHES EAT THE WEAK HUMANS.
AND WE EAT THE WITCHES.
THAT'S AN OBVIOUS NATURAL LAW, DON'T YOU THINK?
YOU LEARNED IT ALL IN SCHOOL, RIGHT? THAT "FOOD CHAIN" THING?
WAIT! NAW, IT COULDN'T BE! YOU DIDN'T GO MAKING A CONTRACT WITH KYUBEY BASED ON SOME WILD IDEAS...
...ABOUT "JUSTICE" AND "RESCUING PEOPLE"! THOSE THINGS ARE A JOKE!
........!

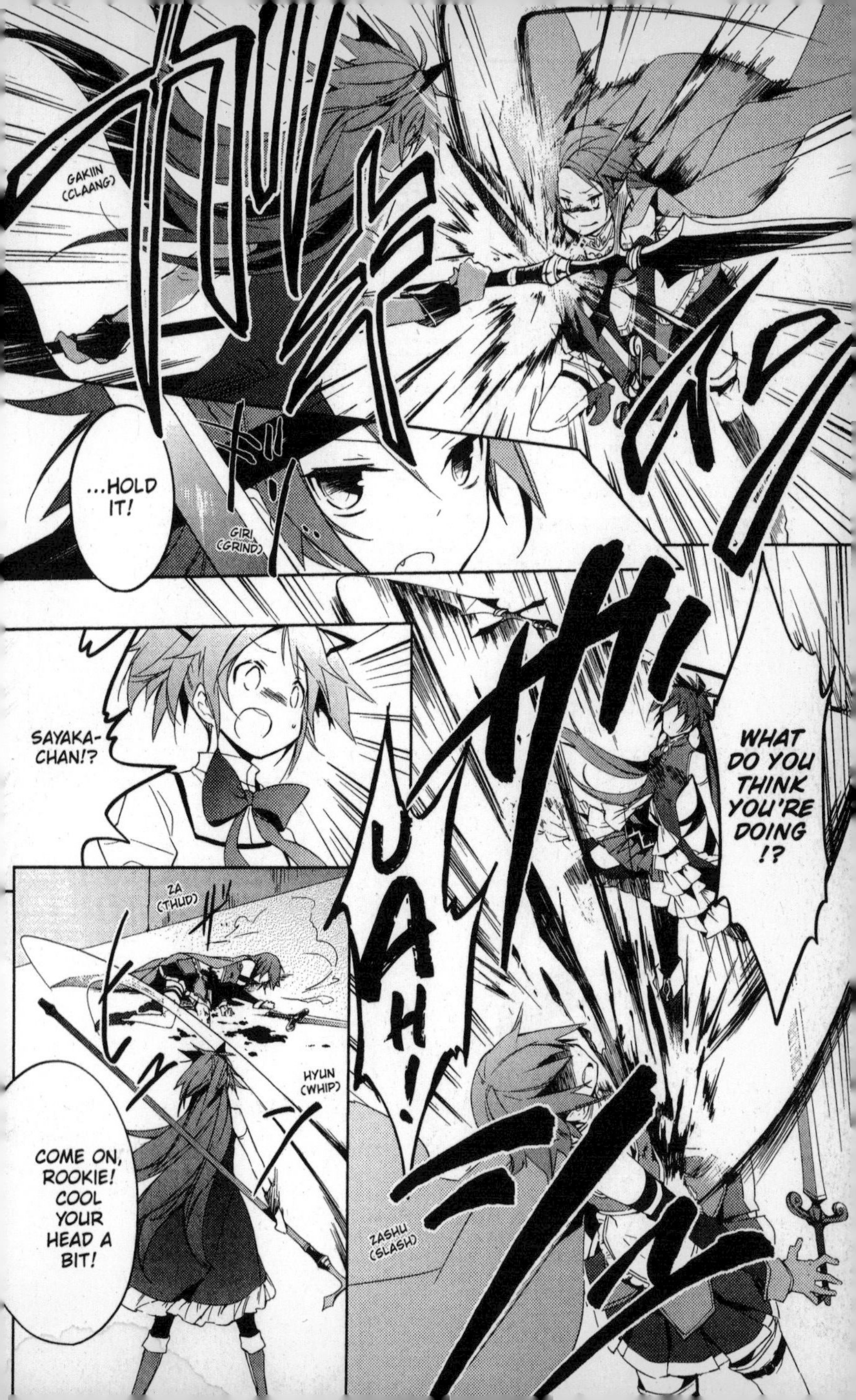
GAKIIN (CLAANG)
...HOLD IT!
GIRI (GRIND)
WHAT DO YOU THINK YOU'RE DOING!?
UAH!!
ZASHU (SLASH)
SAYAKA-CHAN!?
ZA (THUD)
HYUN (WHIP)
COME ON, ROOKIE! COOL YOUR HEAD A BIT!

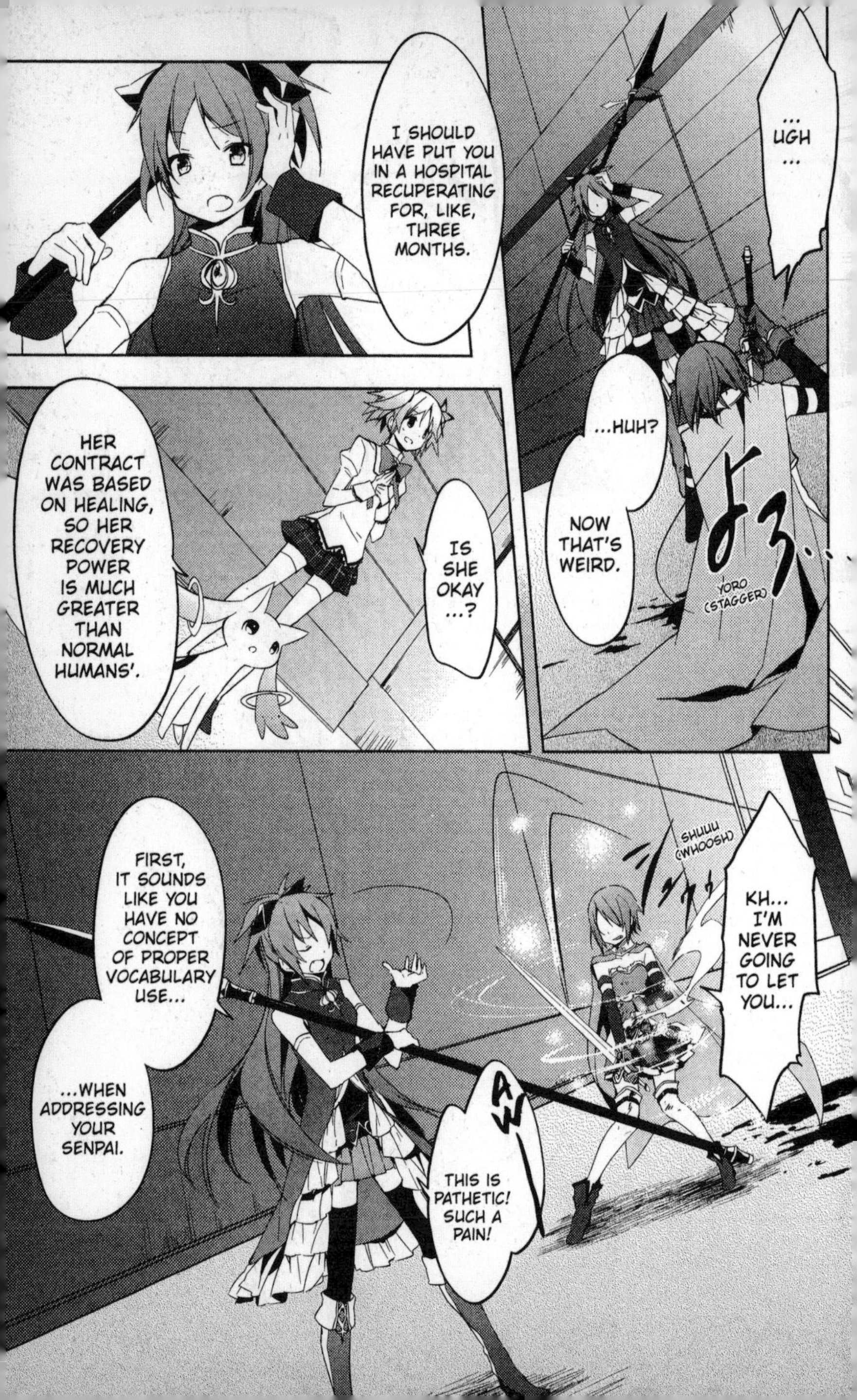
... UGH ...
...HUH?
NOW THAT'S WEIRD.
YORO (STAGGER)
I SHOULD HAVE PUT YOU IN A HOSPITAL RECUPERATING FOR, LIKE, THREE MONTHS.
IS SHE OKAY ...?
HER CONTRACT WAS BASED ON HEALING, SO HER RECOVERY POWER IS MUCH GREATER THAN NORMAL HUMANS'.
KH... I'M NEVER GOING TO LET YOU...
SHUUU (WHOOSH)
AW
THIS IS PATHETIC! SUCH A PAIN!
FIRST, IT SOUNDS LIKE YOU HAVE NO CONCEPT OF PROPER VOCABULARY USE...
...WHEN ADDRESSING YOUR SENPAI.

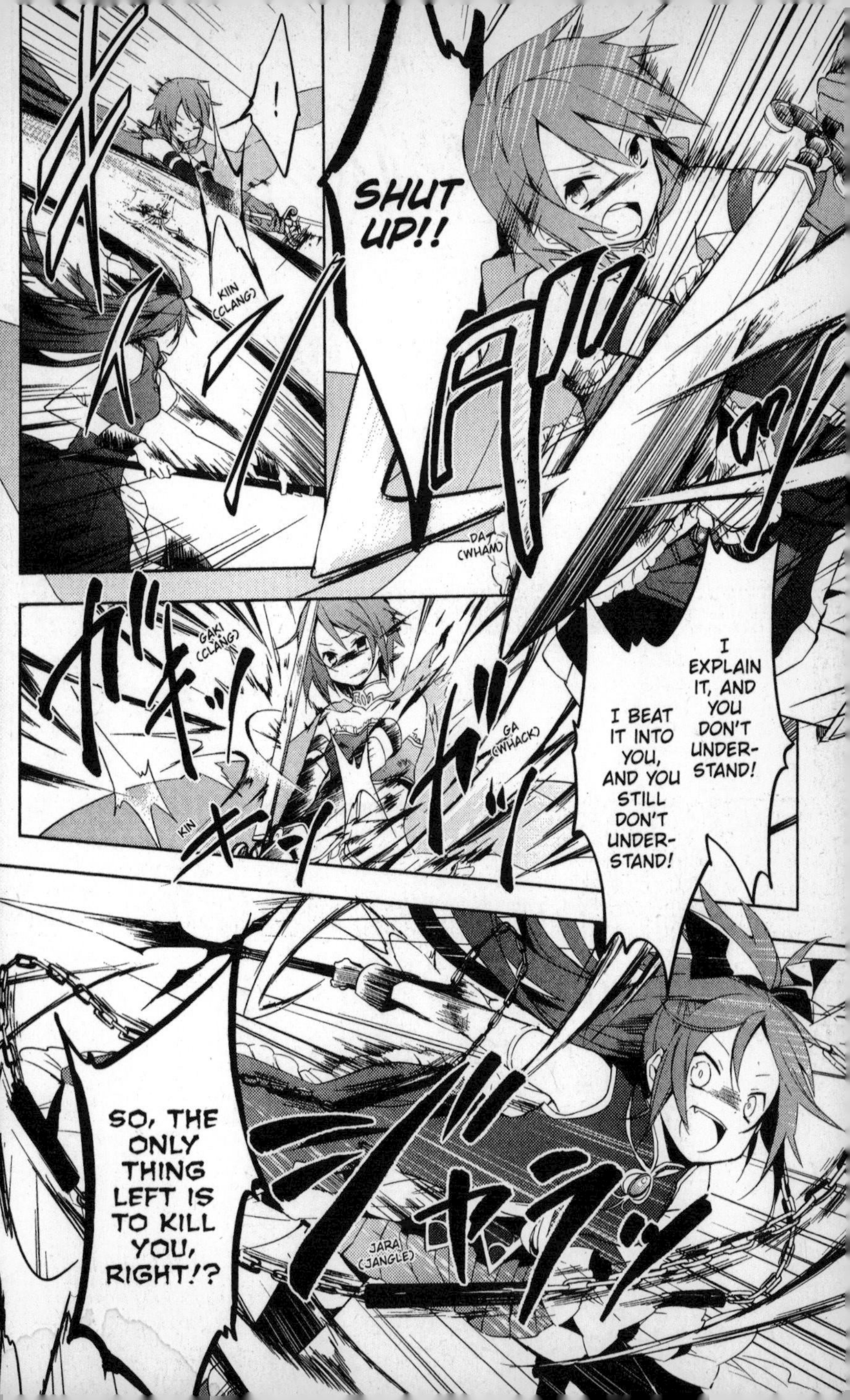
SHUT UP!!
DA (WHAM)
!
KIIN (CLANG)
GA (WHACK)
GAKI (CLANG)
KIN
I EXPLAIN IT, AND YOU DON'T UNDERSTAND!
I BEAT IT INTO YOU, AND YOU STILL DON'T UNDERSTAND!
SO, THE ONLY THING LEFT IS TO KILL YOU, RIGHT!?
JARA (JANGLE)

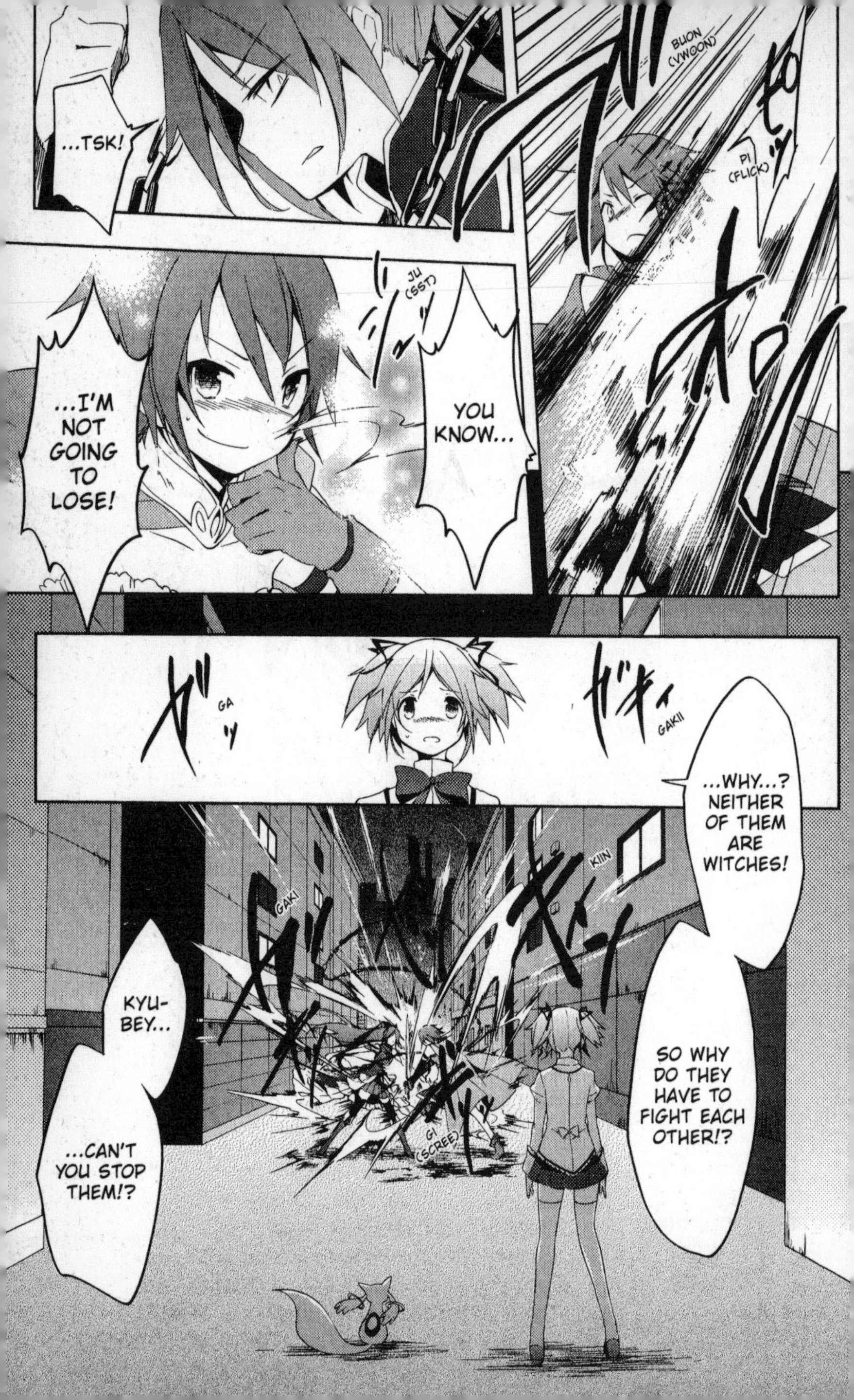

BUON (VWOON)
PI (FLICK)
...TSK!
JU (SST)
YOU KNOW...
...I'M NOT GOING TO LOSE!
GAKII
GA
...WHY...? NEITHER OF THEM ARE WITCHES!
KIIN
GAKI
SO WHY DO THEY HAVE TO FIGHT EACH OTHER!?
GI (SCREE)
KYU-BEY...
...CAN'T YOU STOP THEM!?

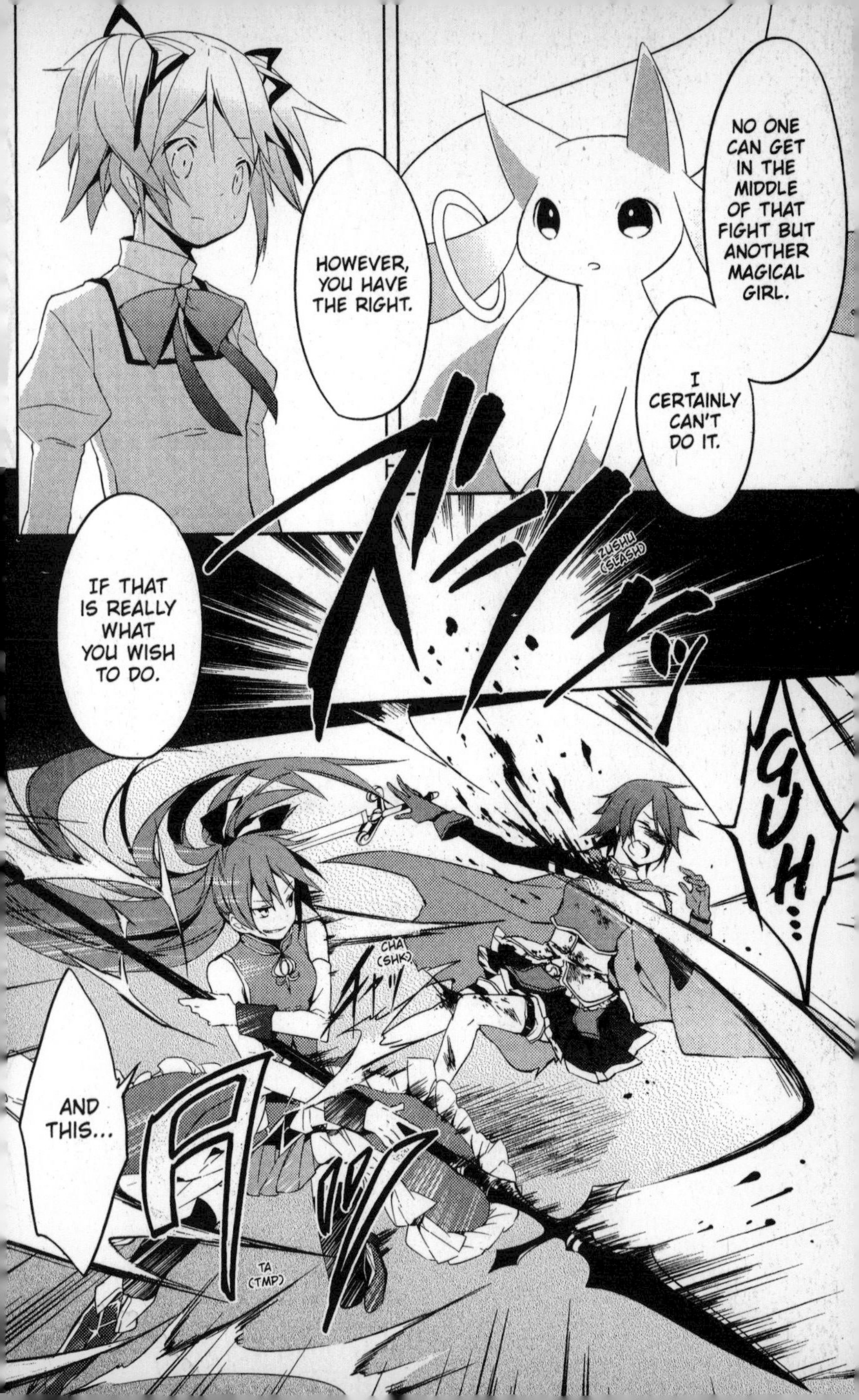
NO ONE CAN GET IN THE MIDDLE OF THAT FIGHT BUT ANOTHER MAGICAL GIRL.
I CERTAINLY CAN'T DO IT.
HOWEVER, YOU HAVE THE RIGHT.
IF THAT IS REALLY WHAT YOU WISH TO DO.
ZUSHU (SLASH)
GUH...
CHA (SHK)
AND THIS...
TA (TMP)

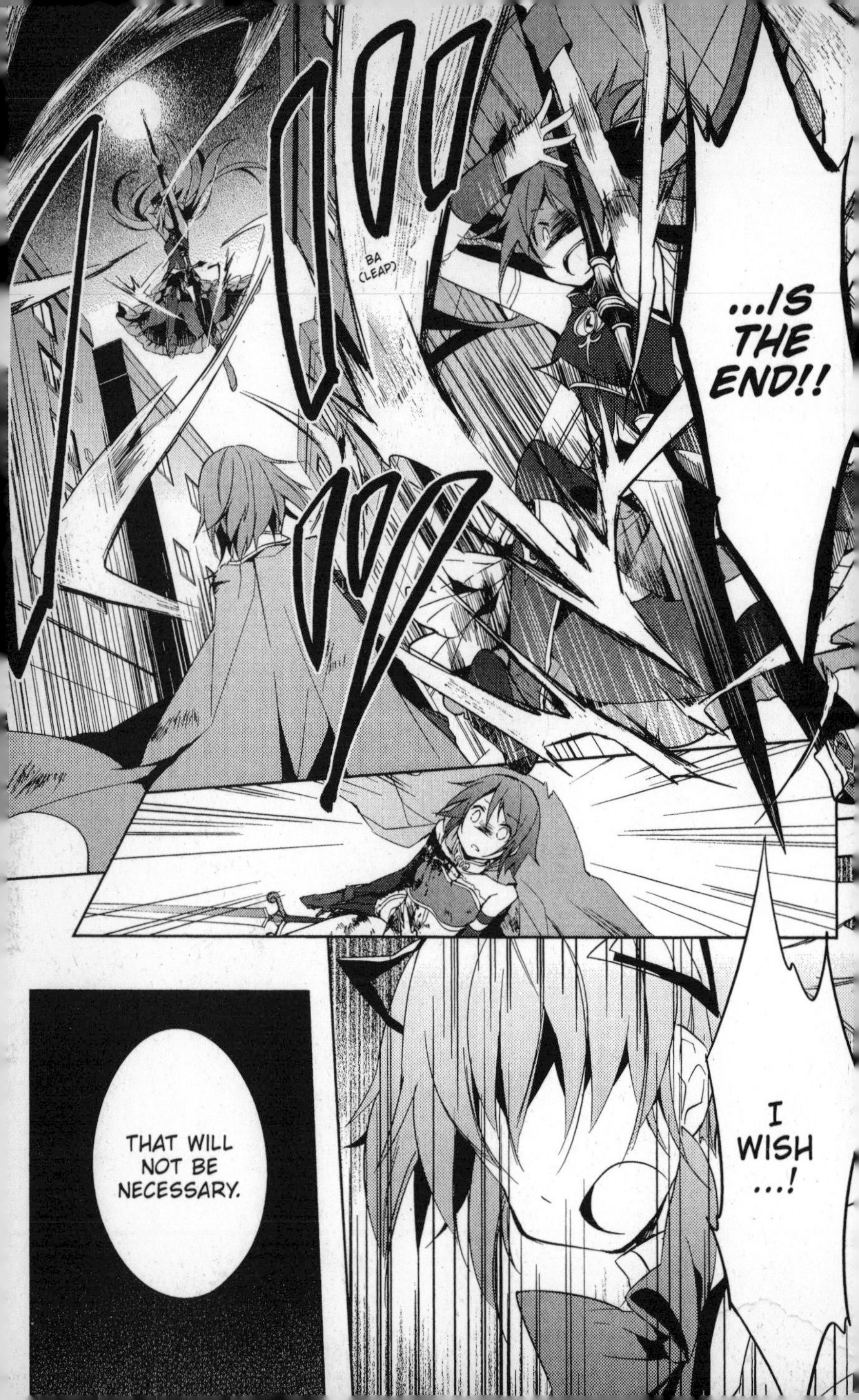
...IS THE END!!
BA (LEAP)
I WISH ...!
THAT WILL NOT BE NECESSARY.

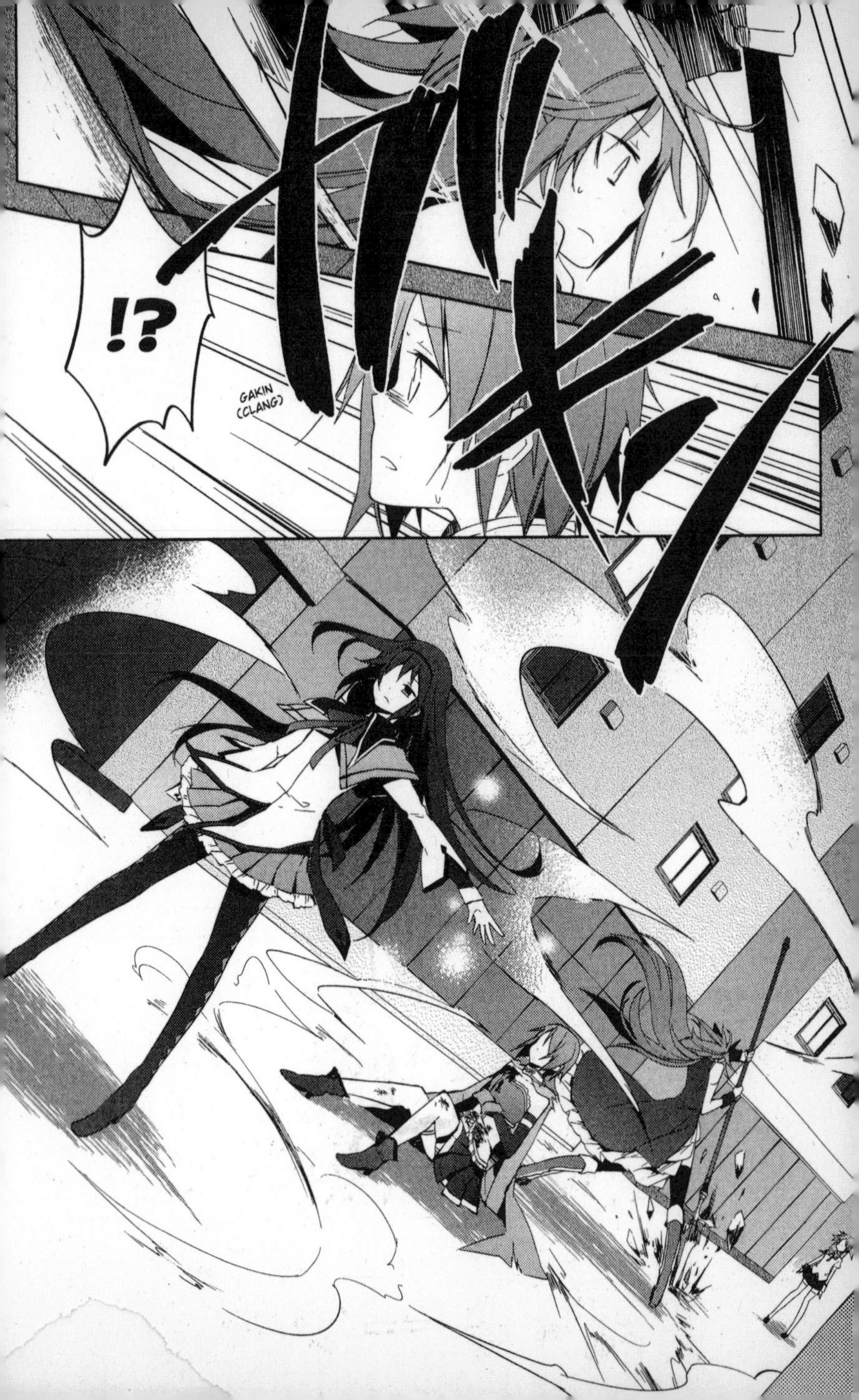
GAKIN (CLANG)
!?

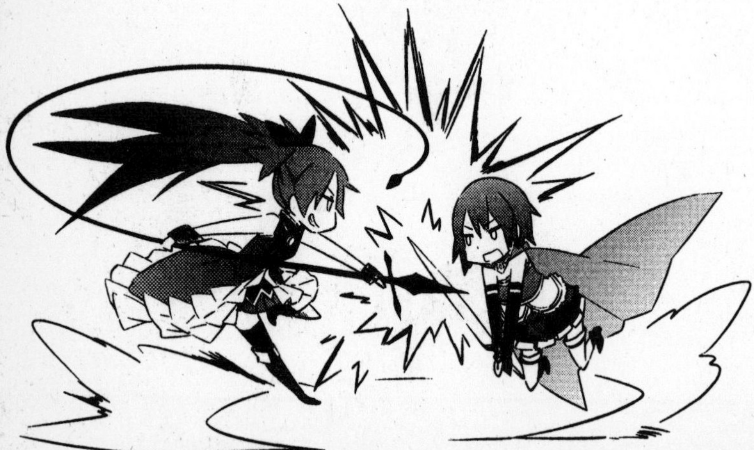

ガッキーン
GAKKIIN (CLAAANG)

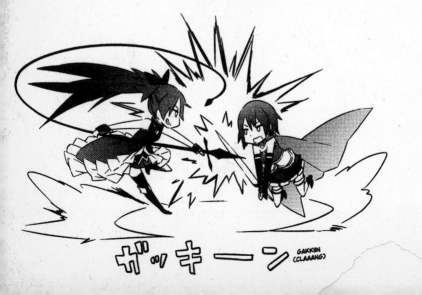

PUELLA MAGI
MADOKA★MAGICA

CHAPTER 6: THIS IS JUST TOO WEIRD

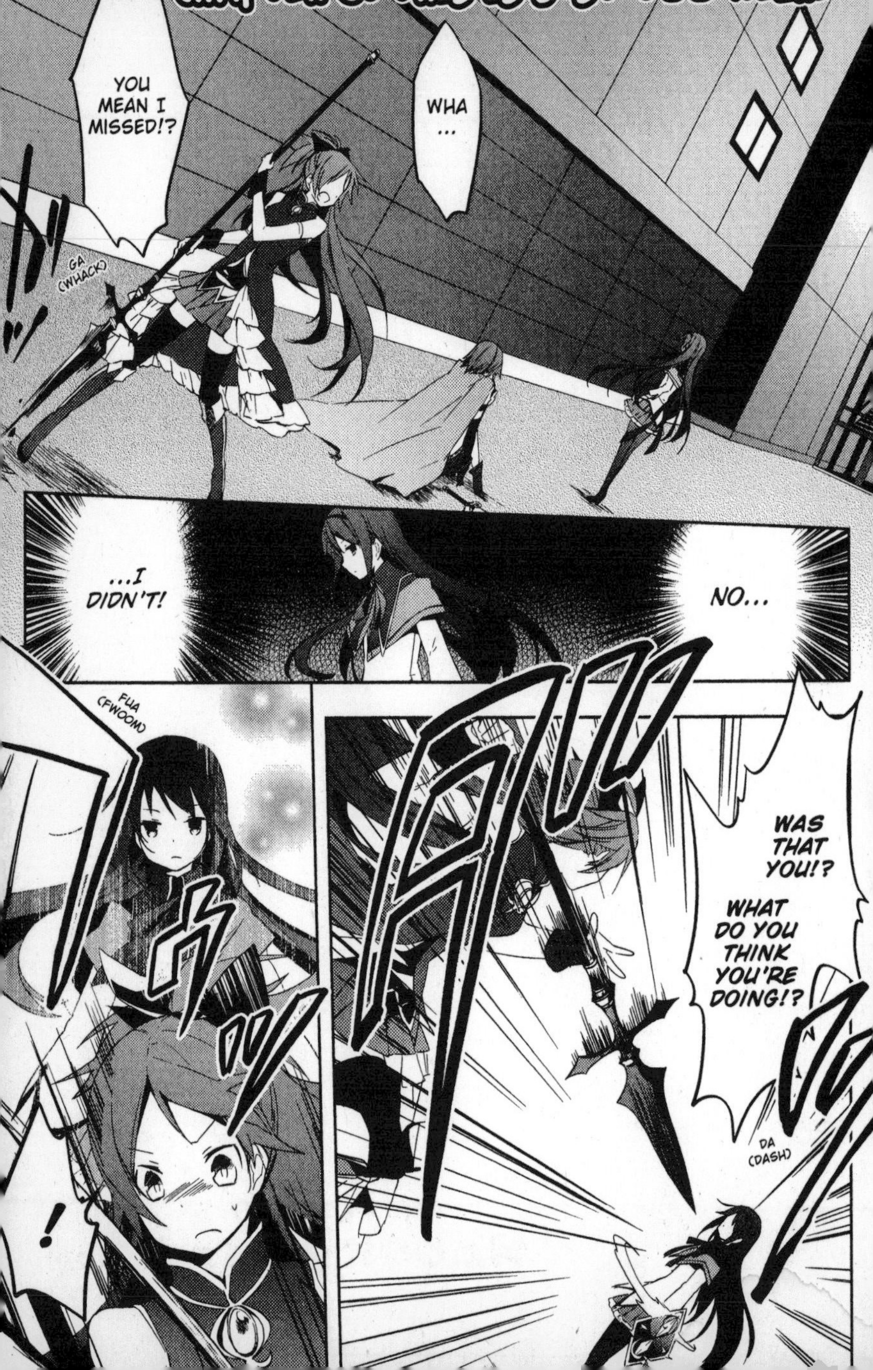
WHA...
YOU MEAN I MISSED!?
GA (WHACK)
NO...
...I DIDN'T!
WAS THAT YOU!?
WHAT DO YOU THINK YOU'RE DOING!?
DA (DASH)
FUA (FWOOM)
!

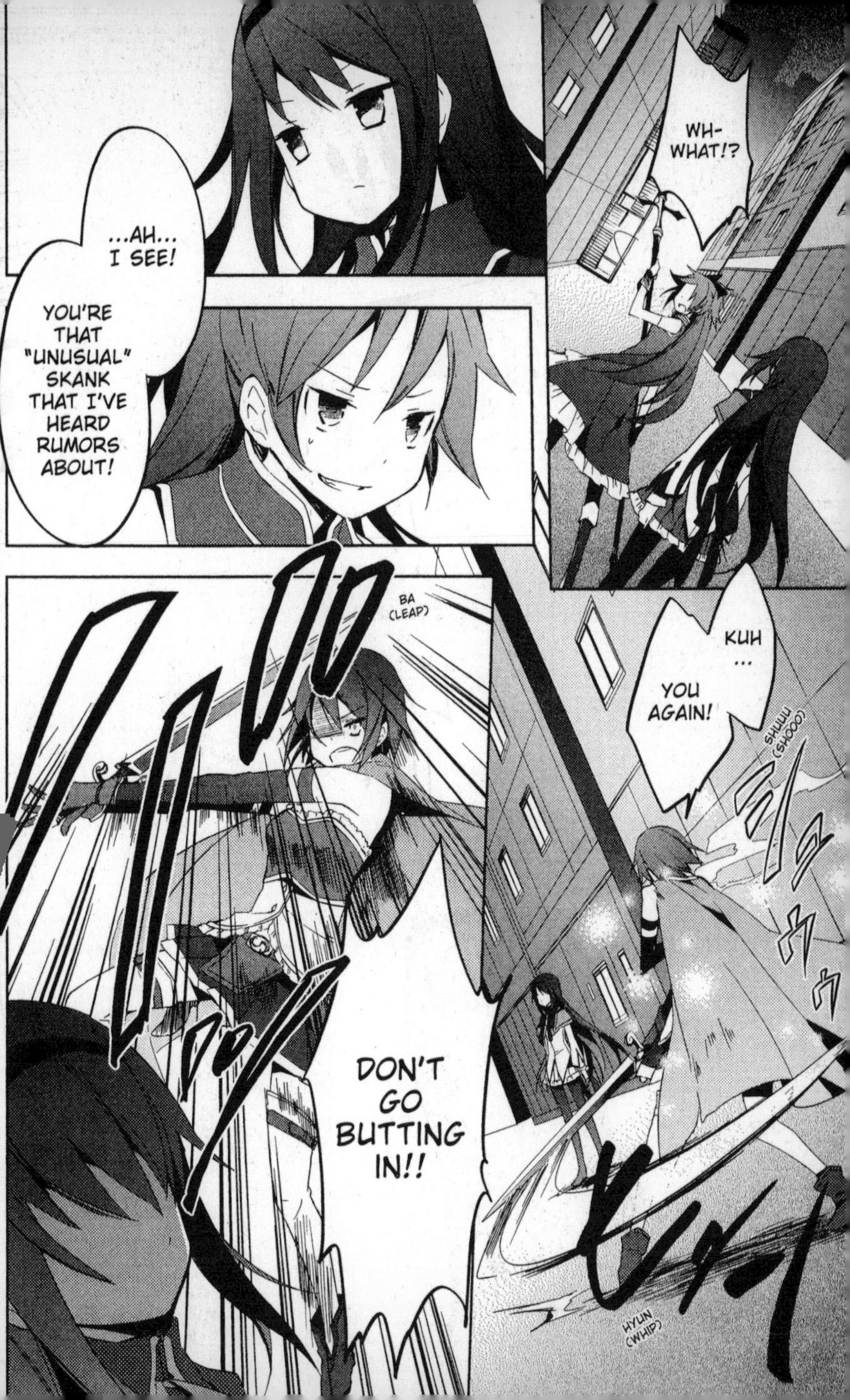
WH-WHAT!?
...AH... I SEE!
YOU'RE THAT "UNUSUAL" SKANK THAT I'VE HEARD RUMORS ABOUT!
KUH ... YOU AGAIN!
SHUUU (SHOOO)
HYUN (WHIP)
BA (LEAP)
DON'T GO BUTTING IN!!

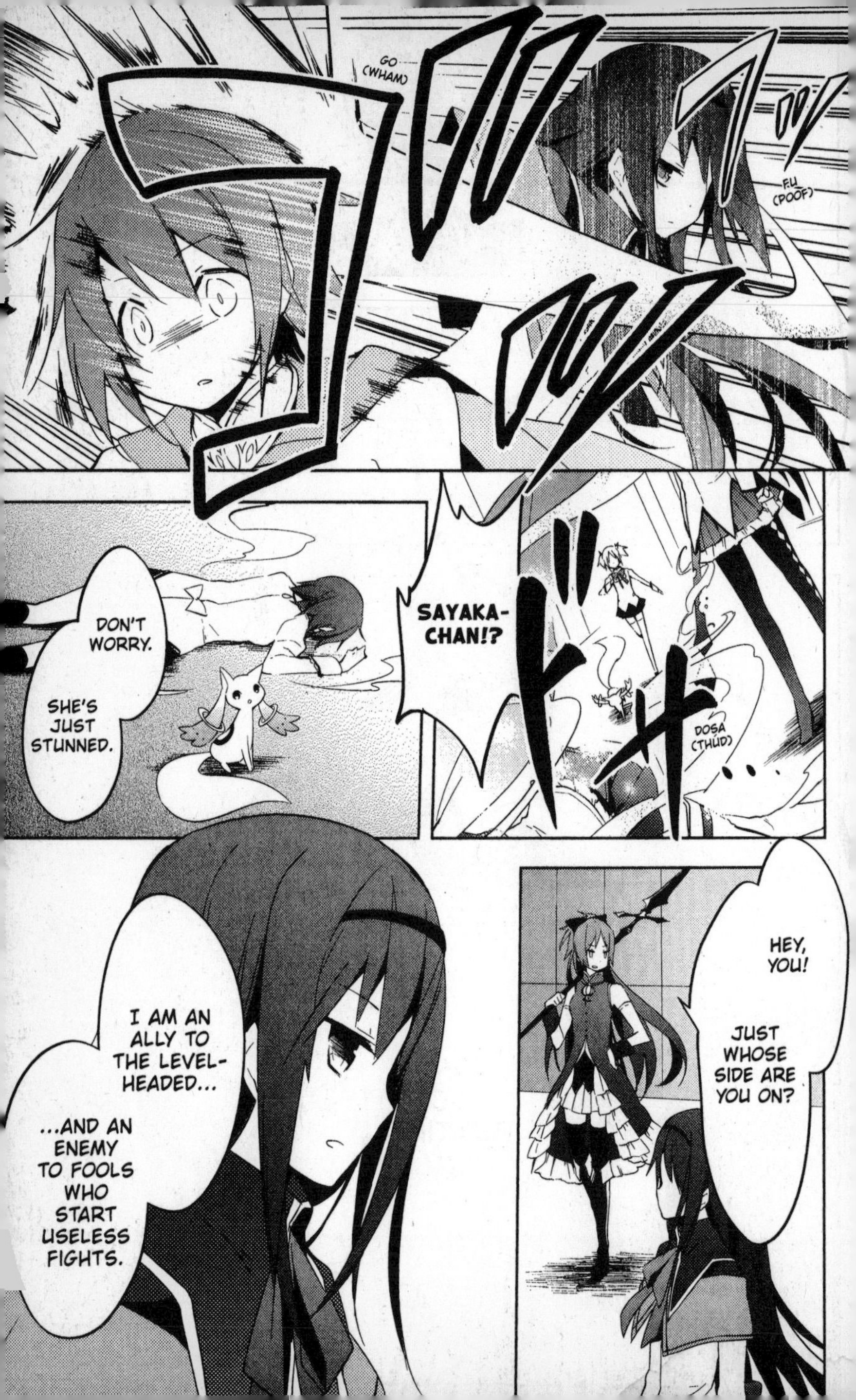
GO (WHAM)
FU (POOF)
DOSA (THUD)
...
SAYAKA-CHAN!?
DON'T WORRY.
SHE'S JUST STUNNED.
HEY, YOU!
JUST WHOSE SIDE ARE YOU ON?
I AM AN ALLY TO THE LEVEL-HEADED...
...AND AN ENEMY TO FOOLS WHO START USELESS FIGHTS.

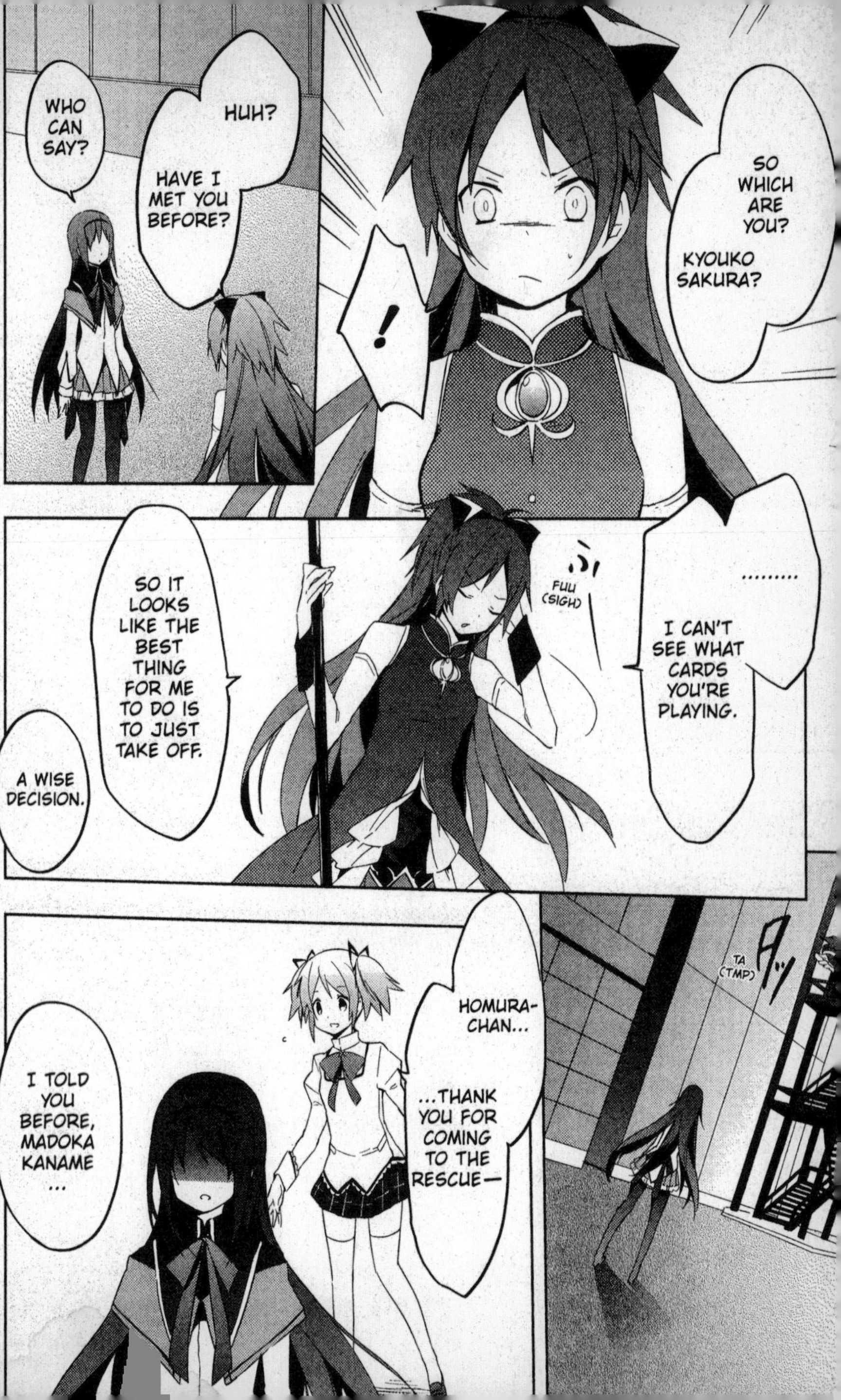
SO WHICH ARE YOU?
KYOUKO SAKURA?
!
HUH?
HAVE I MET YOU BEFORE?
WHO CAN SAY?
....
I CAN'T SEE WHAT CARDS YOU'RE PLAYING.
FUU (SIGH)
SO IT LOOKS LIKE THE BEST THING FOR ME TO DO IS TO JUST TAKE OFF.
A WISE DECISION.
TA (TMP)
HOMURA-CHAN...
...THANK YOU FOR COMING TO THE RESCUE—
I TOLD YOU BEFORE, MADOKA KANAME ...

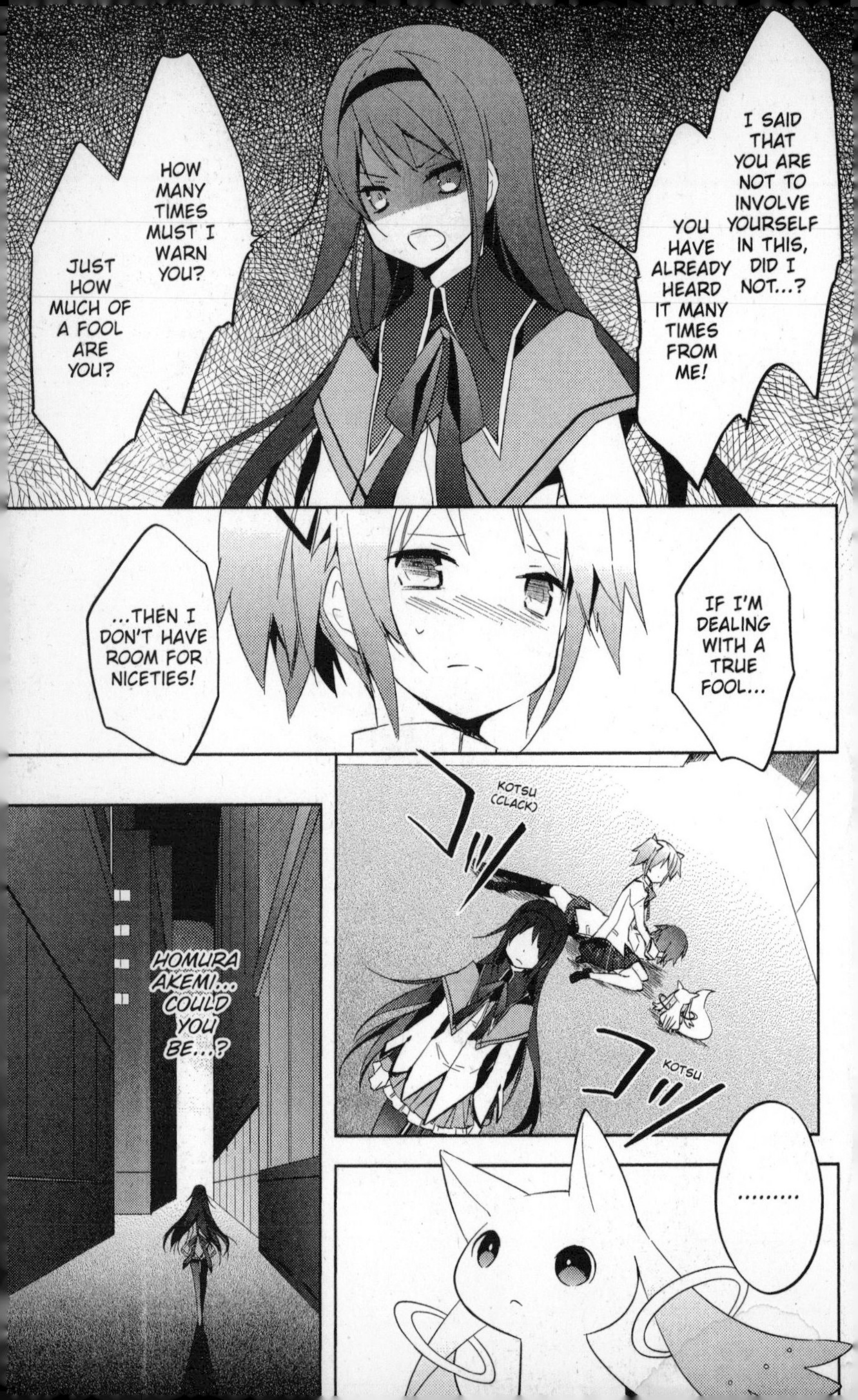
I SAID THAT YOU ARE NOT TO INVOLVE YOURSELF IN THIS, DID I NOT...?
YOU HAVE ALREADY HEARD IT MANY TIMES FROM ME!
HOW MANY TIMES MUST I WARN YOU?
JUST HOW MUCH OF A FOOL ARE YOU?
IF I'M DEALING WITH A TRUE FOOL...
...THEN I DON'T HAVE ROOM FOR NICETIES!
コッ
KOTSU (CLACK)
コッ
KOTSU
....
HOMURA AKEMI... COULD YOU BE...?

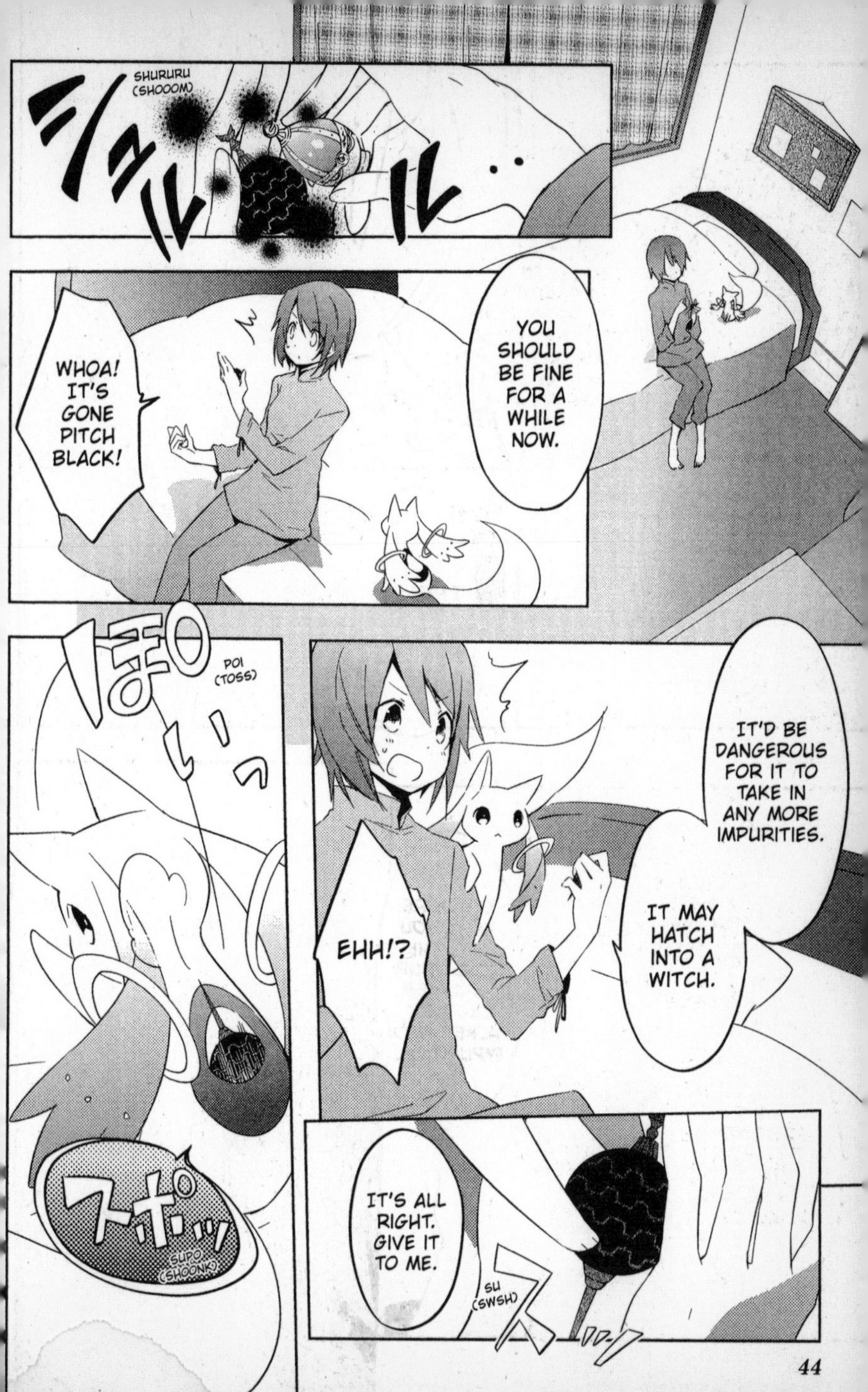
SHURURU (SHOOOM)
YOU SHOULD BE FINE FOR A WHILE NOW.
WHOA! IT'S GONE PITCH BLACK!
IT'D BE DANGEROUS FOR IT TO TAKE IN ANY MORE IMPURITIES.
IT MAY HATCH INTO A WITCH.
EHH!?
IT'S ALL RIGHT. GIVE IT TO ME.
SU (SWSH)
POI (TOSS)
SUPO (SHOONK)

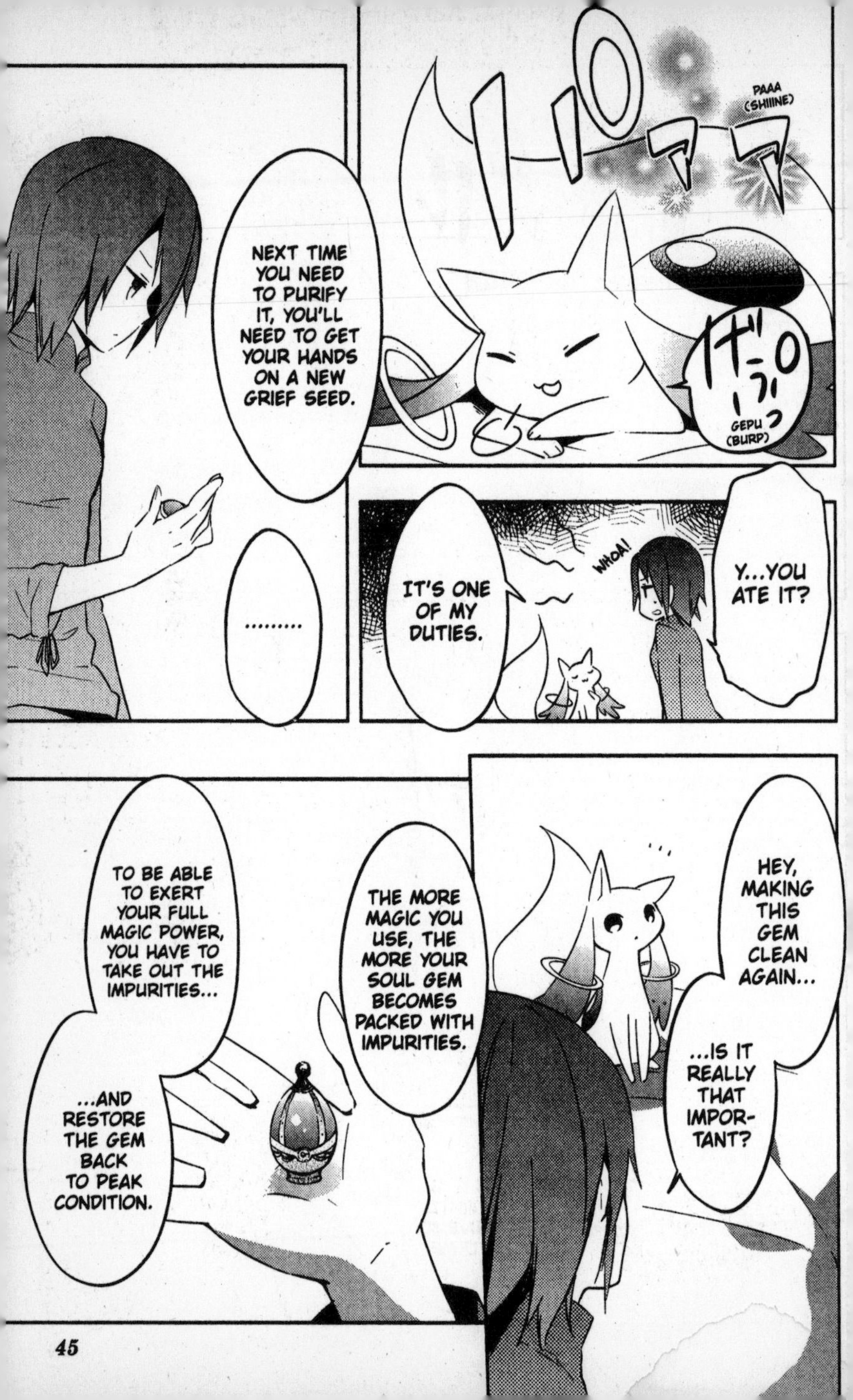
PAAA (SHIIINE)
GEPU (BURP)
Y...YOU ATE IT?
WHOA!
IT'S ONE OF MY DUTIES.
NEXT TIME YOU NEED TO PURIFY IT, YOU'LL NEED TO GET YOUR HANDS ON A NEW GRIEF SEED.
....
HEY, MAKING THIS GEM CLEAN AGAIN...
...IS IT REALLY THAT IMPOR-TANT?
THE MORE MAGIC YOU USE, THE MORE YOUR SOUL GEM BECOMES PACKED WITH IMPURITIES.
TO BE ABLE TO EXERT YOUR FULL MAGIC POWER, YOU HAVE TO TAKE OUT THE IMPURITIES...
...AND RESTORE THE GEM BACK TO PEAK CONDITION.

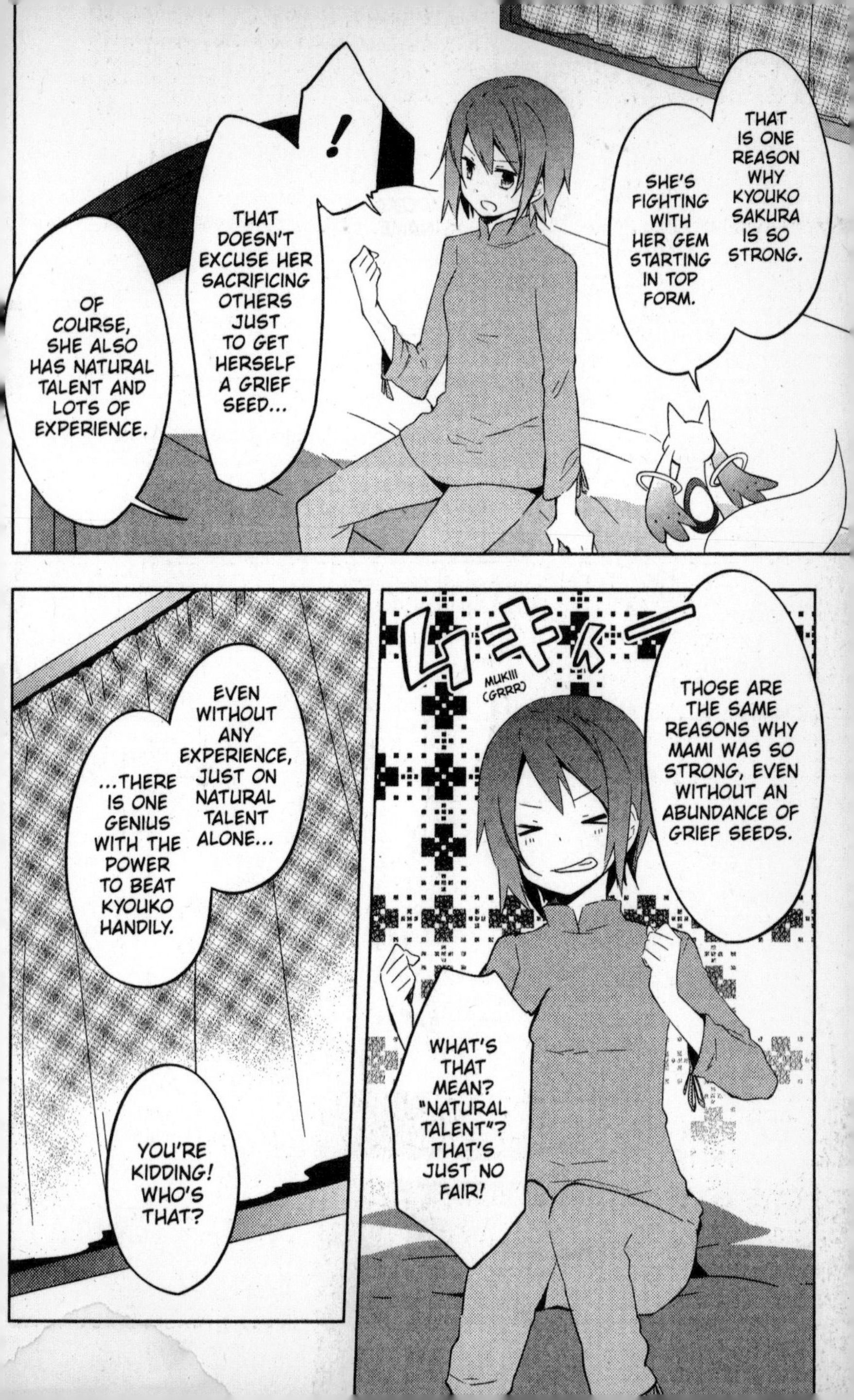

THAT IS ONE REASON WHY KYOUKO SAKURA IS SO STRONG.
SHE'S FIGHTING WITH HER GEM STARTING IN TOP FORM.
!
THAT DOESN'T EXCUSE HER SACRIFICING OTHERS JUST TO GET HERSELF A GRIEF SEED...
OF COURSE, SHE ALSO HAS NATURAL TALENT AND LOTS OF EXPERIENCE.
THOSE ARE THE SAME REASONS WHY MAMI WAS SO STRONG, EVEN WITHOUT AN ABUNDANCE OF GRIEF SEEDS.
ムキィー
MUKIII (GRRR)
WHAT'S THAT MEAN? "NATURAL TALENT"? THAT'S JUST NO FAIR!
EVEN WITHOUT ANY EXPERIENCE, JUST ON NATURAL TALENT ALONE...
...THERE IS ONE GENIUS WITH THE POWER TO BEAT KYOUKO HANDILY.
YOU'RE KIDDING! WHO'S THAT?

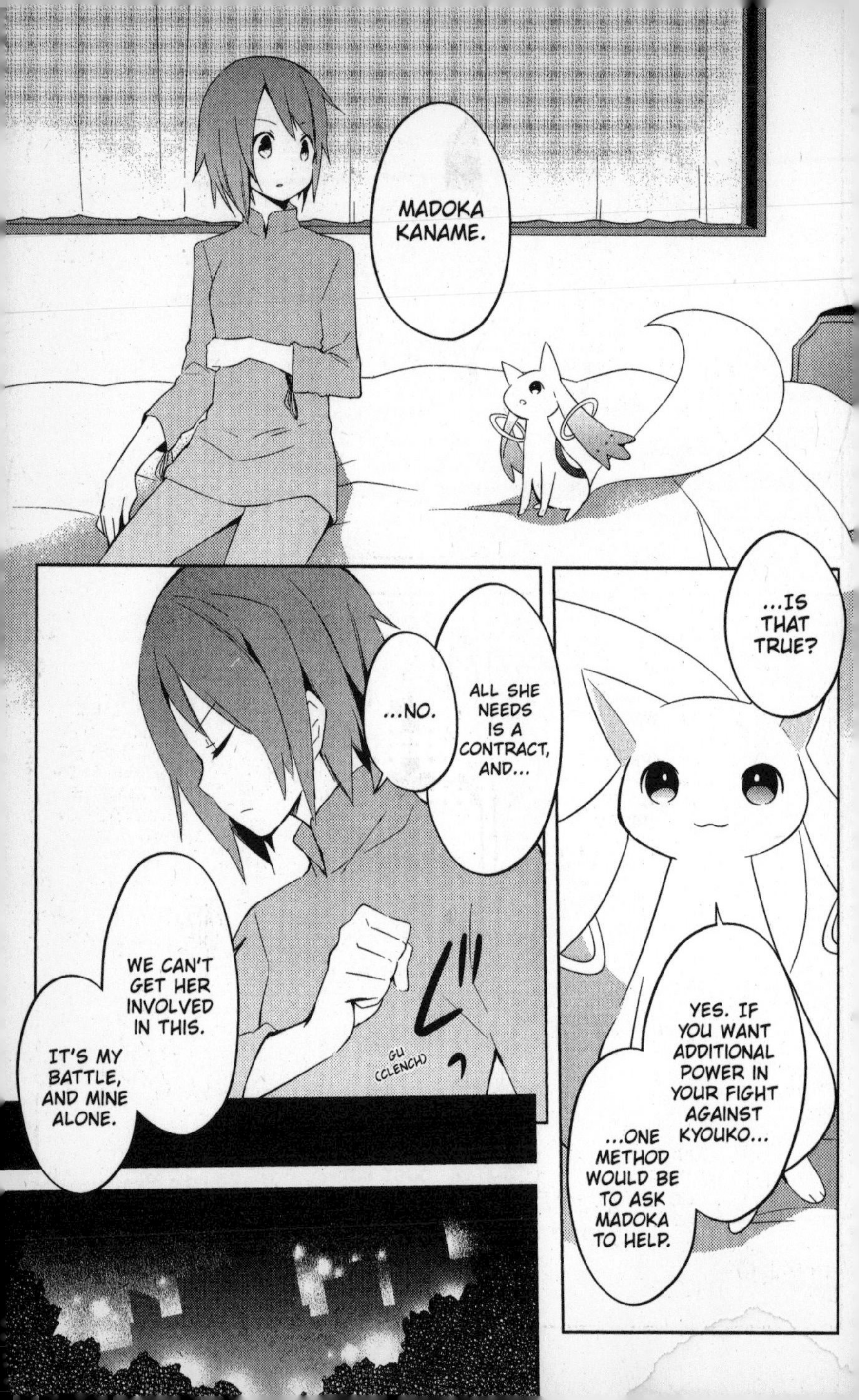
MADOKA KANAME.
...IS THAT TRUE?
YES. IF YOU WANT ADDITIONAL POWER IN YOUR FIGHT AGAINST KYOUKO...
...ONE METHOD WOULD BE TO ASK MADOKA TO HELP.
ALL SHE NEEDS IS A CONTRACT, AND...
...NO.
WE CAN'T GET HER INVOLVED IN THIS.
IT'S MY BATTLE, AND MINE ALONE.
GU (CLENCH)

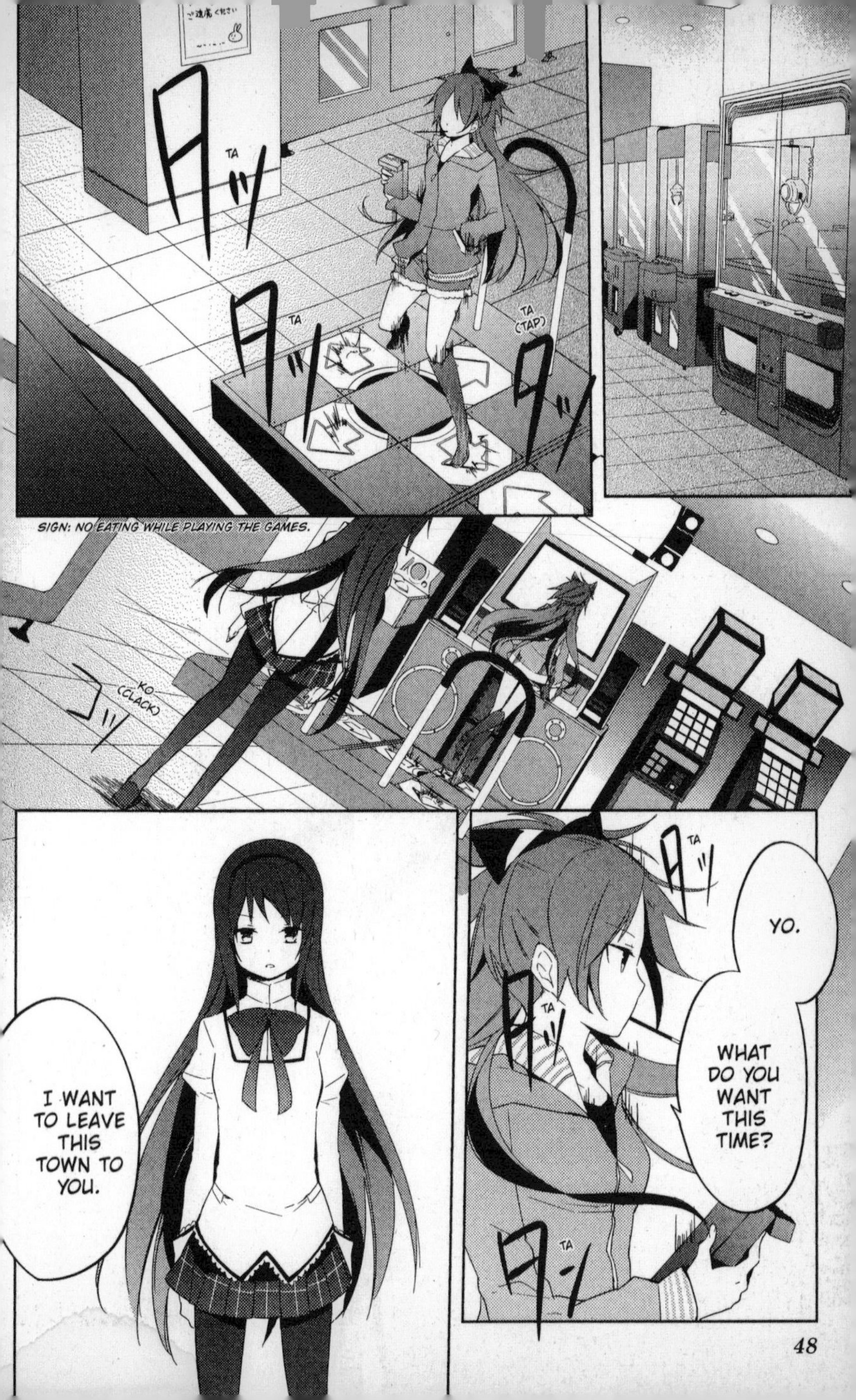
TA
TA
TA (TAP)
SIGN: NO EATING WHILE PLAYING THE GAMES.
KO (CLACK)
TA
YO.
TA
WHAT DO YOU WANT THIS TIME?
TA
I WANT TO LEAVE THIS TOWN TO YOU.

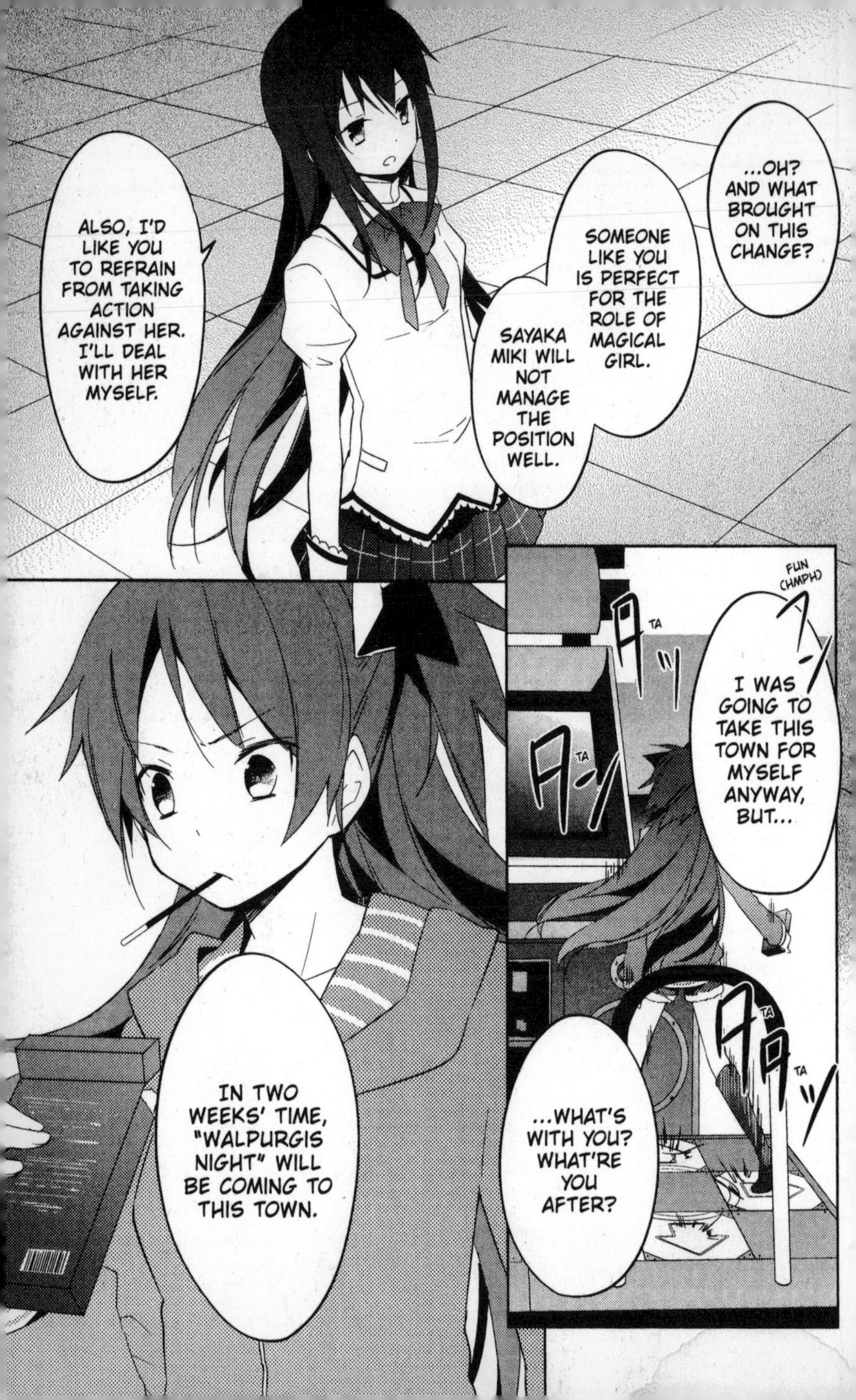
...OH? AND WHAT BROUGHT ON THIS CHANGE?
SOMEONE LIKE YOU IS PERFECT FOR THE ROLE OF MAGICAL GIRL.
SAYAKA MIKI WILL NOT MANAGE THE POSITION WELL.
ALSO, I'D LIKE YOU TO REFRAIN FROM TAKING ACTION AGAINST HER. I'LL DEAL WITH HER MYSELF.
FUN (HMPH)
I WAS GOING TO TAKE THIS TOWN FOR MYSELF ANYWAY, BUT...
TA
TA
TA
TA
...WHAT'S WITH YOU? WHAT'RE YOU AFTER?
IN TWO WEEKS' TIME, "WALPURGIS NIGHT" WILL BE COMING TO THIS TOWN.

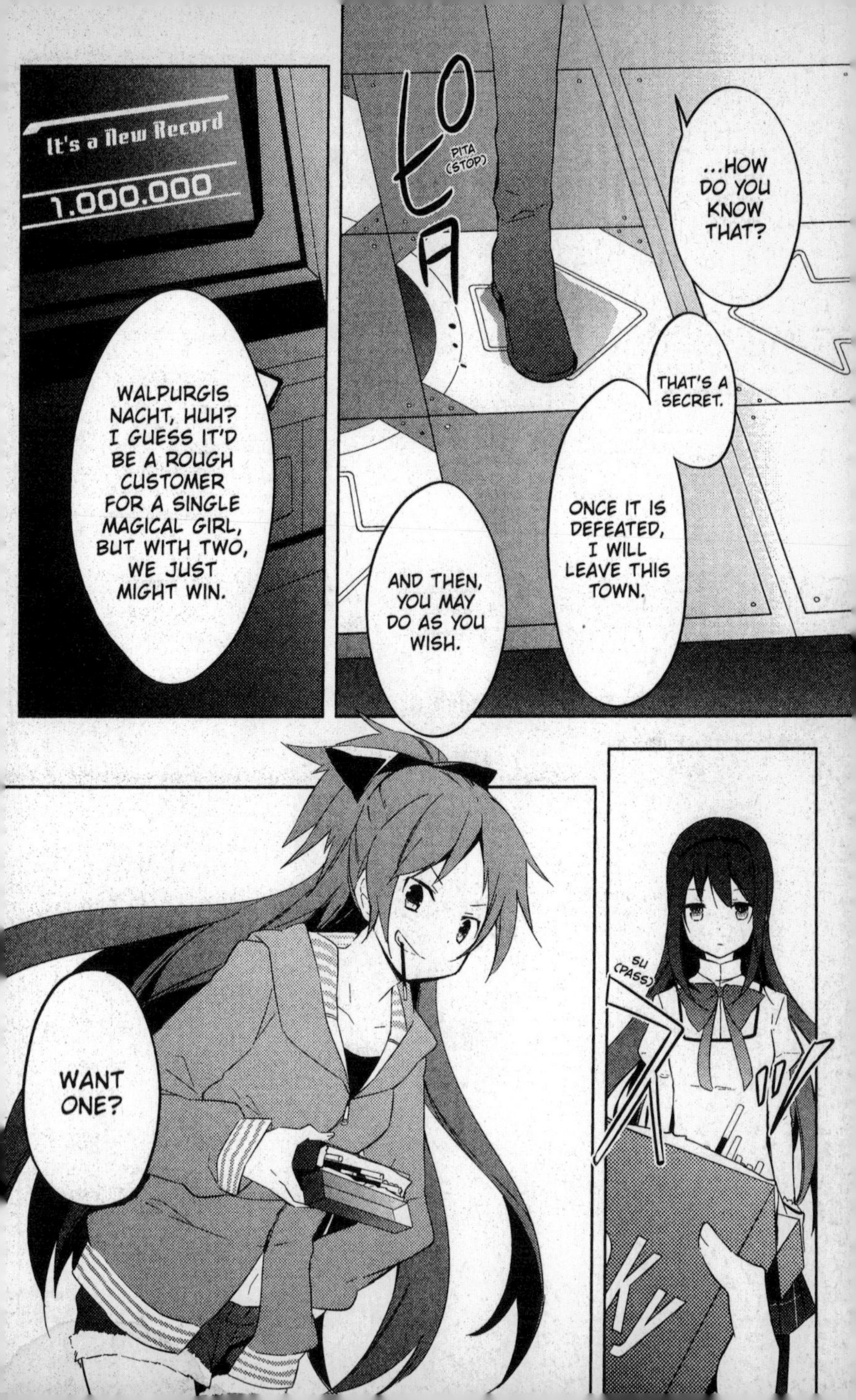
…HOW DO YOU KNOW THAT?
PITA (STOP)
THAT'S A SECRET.
ONCE IT IS DEFEATED, I WILL LEAVE THIS TOWN.
AND THEN, YOU MAY DO AS YOU WISH.
It's a New Record
1.000.000
WALPURGIS NACHT, HUH? I GUESS IT'D BE A ROUGH CUSTOMER FOR A SINGLE MAGICAL GIRL, BUT WITH TWO, WE JUST MIGHT WIN.
SU (PASS)
WANT ONE?

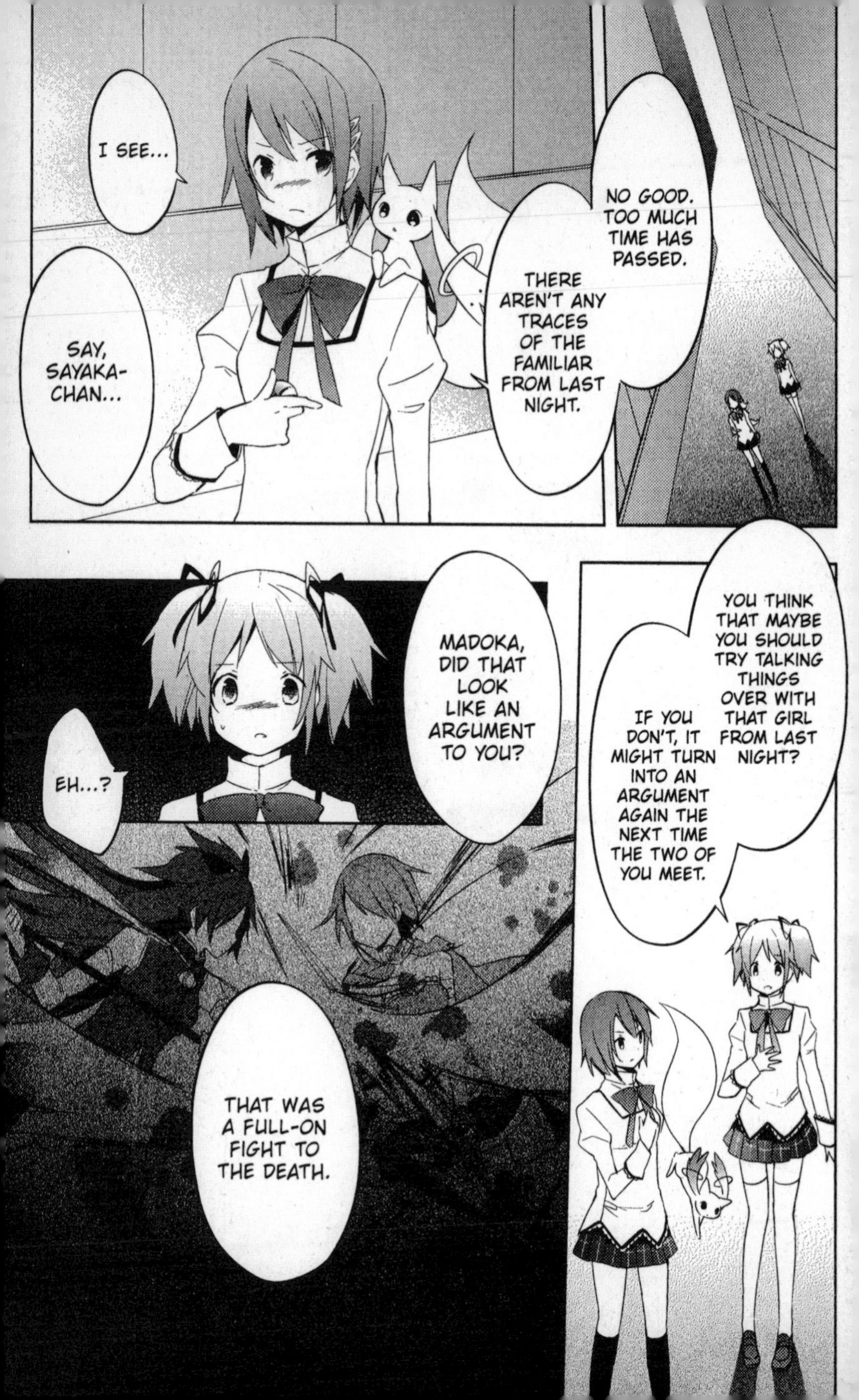
NO GOOD. TOO MUCH TIME HAS PASSED.
THERE AREN'T ANY TRACES OF THE FAMILIAR FROM LAST NIGHT.
I SEE...
SAY, SAYAKA-CHAN...
YOU THINK THAT MAYBE YOU SHOULD TRY TALKING THINGS OVER WITH THAT GIRL FROM LAST NIGHT?
IF YOU DON'T, IT MIGHT TURN INTO AN ARGUMENT AGAIN THE NEXT TIME THE TWO OF YOU MEET.
MADOKA, DID THAT LOOK LIKE AN ARGUMENT TO YOU?
EH...?
THAT WAS A FULL-ON FIGHT TO THE DEATH.

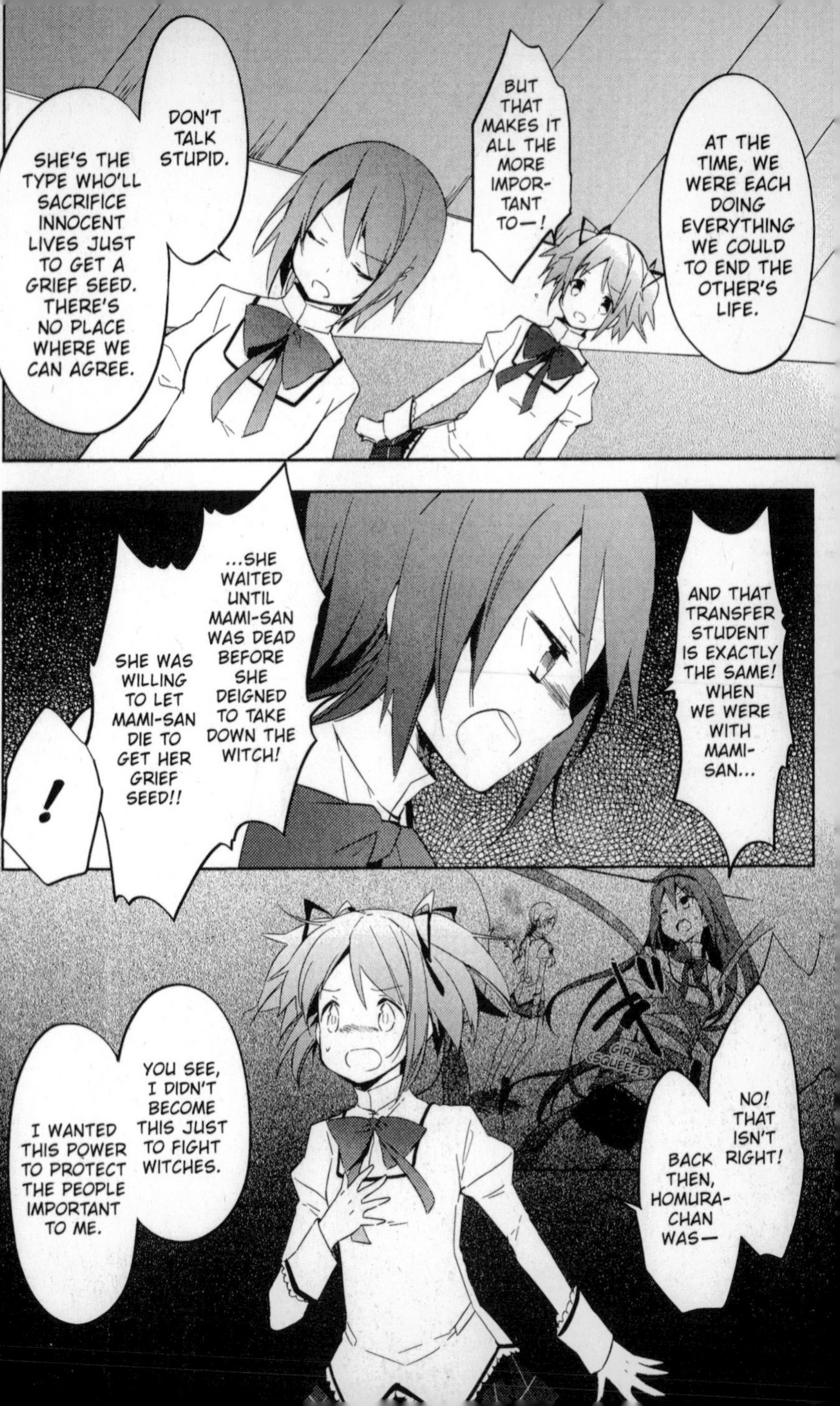
AT THE TIME, WE WERE EACH DOING EVERYTHING WE COULD TO END THE OTHER'S LIFE.
BUT THAT MAKES IT ALL THE MORE IMPORTANT TO—!
DON'T TALK STUPID.
SHE'S THE TYPE WHO'LL SACRIFICE INNOCENT LIVES JUST TO GET A GRIEF SEED. THERE'S NO PLACE WHERE WE CAN AGREE.
AND THAT TRANSFER STUDENT IS EXACTLY THE SAME! WHEN WE WERE WITH MAMI-SAN...
...SHE WAITED UNTIL MAMI-SAN WAS DEAD BEFORE SHE DEIGNED TO TAKE DOWN THE WITCH!
SHE WAS WILLING TO LET MAMI-SAN DIE TO GET HER GRIEF SEED!!
!
NO! THAT ISN'T RIGHT!
BACK THEN, HOMURA-CHAN WAS—
GIRI (SQUEEZE)
YOU SEE, I DIDN'T BECOME THIS JUST TO FIGHT WITCHES.
I WANTED THIS POWER TO PROTECT THE PEOPLE IMPORTANT TO ME.

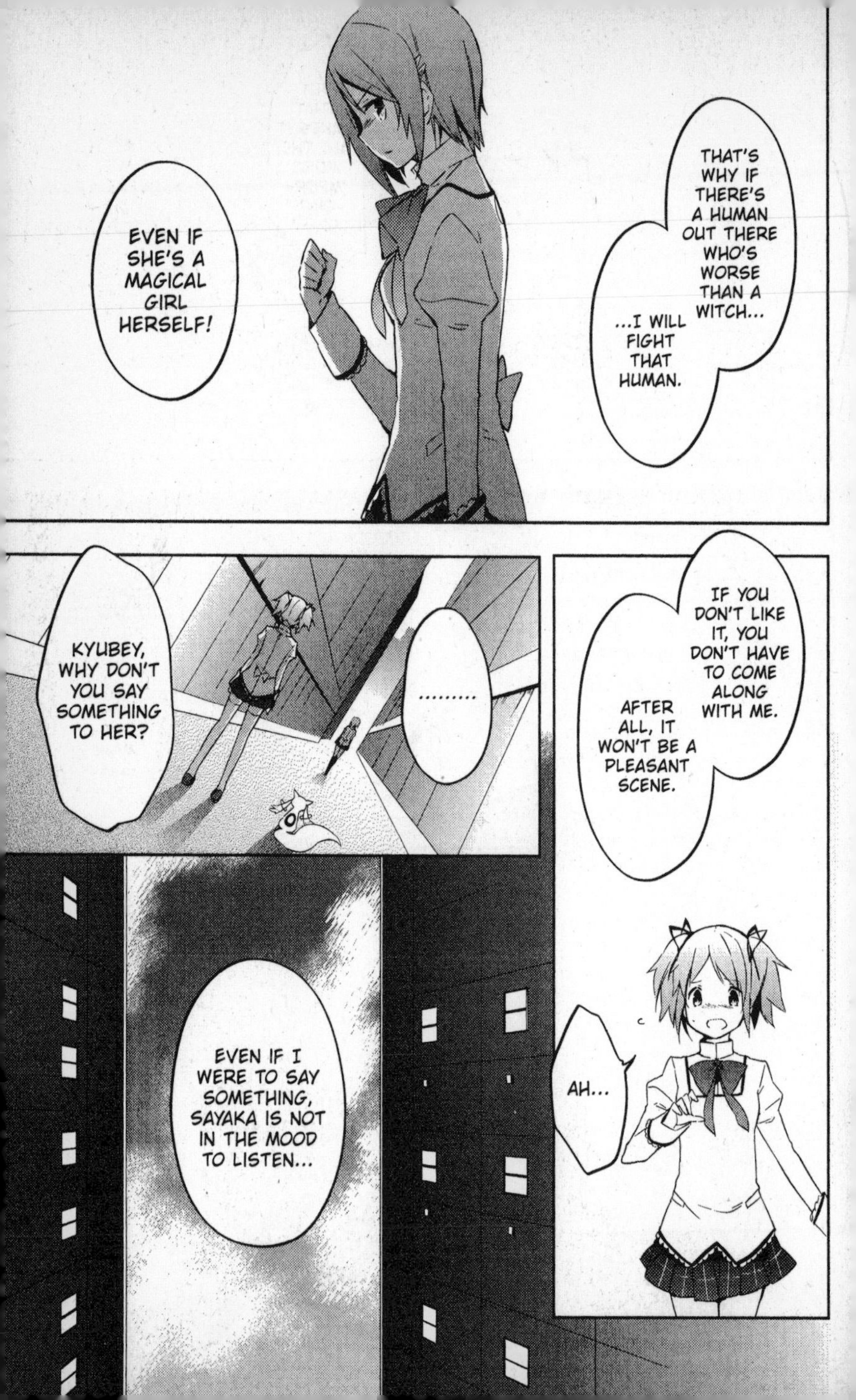
THAT'S WHY IF THERE'S A HUMAN OUT THERE WHO'S WORSE THAN A WITCH...
...I WILL FIGHT THAT HUMAN.
EVEN IF SHE'S A MAGICAL GIRL HERSELF!
IF YOU DON'T LIKE IT, YOU DON'T HAVE TO COME ALONG WITH ME.
AFTER ALL, IT WON'T BE A PLEASANT SCENE.
AH...
....
KYUBEY, WHY DON'T YOU SAY SOMETHING TO HER?
EVEN IF I WERE TO SAY SOMETHING, SAYAKA IS NOT IN THE MOOD TO LISTEN...

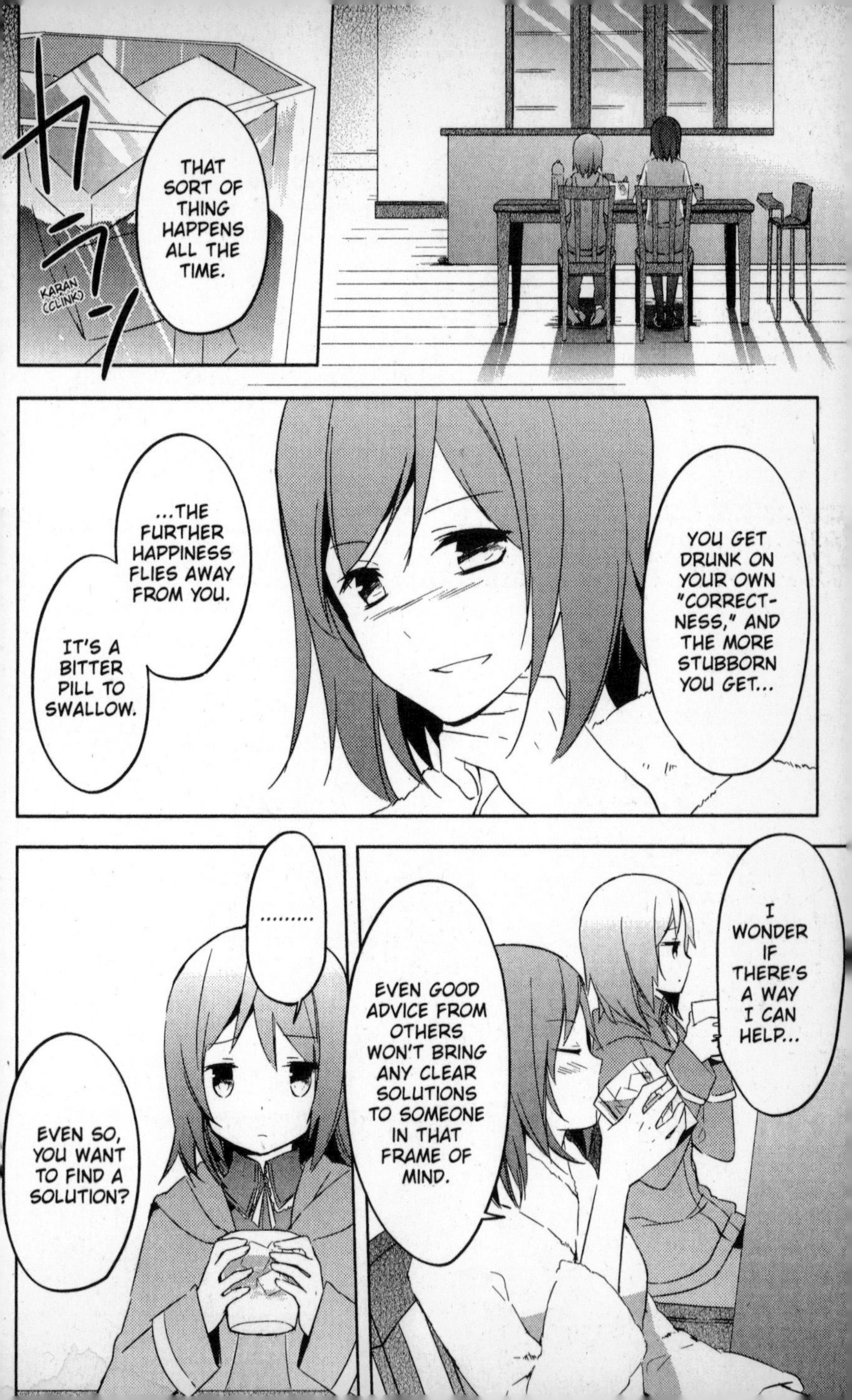

THAT SORT OF THING HAPPENS ALL THE TIME.
KARAN (CLINK)
YOU GET DRUNK ON YOUR OWN "CORRECTNESS," AND THE MORE STUBBORN YOU GET...
...THE FURTHER HAPPINESS FLIES AWAY FROM YOU.
IT'S A BITTER PILL TO SWALLOW.
I WONDER IF THERE'S A WAY I CAN HELP...
EVEN GOOD ADVICE FROM OTHERS WON'T BRING ANY CLEAR SOLUTIONS TO SOMEONE IN THAT FRAME OF MIND.
....
EVEN SO, YOU WANT TO FIND A SOLUTION?

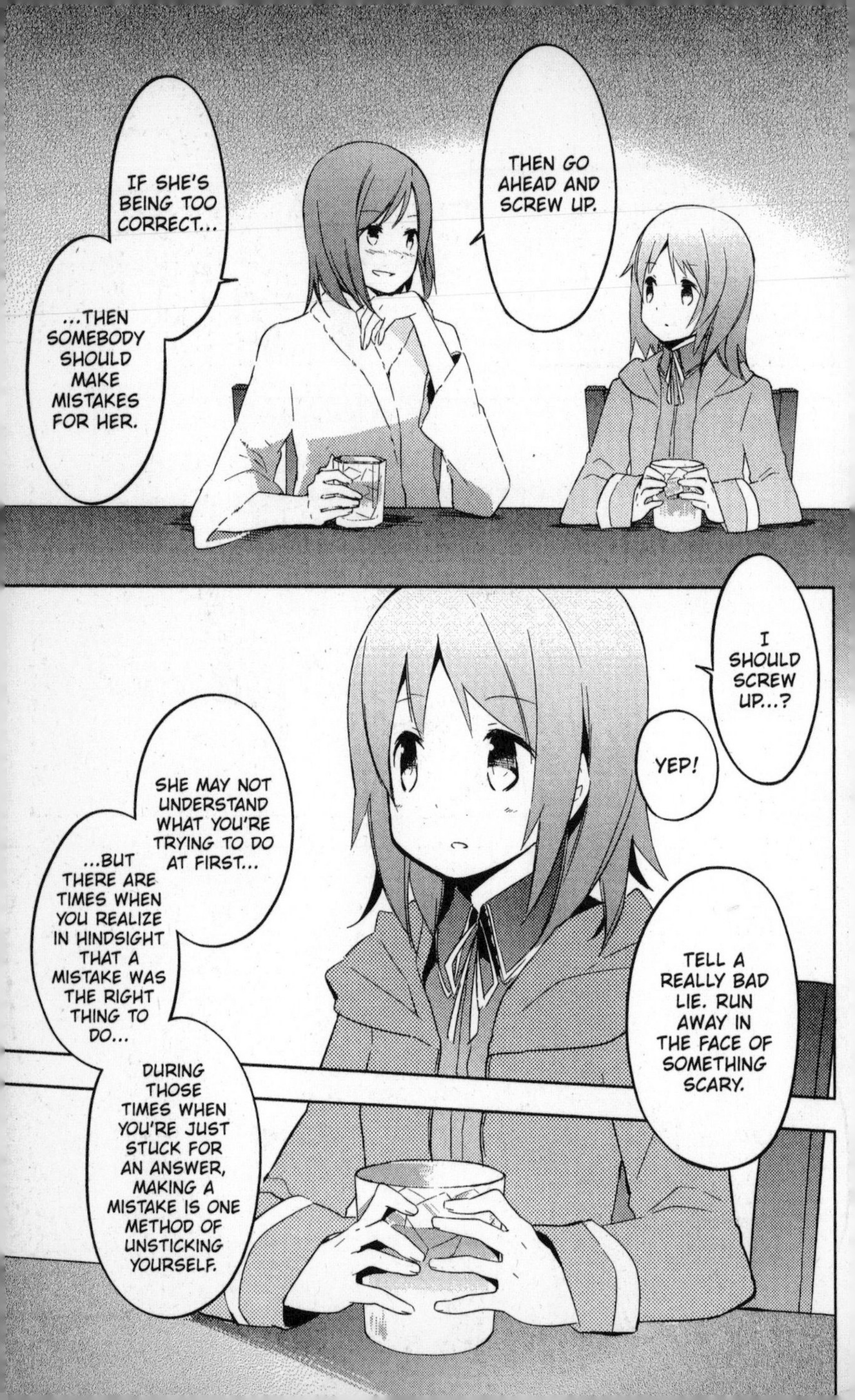
THEN GO AHEAD AND SCREW UP.
IF SHE'S BEING TOO CORRECT...
...THEN SOMEBODY SHOULD MAKE MISTAKES FOR HER.
I SHOULD SCREW UP...?
YEP!
TELL A REALLY BAD LIE. RUN AWAY IN THE FACE OF SOMETHING SCARY.
SHE MAY NOT UNDERSTAND WHAT YOU'RE TRYING TO DO AT FIRST...
...BUT THERE ARE TIMES WHEN YOU REALIZE IN HINDSIGHT THAT A MISTAKE WAS THE RIGHT THING TO DO...
DURING THOSE TIMES WHEN YOU'RE JUST STUCK FOR AN ANSWER, MAKING A MISTAKE IS ONE METHOD OF UNSTICKING YOURSELF.

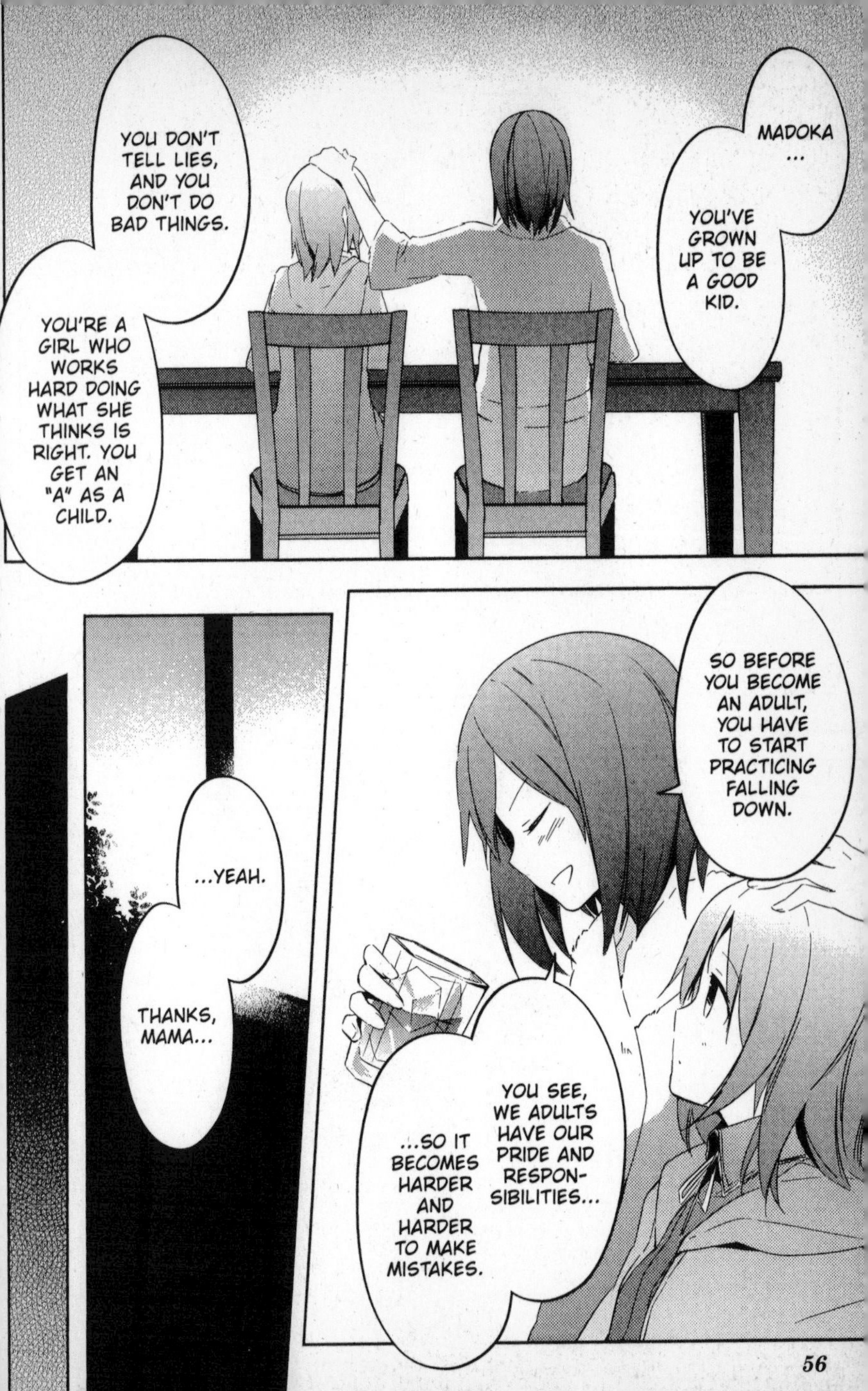
MADOKA ...
YOU'VE GROWN UP TO BE A GOOD KID.
YOU DON'T TELL LIES, AND YOU DON'T DO BAD THINGS.
YOU'RE A GIRL WHO WORKS HARD DOING WHAT SHE THINKS IS RIGHT. YOU GET AN "A" AS A CHILD.
SO BEFORE YOU BECOME AN ADULT, YOU HAVE TO START PRACTICING FALLING DOWN.
YOU SEE, WE ADULTS HAVE OUR PRIDE AND RESPON-SIBILITIES...
...SO IT BECOMES HARDER AND HARDER TO MAKE MISTAKES.
...YEAH.
THANKS, MAMA...

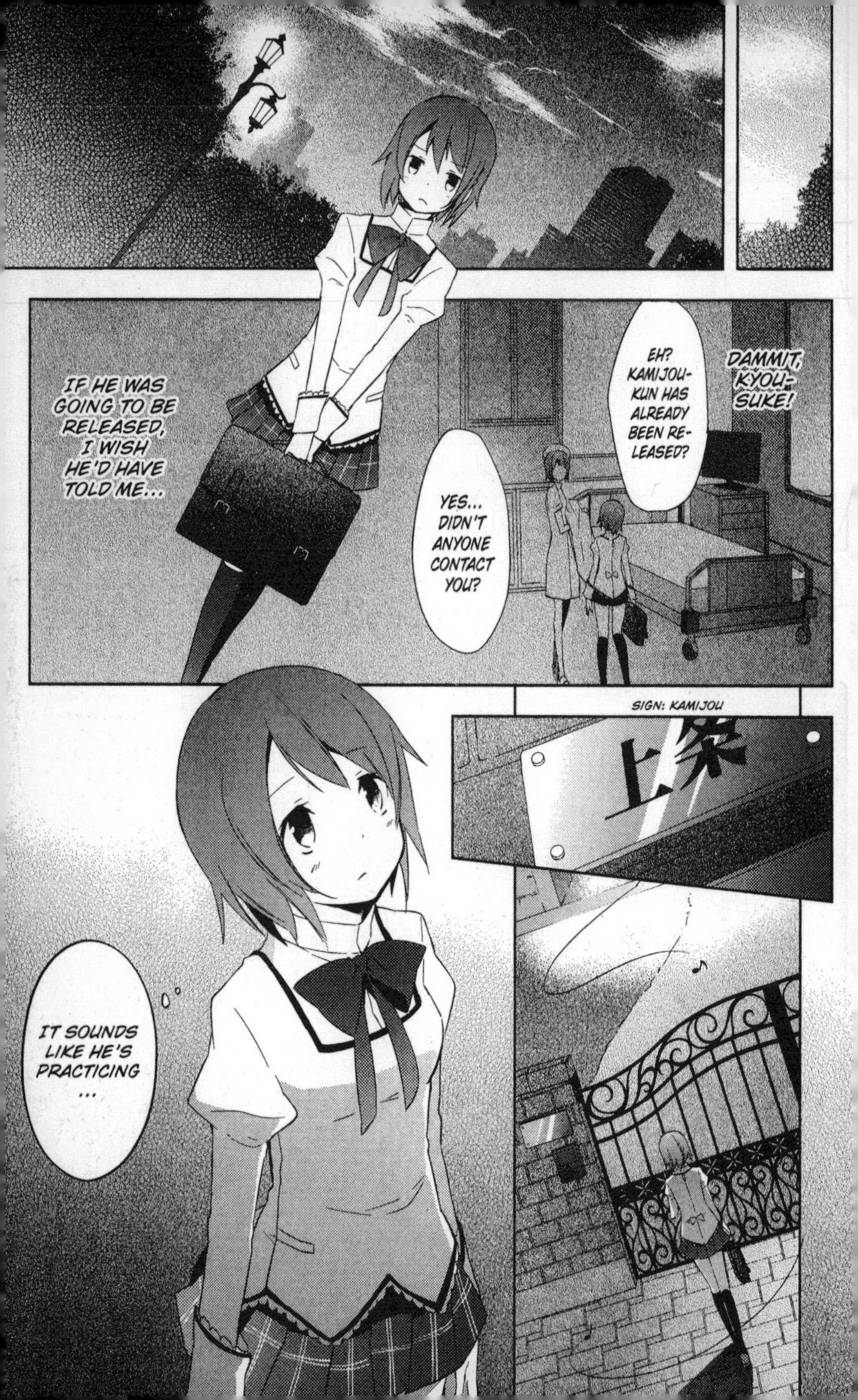
DAMMIT, KYOU-SUKE!
EH? KAMIJOU-KUN HAS ALREADY BEEN RE-LEASED?
YES... DIDN'T ANYONE CONTACT YOU?
IF HE WAS GOING TO BE RELEASED, I WISH HE'D HAVE TOLD ME...
SIGN: KAMIJOU
上条
IT SOUNDS LIKE HE'S PRACTICING ...

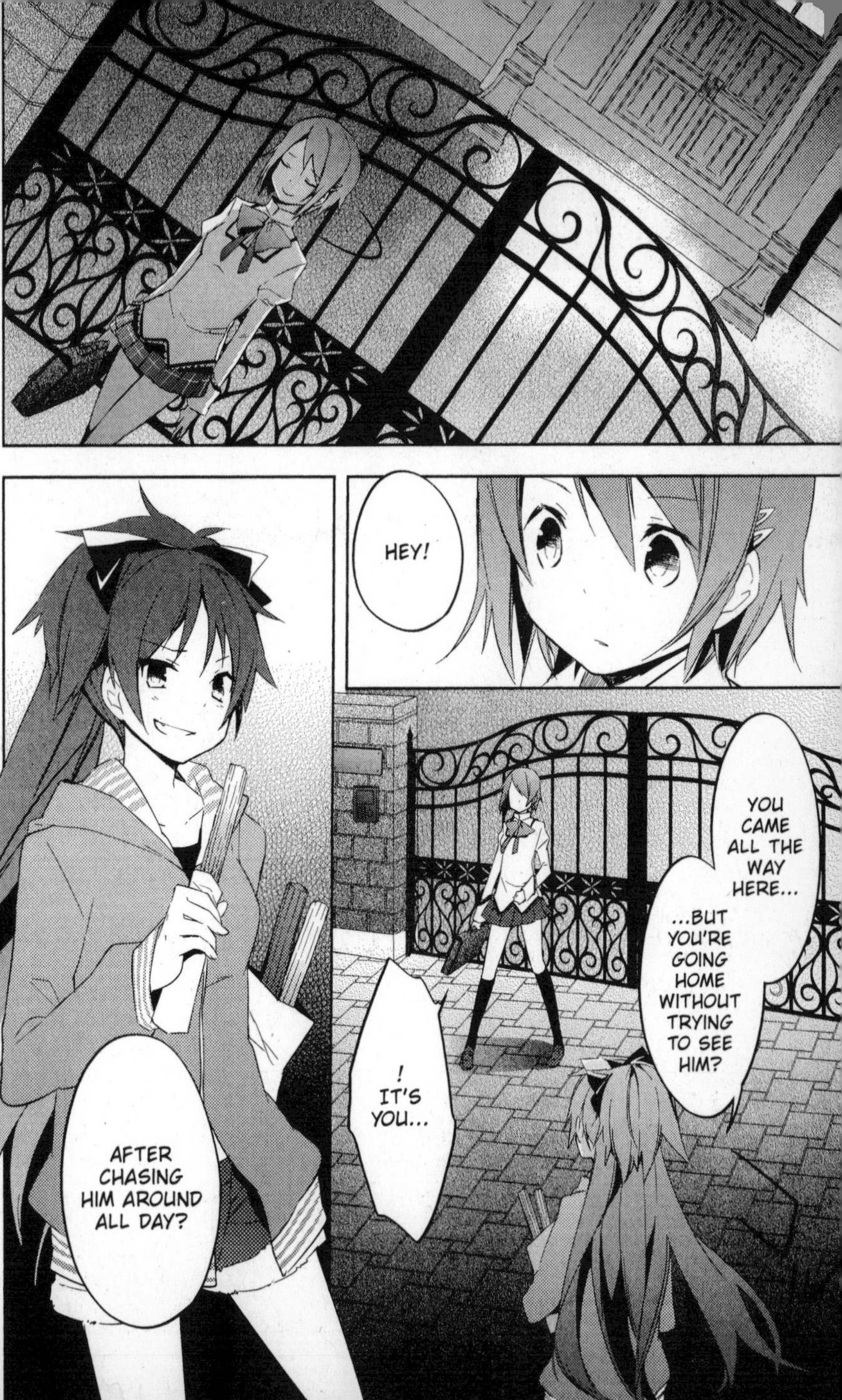
HEY!
YOU CAME ALL THE WAY HERE...
...BUT YOU'RE GOING HOME WITHOUT TRYING TO SEE HIM?
! IT'S YOU...
AFTER CHASING HIM AROUND ALL DAY?

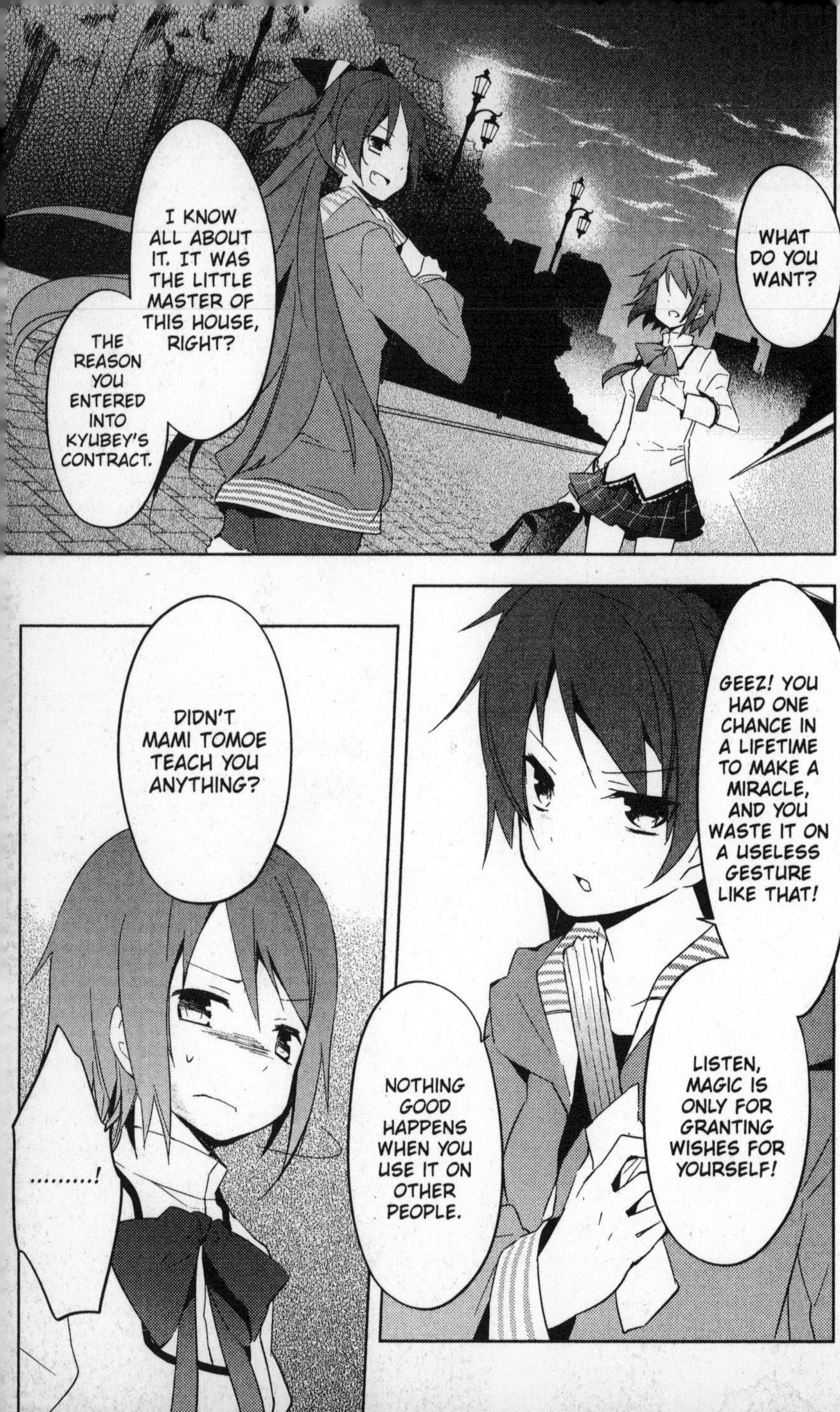
WHAT DO YOU WANT?
I KNOW ALL ABOUT IT. IT WAS THE LITTLE MASTER OF THIS HOUSE, RIGHT?
THE REASON YOU ENTERED INTO KYUBEY'S CONTRACT.
GEEZ! YOU HAD ONE CHANCE IN A LIFETIME TO MAKE A MIRACLE, AND YOU WASTE IT ON A USELESS GESTURE LIKE THAT!
LISTEN, MAGIC IS ONLY FOR GRANTING WISHES FOR YOURSELF!
NOTHING GOOD HAPPENS WHEN YOU USE IT ON OTHER PEOPLE.
DIDN'T MAMI TOMOE TEACH YOU ANYTHING?
.........!

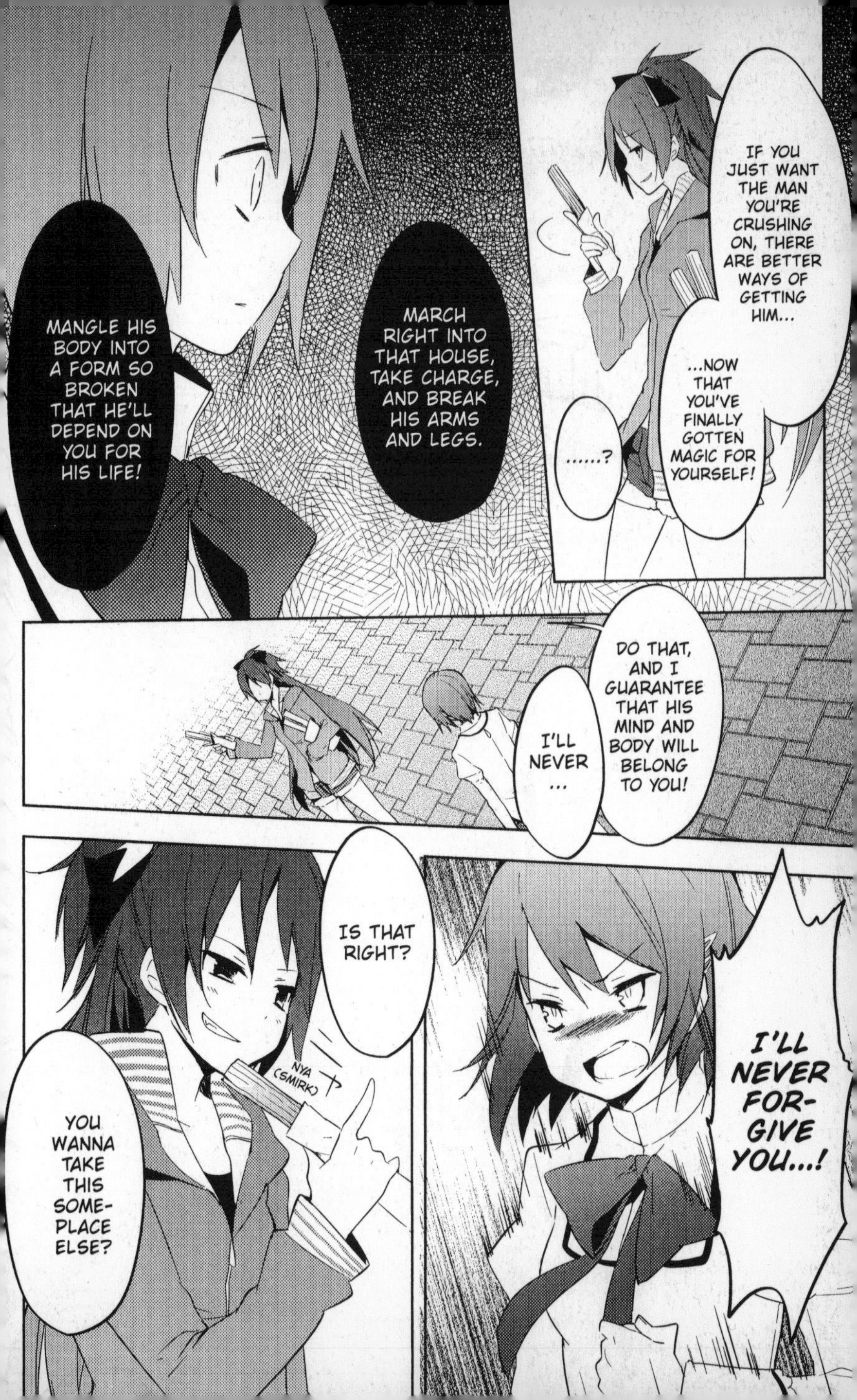
IF YOU JUST WANT THE MAN YOU'RE CRUSHING ON, THERE ARE BETTER WAYS OF GETTING HIM...
...NOW THAT YOU'VE FINALLY GOTTEN MAGIC FOR YOURSELF!
......?
MARCH RIGHT INTO THAT HOUSE, TAKE CHARGE, AND BREAK HIS ARMS AND LEGS.
MANGLE HIS BODY INTO A FORM SO BROKEN THAT HE'LL DEPEND ON YOU FOR HIS LIFE!
DO THAT, AND I GUARANTEE THAT HIS MIND AND BODY WILL BELONG TO YOU!
I'LL NEVER ...
I'LL NEVER FOR-GIVE YOU...!
IS THAT RIGHT?
NYA (SMIRK)
YOU WANNA TAKE THIS SOME-PLACE ELSE?

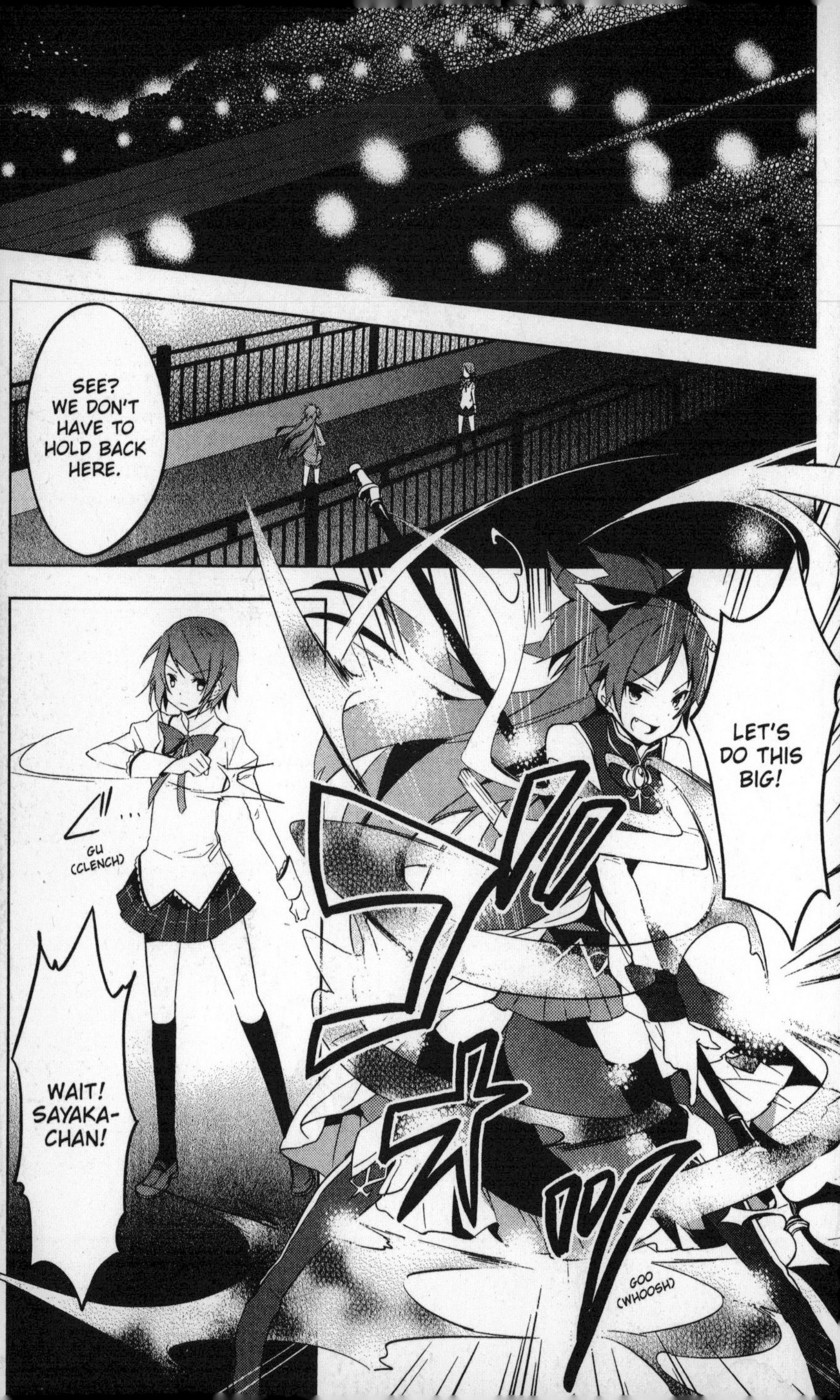
SEE? WE DON'T HAVE TO HOLD BACK HERE.
LET'S DO THIS BIG!
GU (CLENCH)
WAIT! SAYAKA-CHAN!
GOO (WHOOSH)

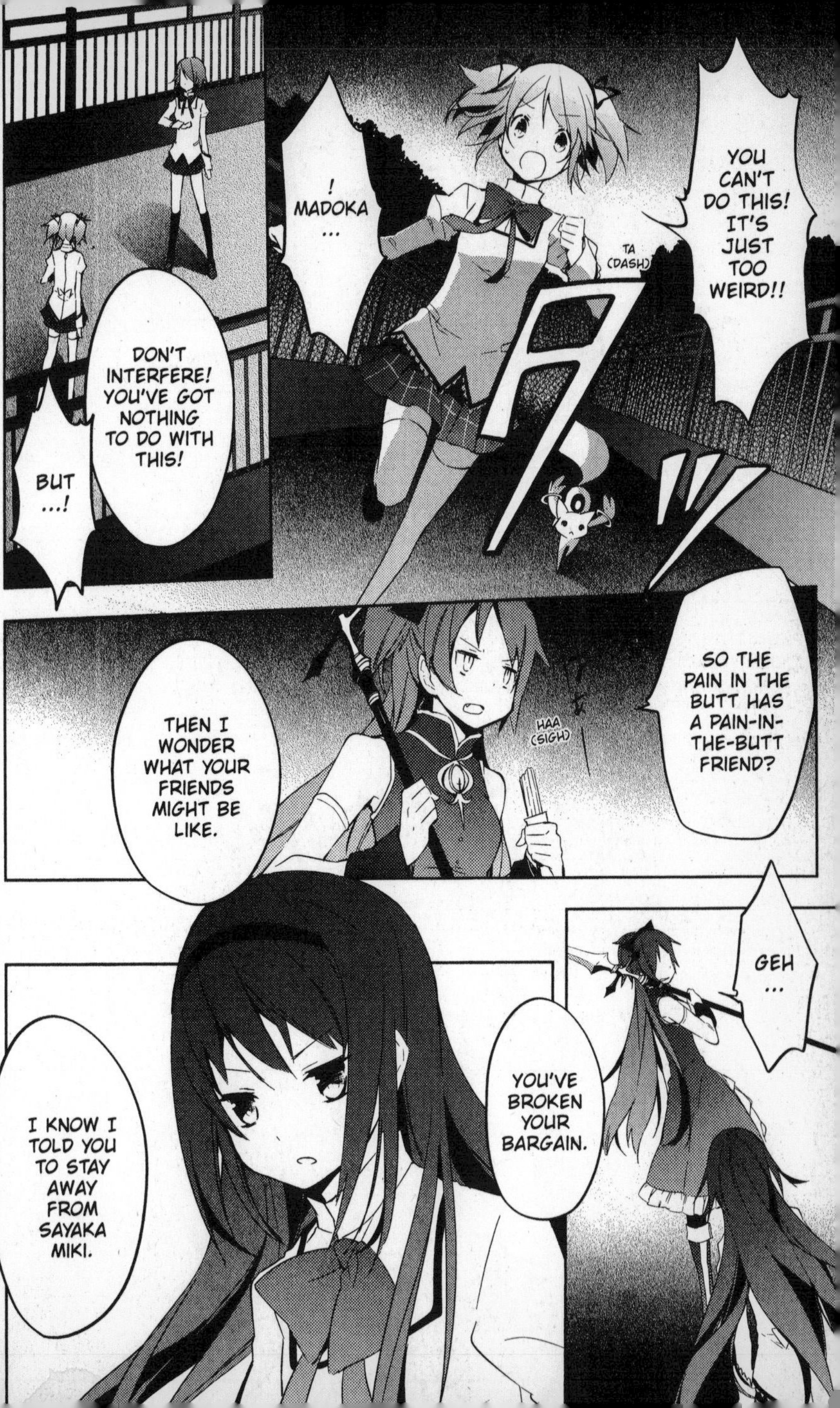
YOU CAN'T DO THIS! IT'S JUST TOO WEIRD!!
TA (DASH)
! MADOKA ...
DON'T INTERFERE! YOU'VE GOT NOTHING TO DO WITH THIS!
BUT ...!
SO THE PAIN IN THE BUTT HAS A PAIN-IN-THE-BUTT FRIEND?
HAA (SIGH)
THEN I WONDER WHAT YOUR FRIENDS MIGHT BE LIKE.
GEH ...
YOU'VE BROKEN YOUR BARGAIN.
I KNOW I TOLD YOU TO STAY AWAY FROM SAYAKA MIKI.

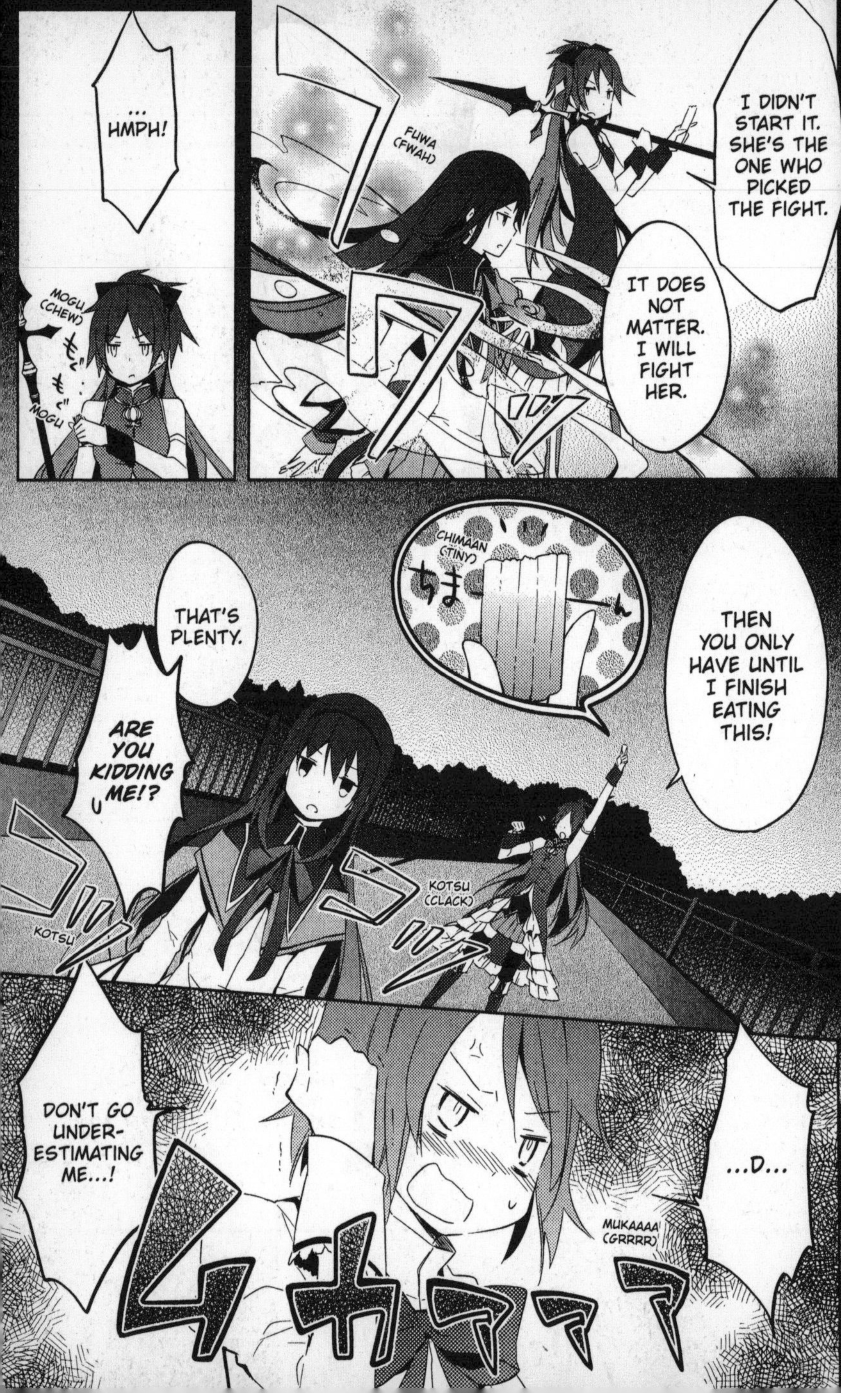
I DIDN'T START IT. SHE'S THE ONE WHO PICKED THE FIGHT.
FUWA (FWAH)
IT DOES NOT MATTER. I WILL FIGHT HER.
... HMPH!
MOGU (CHEW)
もぐ もぐ
MOGU
THEN YOU ONLY HAVE UNTIL I FINISH EATING THIS!
CHIMAAN (TINY)
ちまーーん
THAT'S PLENTY.
ARE YOU KIDDING ME!?
KOTSU (CLACK)
KOTSU
...D...
DON'T GO UNDER-ESTIMATING ME...!
MUKAAAA (GRRRR)
ムカァァァ

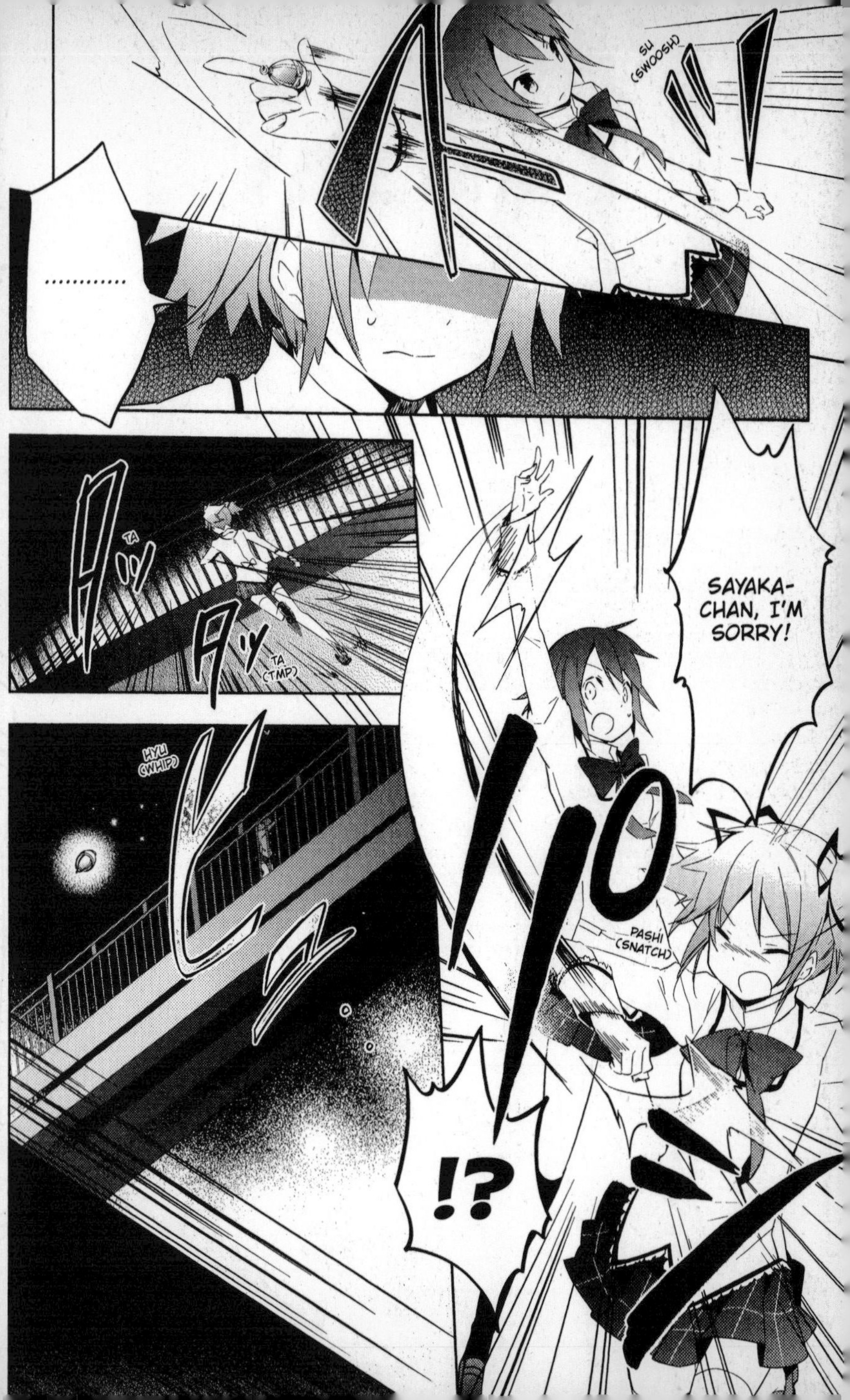
SU (SWOOSH)
....
SAYAKA-CHAN, I'M SORRY!
TA
TA (TMP)
PASHI (SNATCH)
!?
HYU (WHIP)

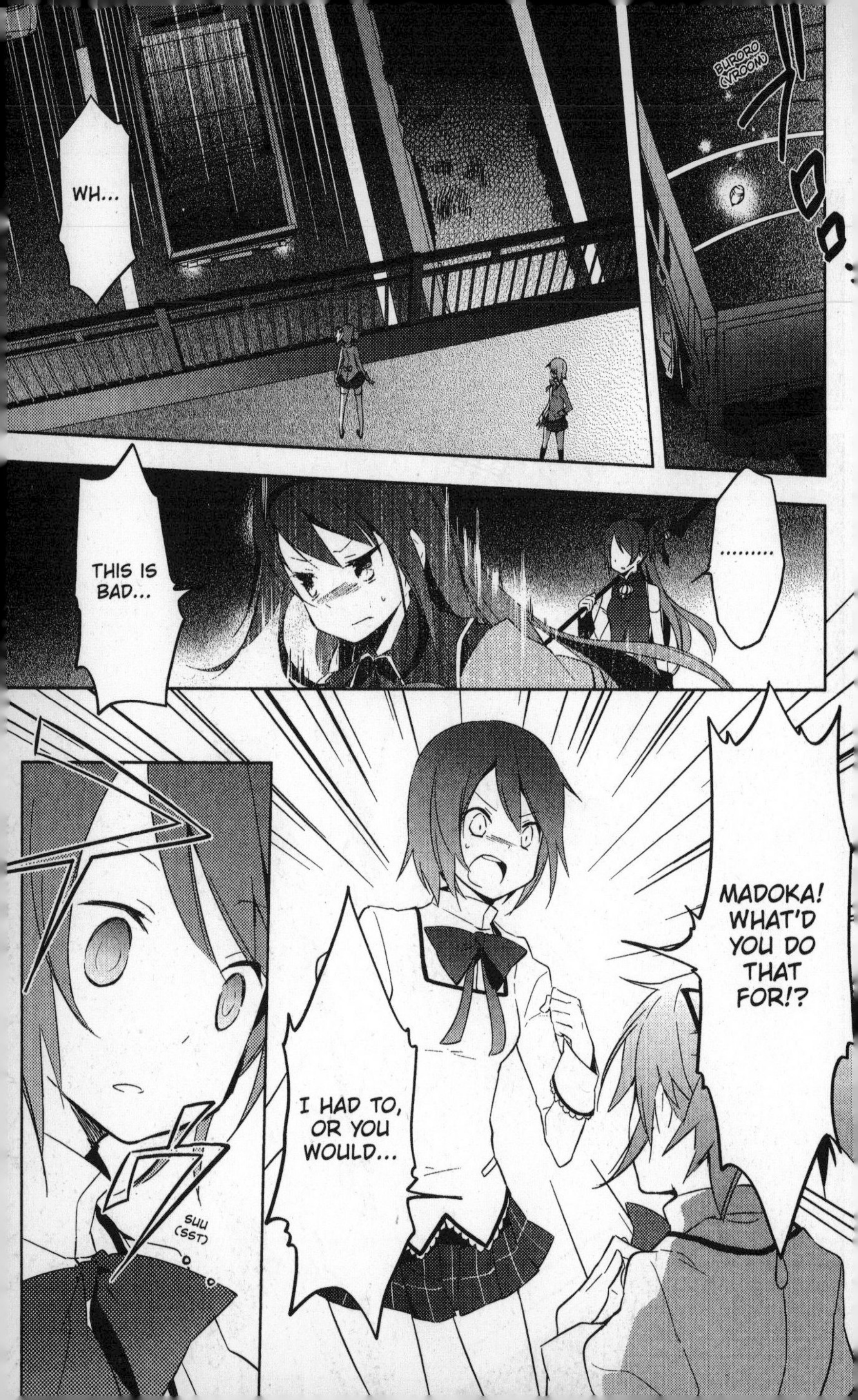

BURORO (VROOM)
WH...
....
THIS IS BAD...
MADOKA! WHAT'D YOU DO THAT FOR!?
I HAD TO, OR YOU WOULD...
SUU (SST)

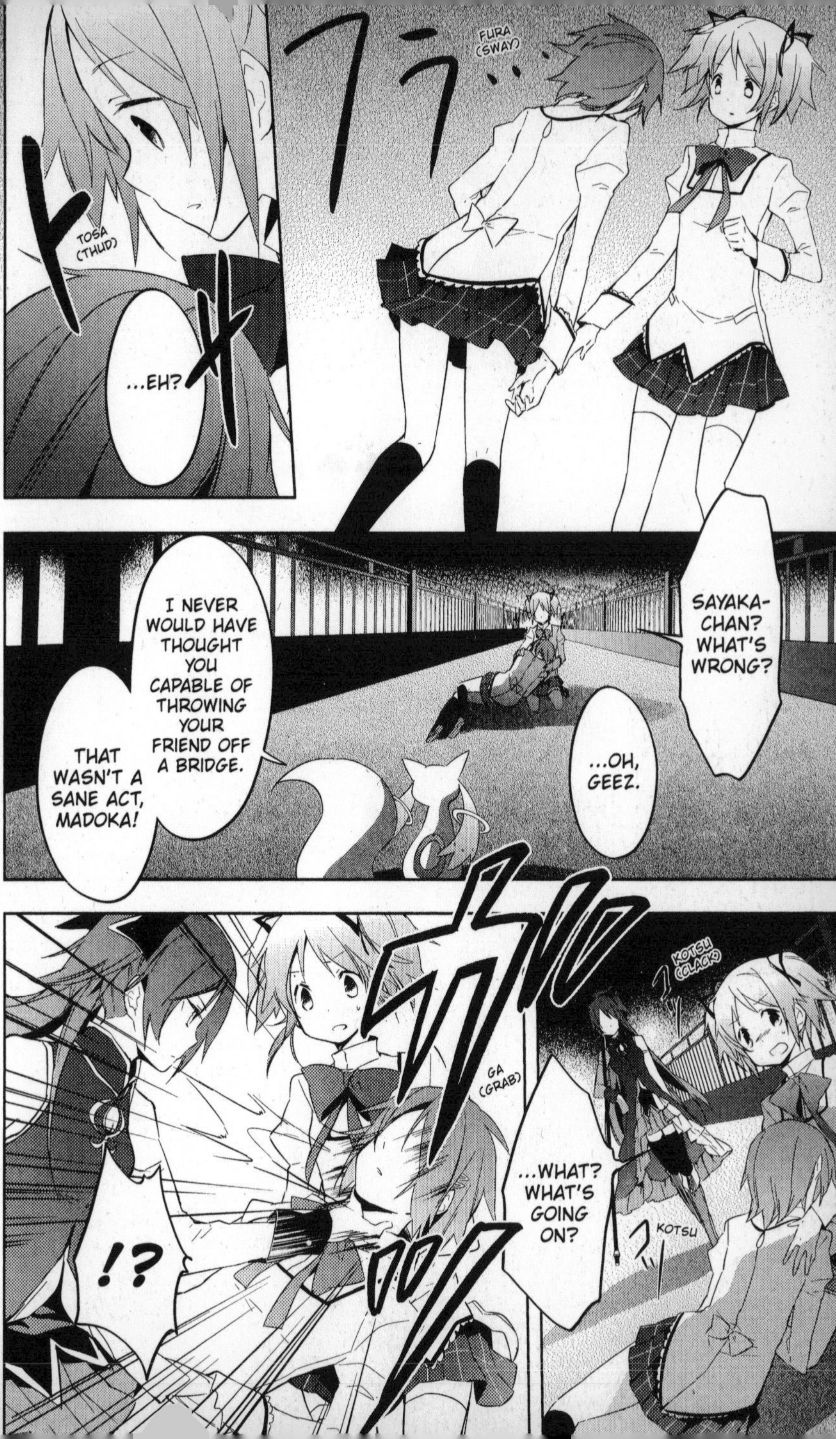
FURA (SWAY)
TOSA (THUD)
...EH?
SAYAKA-CHAN? WHAT'S WRONG?
...OH, GEEZ.
I NEVER WOULD HAVE THOUGHT YOU CAPABLE OF THROWING YOUR FRIEND OFF A BRIDGE.
THAT WASN'T A SANE ACT, MADOKA!
KOTSU (CLACK)
...WHAT? WHAT'S GOING ON?
KOTSU
GA (GRAB)
!?

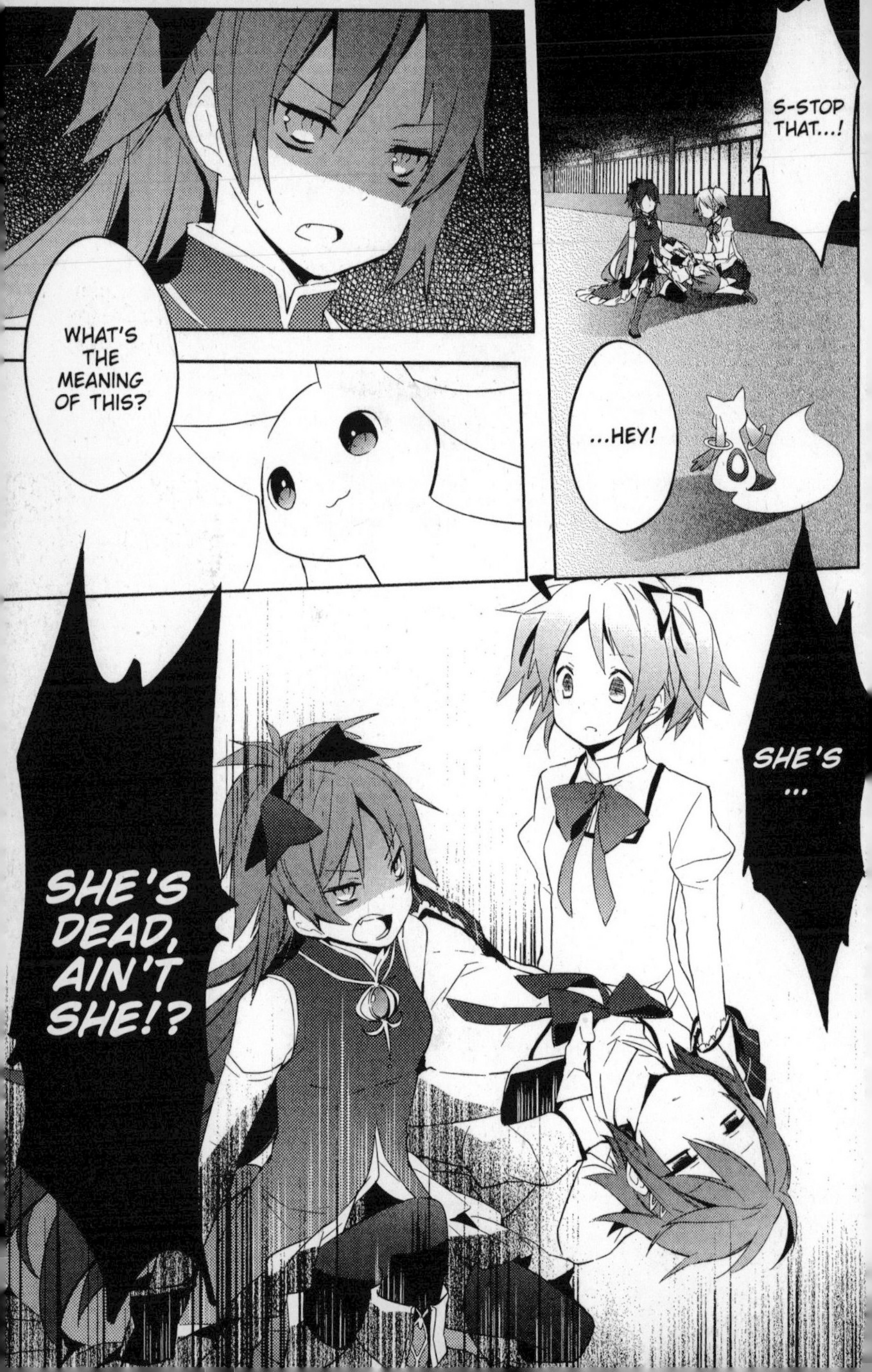
S-STOP THAT...!
...HEY!
WHAT'S THE MEANING OF THIS?
SHE'S ...
SHE'S DEAD, AIN'T SHE!?

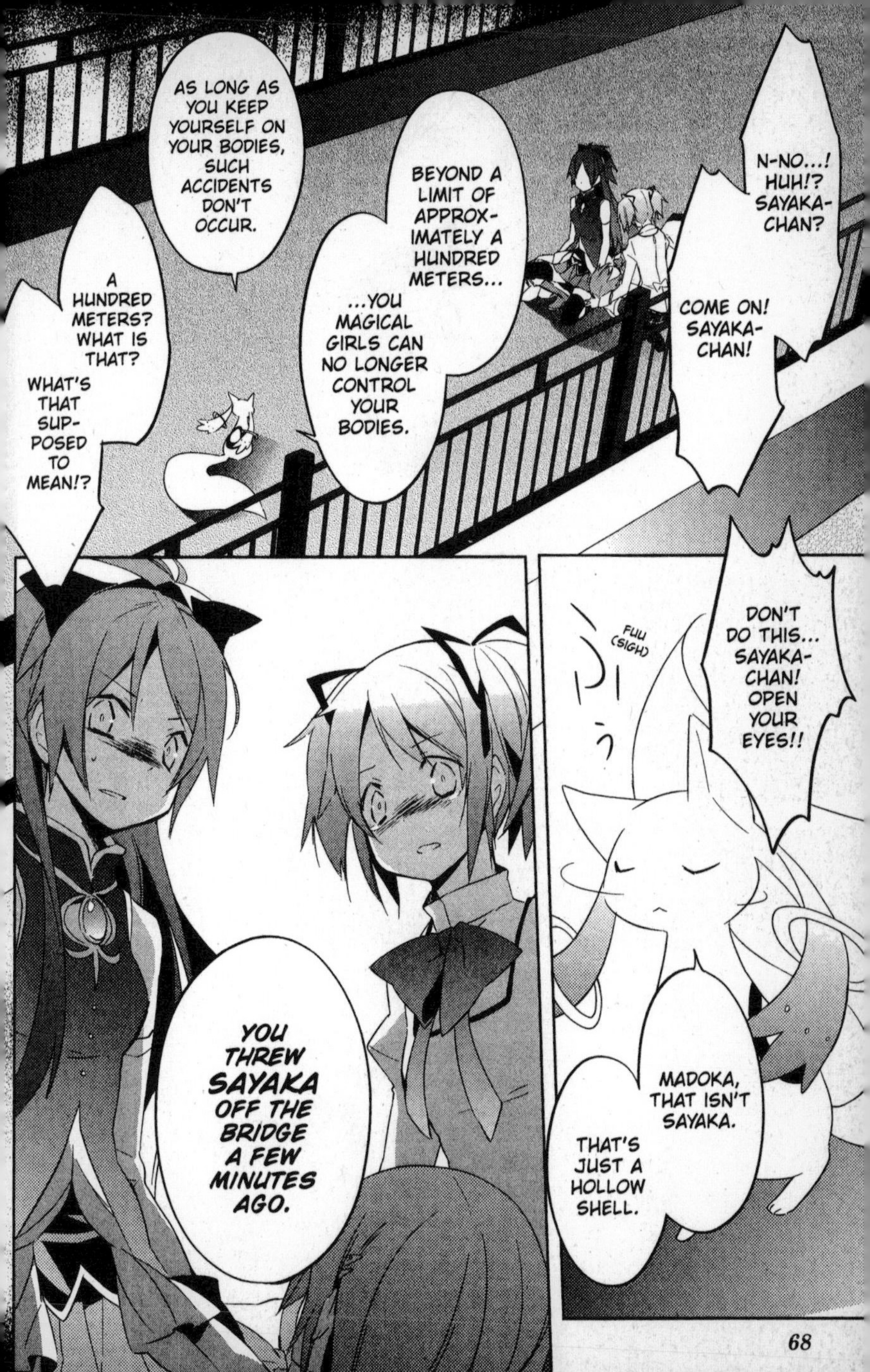
N-NO...! HUH!? SAYAKA-CHAN?
COME ON! SAYAKA-CHAN!
BEYOND A LIMIT OF APPROX-IMATELY A HUNDRED METERS...
...YOU MAGICAL GIRLS CAN NO LONGER CONTROL YOUR BODIES.
AS LONG AS YOU KEEP YOURSELF ON YOUR BODIES, SUCH ACCIDENTS DON'T OCCUR.
A HUNDRED METERS? WHAT IS THAT?
WHAT'S THAT SUP-POSED TO MEAN!?
DON'T DO THIS... SAYAKA-CHAN! OPEN YOUR EYES!!
FUU (SIGH)
MADOKA, THAT ISN'T SAYAKA.
THAT'S JUST A HOLLOW SHELL.
YOU THREW SAYAKA OFF THE BRIDGE A FEW MINUTES AGO.

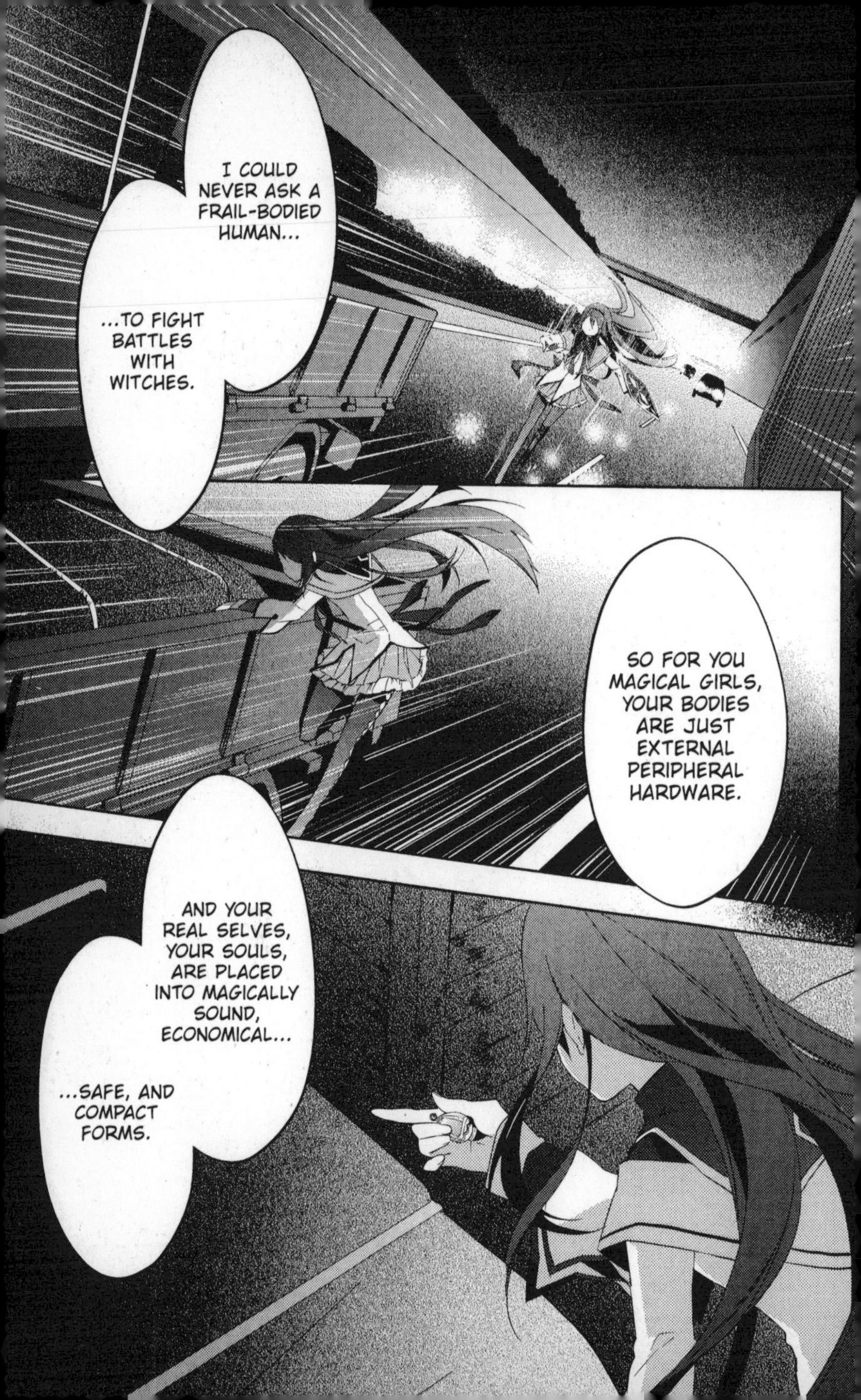
I COULD NEVER ASK A FRAIL-BODIED HUMAN...
...TO FIGHT BATTLES WITH WITCHES.
SO FOR YOU MAGICAL GIRLS, YOUR BODIES ARE JUST EXTERNAL PERIPHERAL HARDWARE.
AND YOUR REAL SELVES, YOUR SOULS, ARE PLACED INTO MAGICALLY SOUND, ECONOMICAL...
...SAFE, AND COMPACT FORMS.

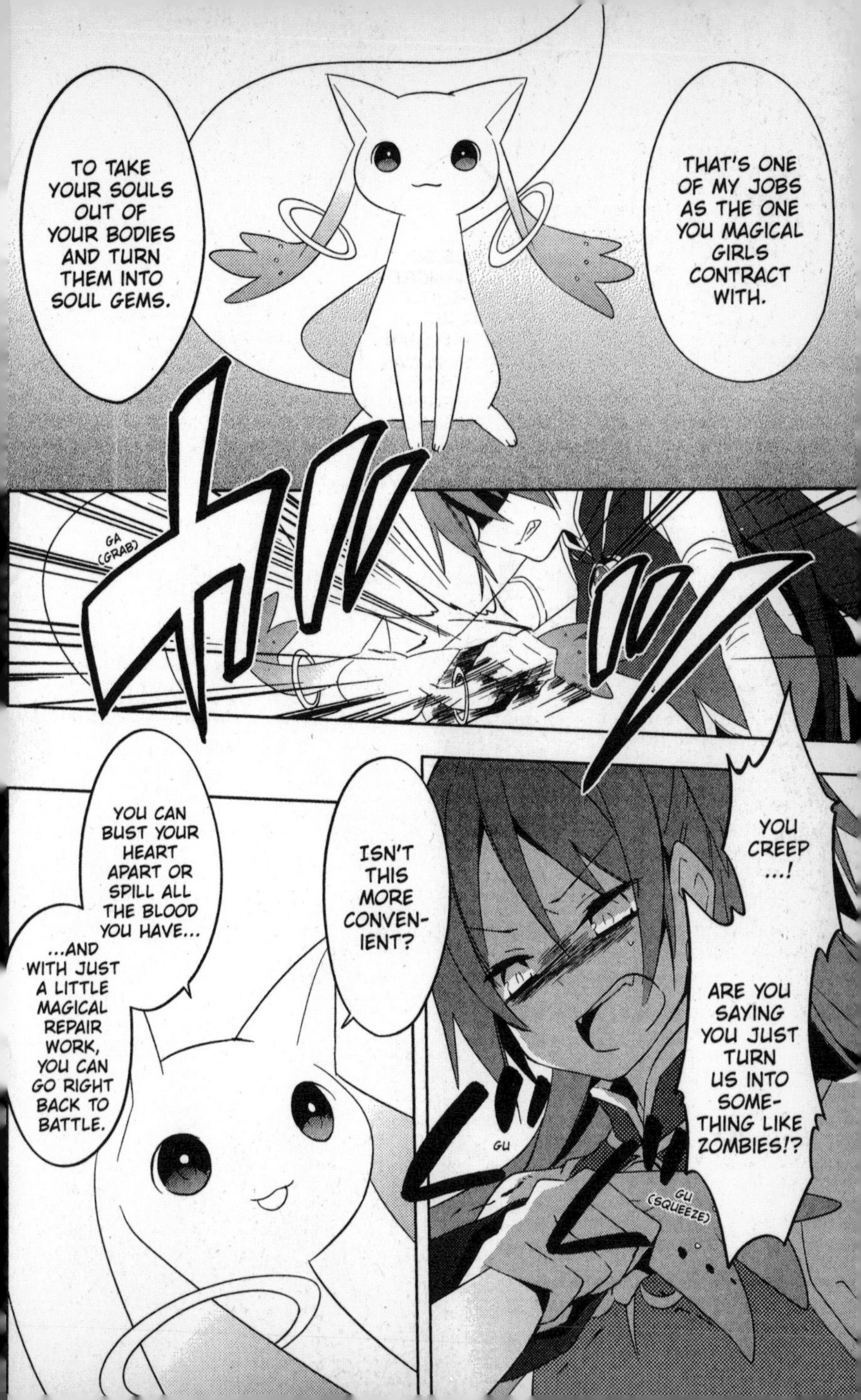
THAT'S ONE OF MY JOBS AS THE ONE YOU MAGICAL GIRLS CONTRACT WITH.
TO TAKE YOUR SOULS OUT OF YOUR BODIES AND TURN THEM INTO SOUL GEMS.
GA (GRAB)
YOU CREEP ...!
ARE YOU SAYING YOU JUST TURN US INTO SOMETHING LIKE ZOMBIES!?
GU
GU (SQUEEZE)
ISN'T THIS MORE CONVENIENT?
YOU CAN BUST YOUR HEART APART OR SPILL ALL THE BLOOD YOU HAVE...
...AND WITH JUST A LITTLE MAGICAL REPAIR WORK, YOU CAN GO RIGHT BACK TO BATTLE.

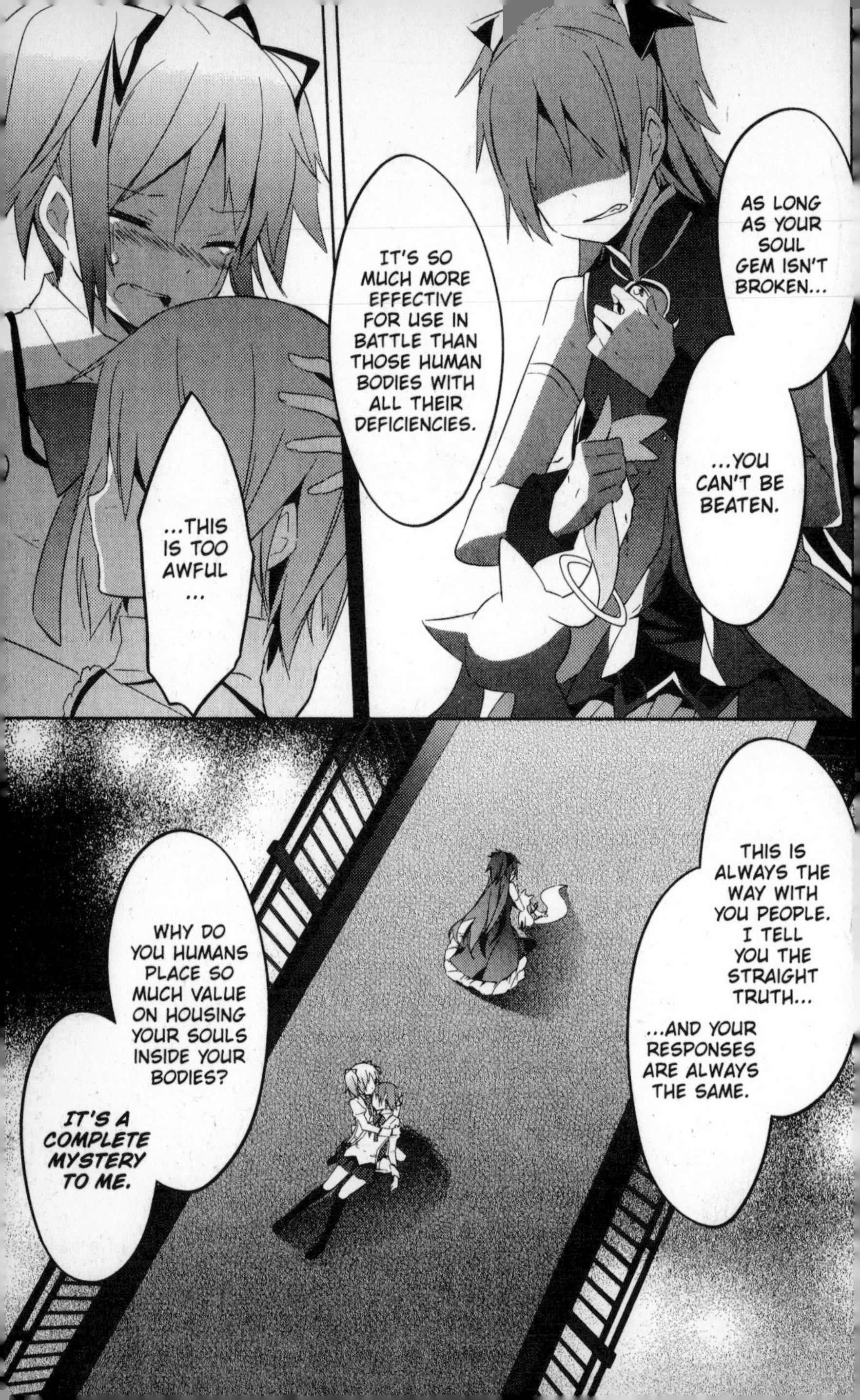
AS LONG AS YOUR SOUL GEM ISN'T BROKEN...
...YOU CAN'T BE BEATEN.
IT'S SO MUCH MORE EFFECTIVE FOR USE IN BATTLE THAN THOSE HUMAN BODIES WITH ALL THEIR DEFICIENCIES.
...THIS IS TOO AWFUL ...
THIS IS ALWAYS THE WAY WITH YOU PEOPLE. I TELL YOU THE STRAIGHT TRUTH...
...AND YOUR RESPONSES ARE ALWAYS THE SAME.
WHY DO YOU HUMANS PLACE SO MUCH VALUE ON HOUSING YOUR SOULS INSIDE YOUR BODIES?
IT'S A COMPLETE MYSTERY TO ME.

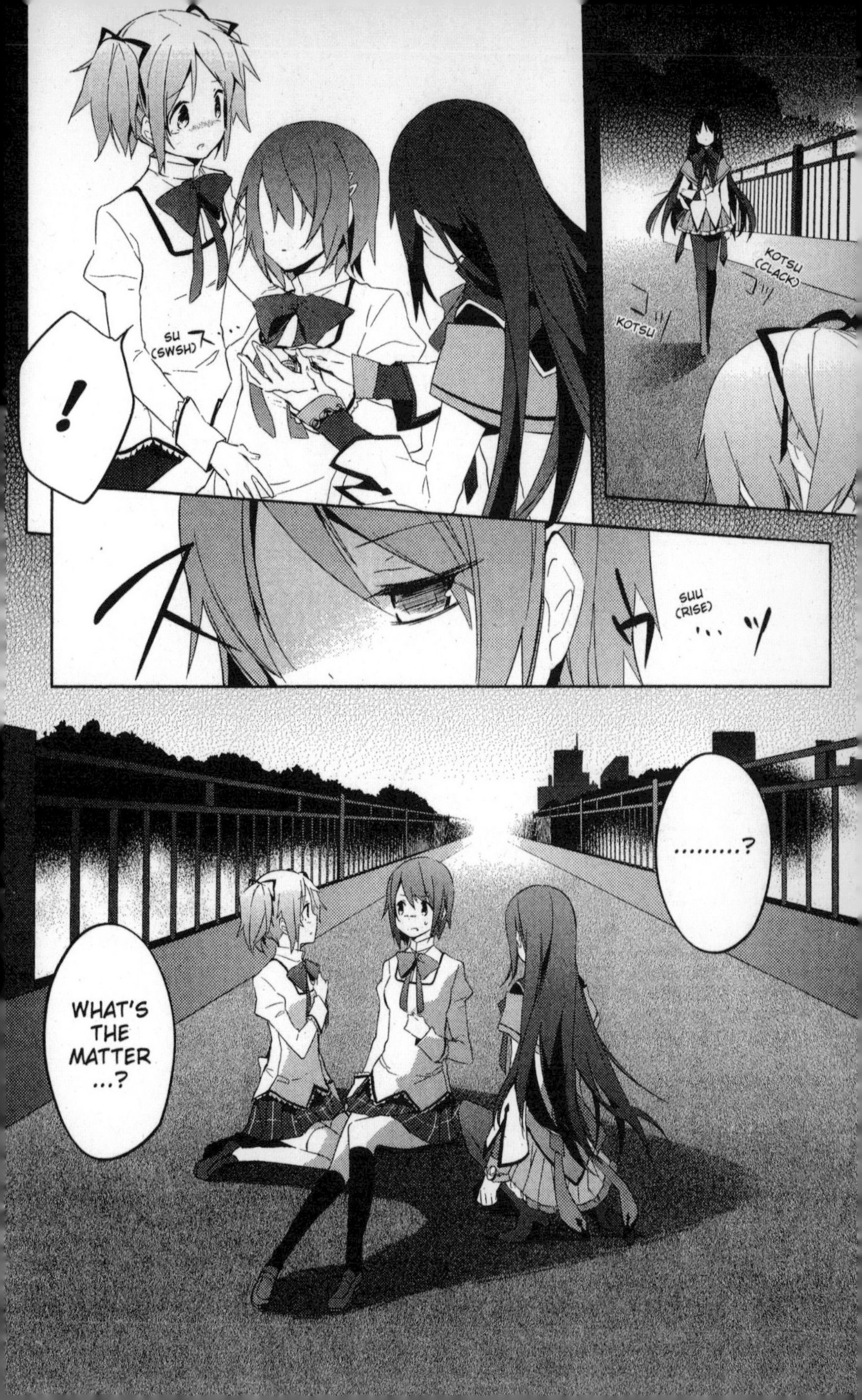
KOTSU (CLACK)
KOTSU
!
SU (SWSH)
SUU (RISE)
.........?
WHAT'S THE MATTER ...?

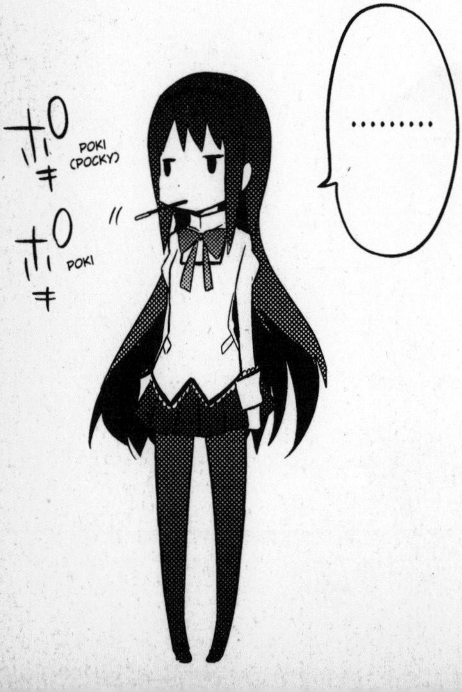
....
ポキ
POKI (POCKY)
ポキ
POKI

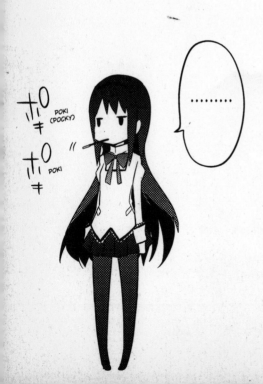

PUELLA MAGI
MADOKA★MAGICA

CHAPTER 7
CAN YOU TRULY FACE YOUR FEELINGS?

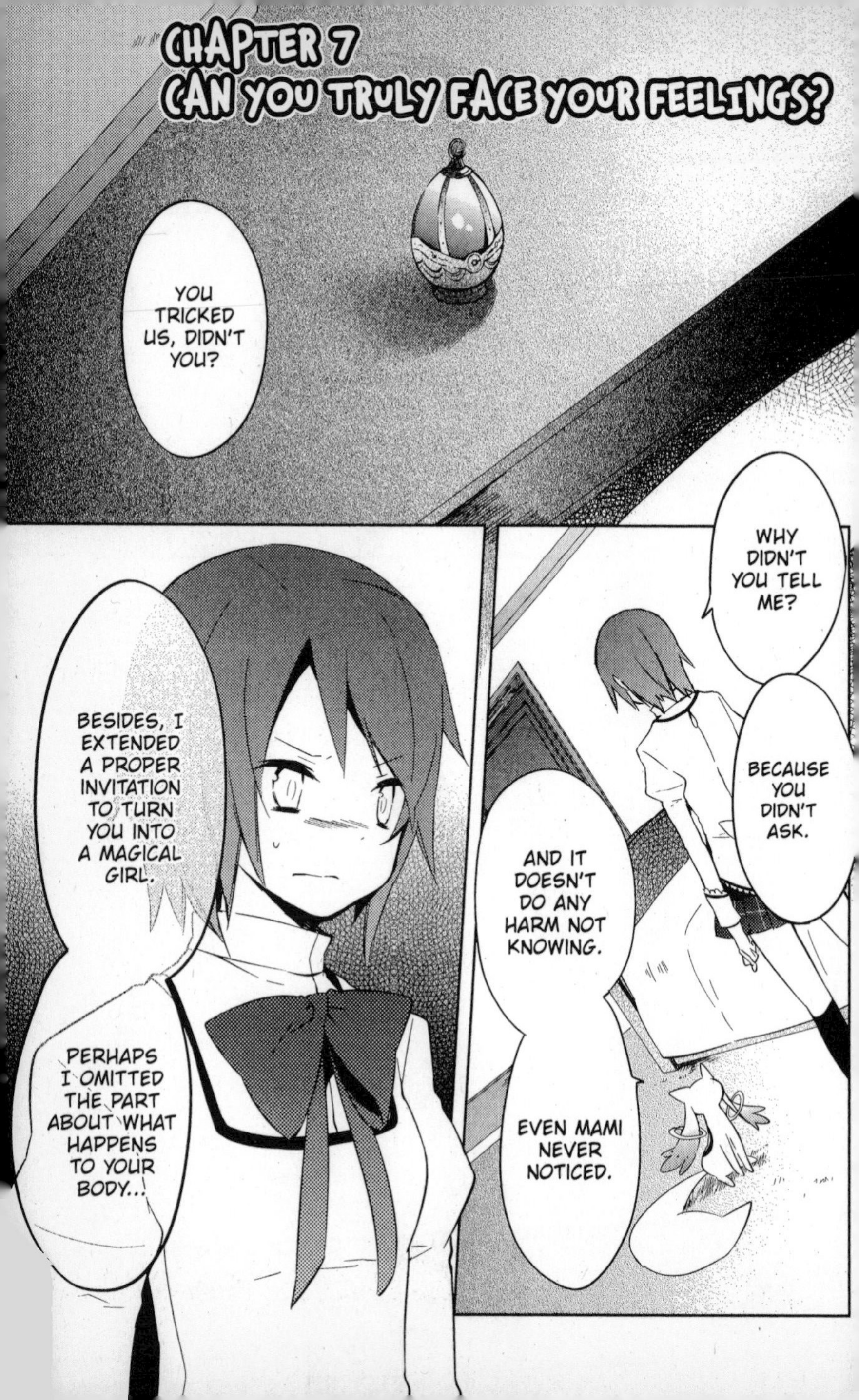
YOU TRICKED US, DIDN'T YOU?
WHY DIDN'T YOU TELL ME?
BECAUSE YOU DIDN'T ASK.
AND IT DOESN'T DO ANY HARM NOT KNOWING.
EVEN MAMI NEVER NOTICED.
BESIDES, I EXTENDED A PROPER INVITATION TO TURN YOU INTO A MAGICAL GIRL.
PERHAPS I OMITTED THE PART ABOUT WHAT HAPPENS TO YOUR BODY...

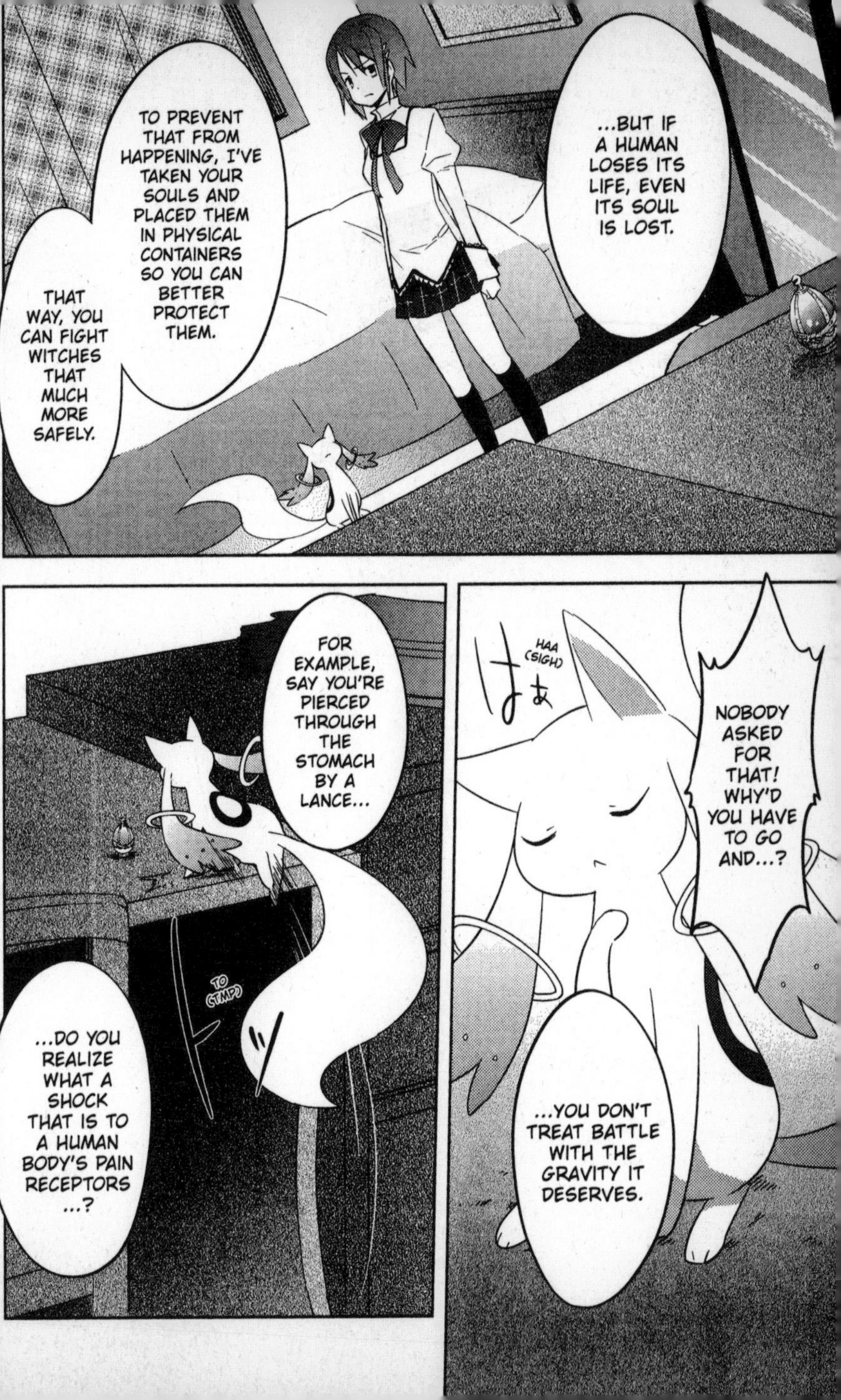
...BUT IF A HUMAN LOSES ITS LIFE, EVEN ITS SOUL IS LOST.
TO PREVENT THAT FROM HAPPENING, I'VE TAKEN YOUR SOULS AND PLACED THEM IN PHYSICAL CONTAINERS SO YOU CAN BETTER PROTECT THEM.
THAT WAY, YOU CAN FIGHT WITCHES THAT MUCH MORE SAFELY.
NOBODY ASKED FOR THAT! WHY'D YOU HAVE TO GO AND...?
HAA (SIGH)
はぁ
...YOU DON'T TREAT BATTLE WITH THE GRAVITY IT DESERVES.
FOR EXAMPLE, SAY YOU'RE PIERCED THROUGH THE STOMACH BY A LANCE...
TO (TMP)
...DO YOU REALIZE WHAT A SHOCK THAT IS TO A HUMAN BODY'S PAIN RECEPTORS ...?

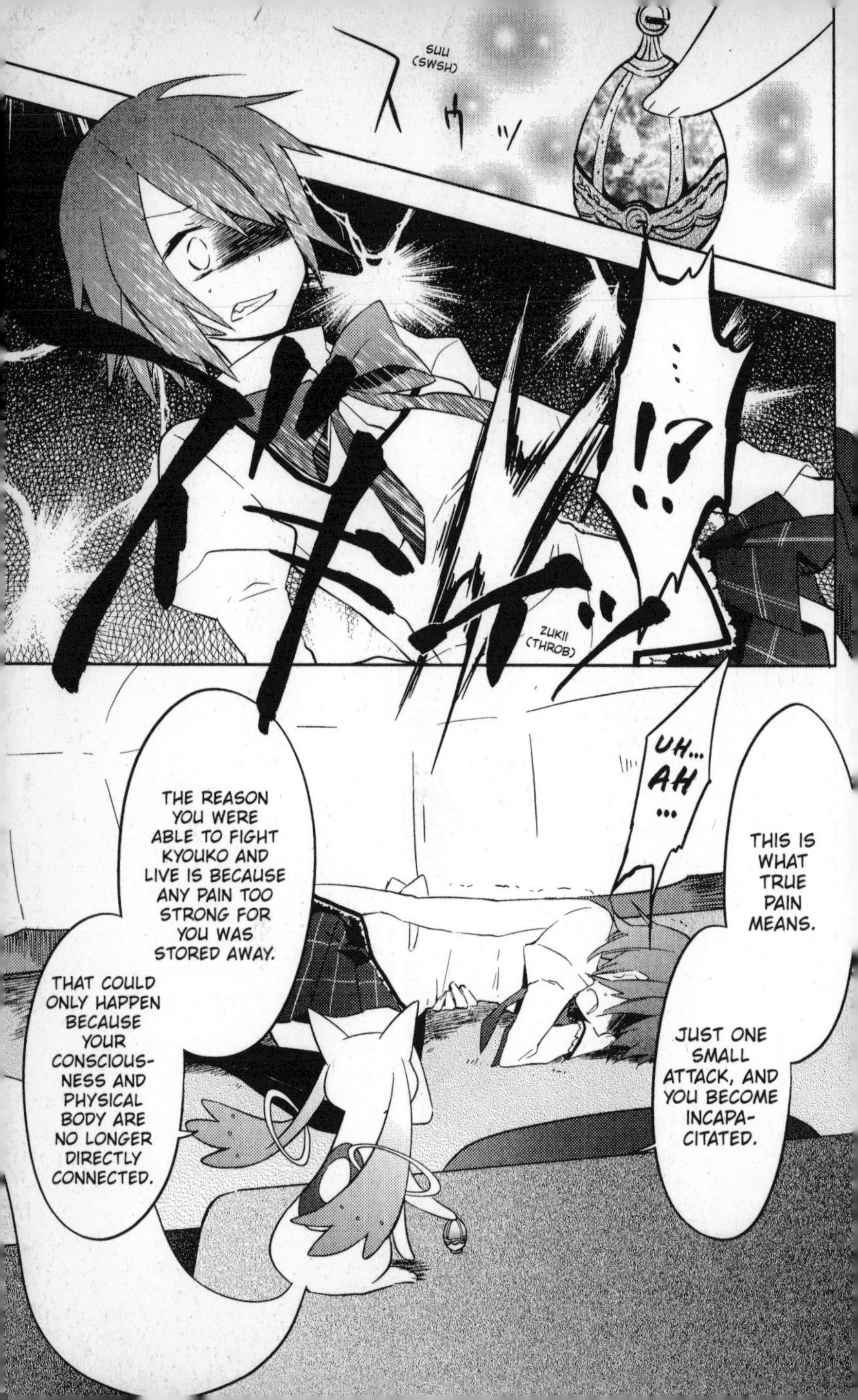
SUU (SWSH)
...!?
ZUKII (THROB)
UH... AH ...
THIS IS WHAT TRUE PAIN MEANS.
JUST ONE SMALL ATTACK, AND YOU BECOME INCAPACITATED.
THE REASON YOU WERE ABLE TO FIGHT KYOUKO AND LIVE IS BECAUSE ANY PAIN TOO STRONG FOR YOU WAS STORED AWAY.
THAT COULD ONLY HAPPEN BECAUSE YOUR CONSCIOUSNESS AND PHYSICAL BODY ARE NO LONGER DIRECTLY CONNECTED.

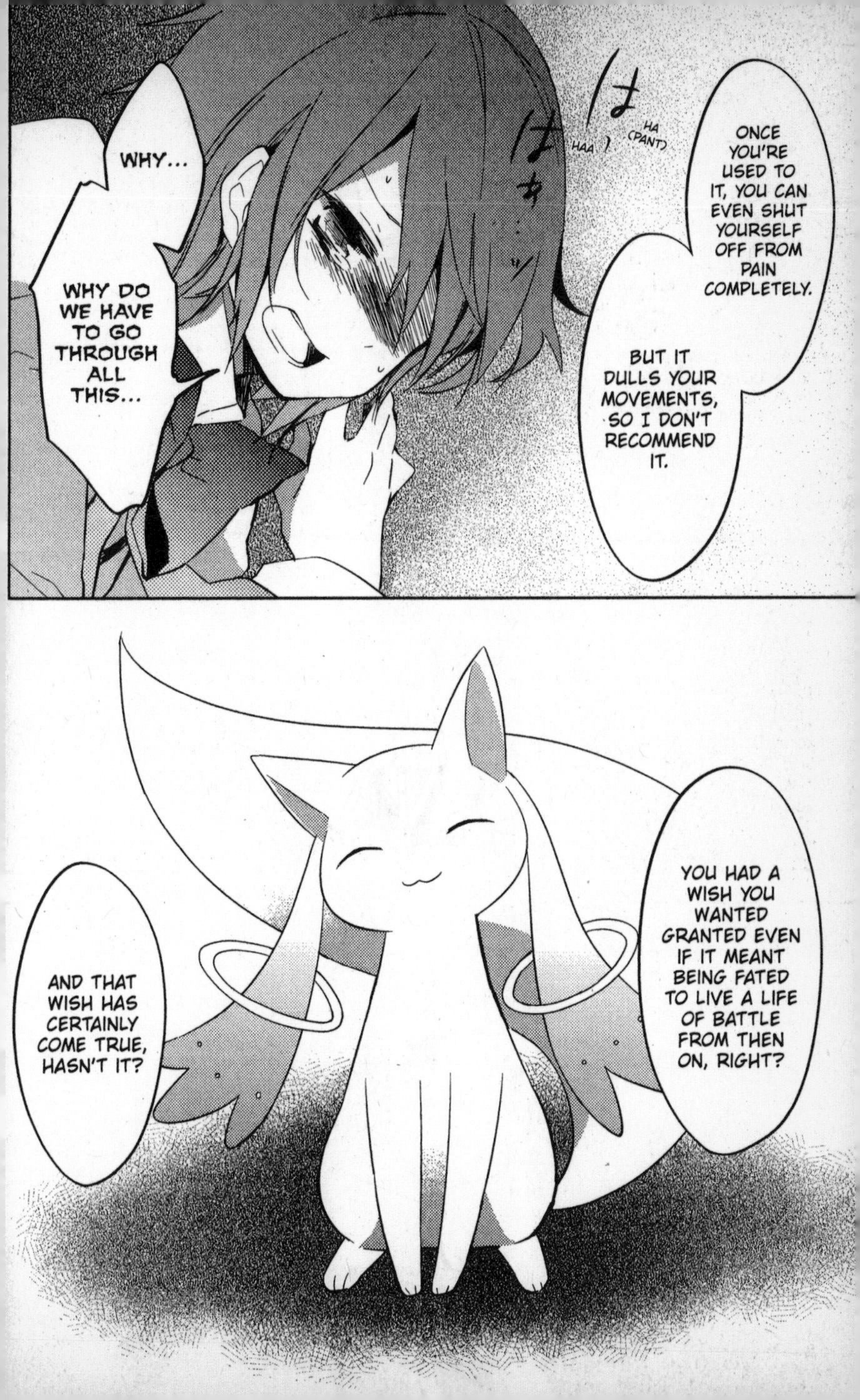
HA HAA (PANT)
ONCE YOU'RE USED TO IT, YOU CAN EVEN SHUT YOURSELF OFF FROM PAIN COMPLETELY.
BUT IT DULLS YOUR MOVEMENTS, SO I DON'T RECOMMEND IT.
WHY...
WHY DO WE HAVE TO GO THROUGH ALL THIS...
YOU HAD A WISH YOU WANTED GRANTED EVEN IF IT MEANT BEING FATED TO LIVE A LIFE OF BATTLE FROM THEN ON, RIGHT?
AND THAT WISH HAS CERTAINLY COME TRUE, HASN'T IT?

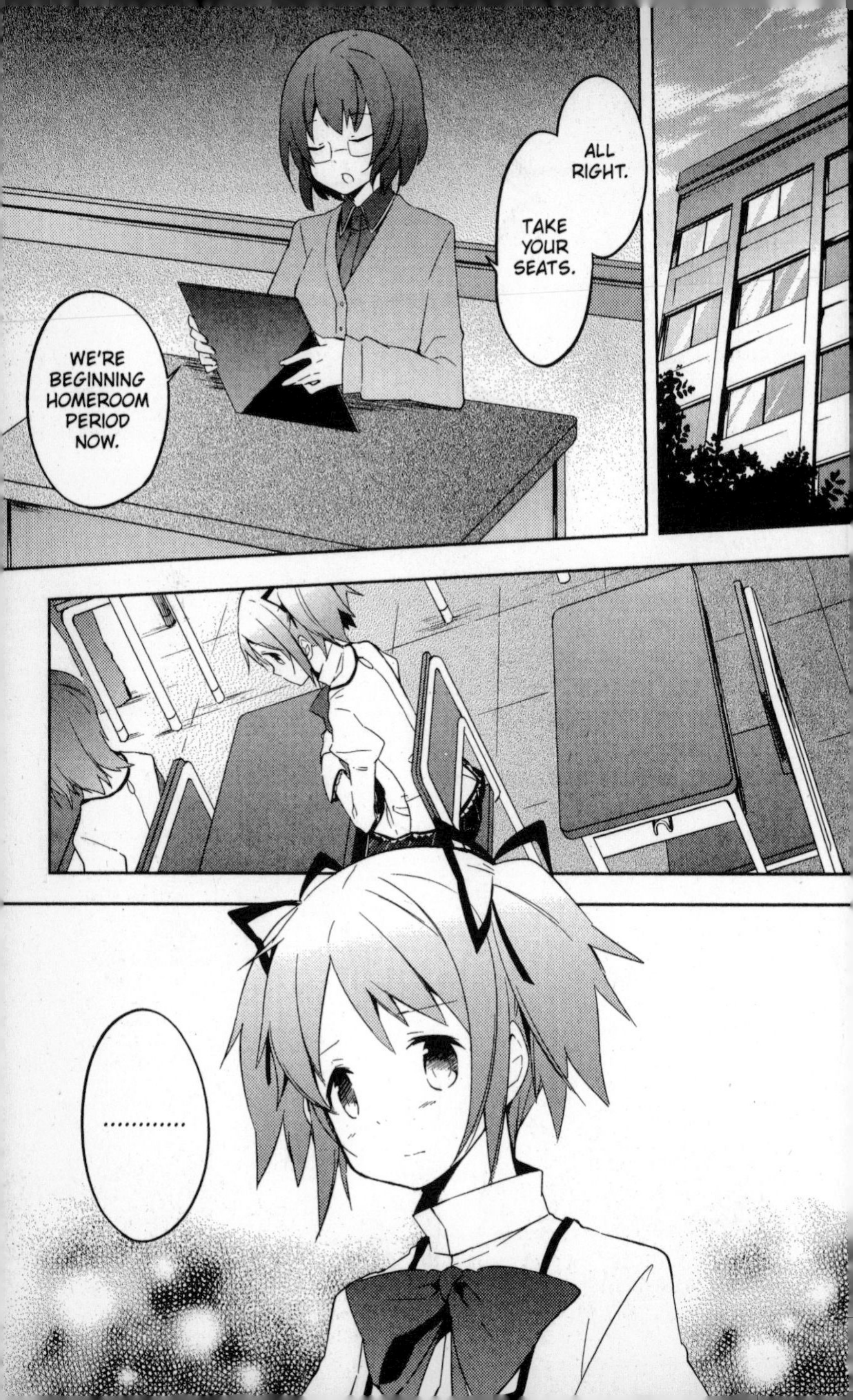
ALL RIGHT.
TAKE YOUR SEATS.
WE'RE BEGINNING HOMEROOM PERIOD NOW.
....

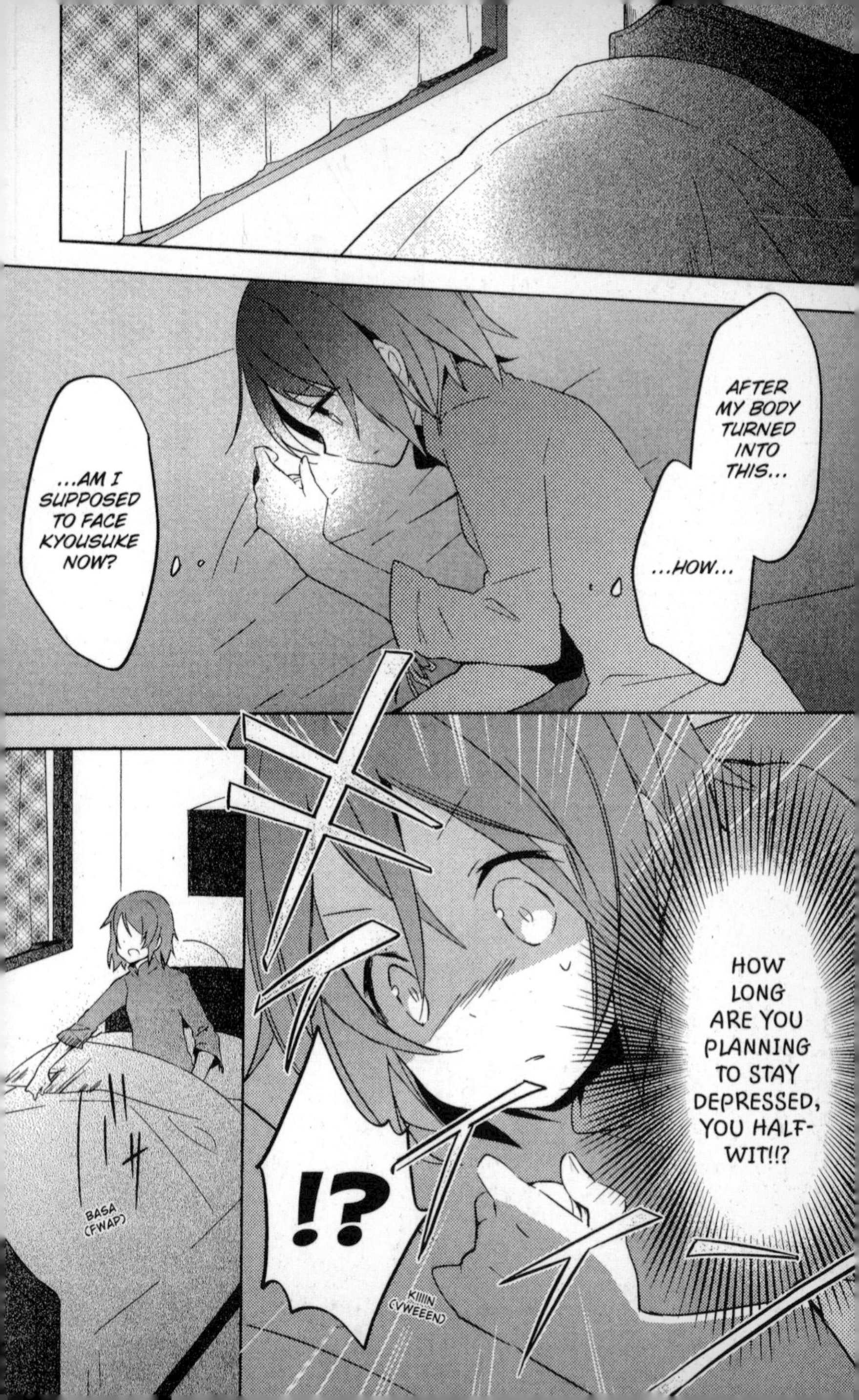
AFTER MY BODY TURNED INTO THIS...
...HOW...
...AM I SUPPOSED TO FACE KYOUSUKE NOW?
HOW LONG ARE YOU PLANNING TO STAY DEPRESSED, YOU HALF-WIT!!?
!?
KIIIN (VWEEEN)
BASA (FWAP)

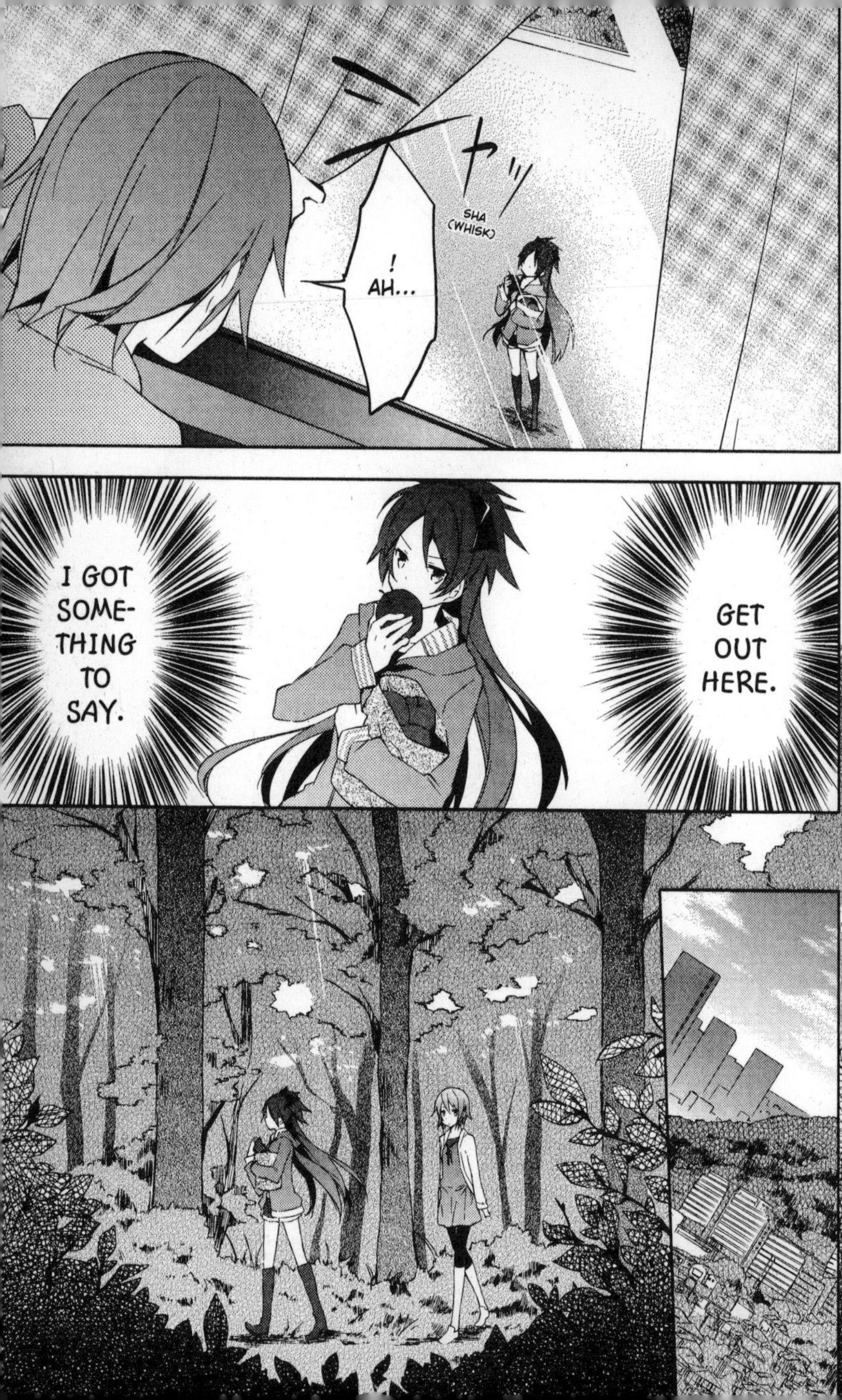
SHA (WHISK)
! AH...
GET OUT HERE.
I GOT SOME-THING TO SAY.

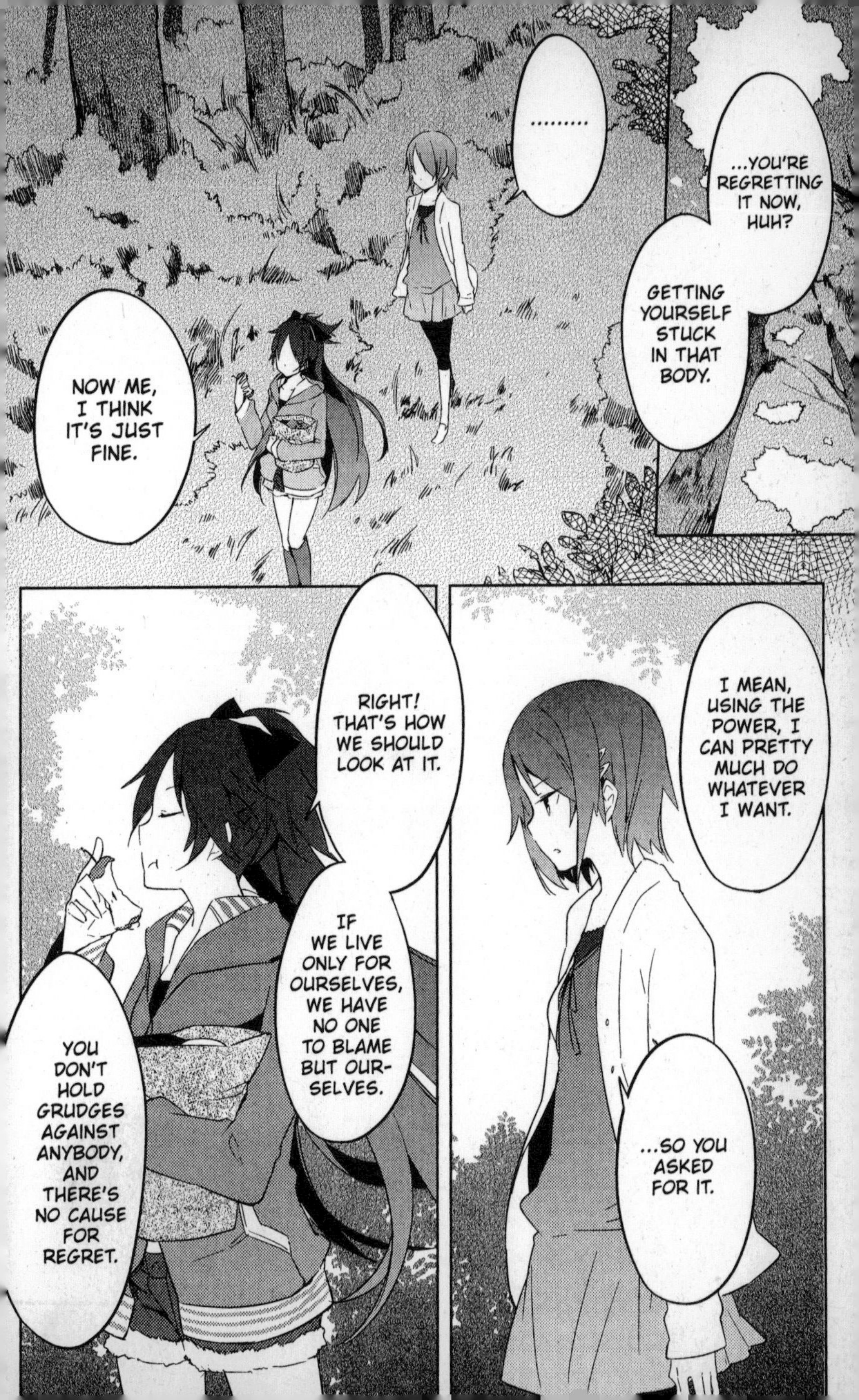
...YOU'RE REGRETTING IT NOW, HUH?
GETTING YOURSELF STUCK IN THAT BODY.
....
NOW ME, I THINK IT'S JUST FINE.
I MEAN, USING THE POWER, I CAN PRETTY MUCH DO WHATEVER I WANT.
...SO YOU ASKED FOR IT.
RIGHT! THAT'S HOW WE SHOULD LOOK AT IT.
IF WE LIVE ONLY FOR OURSELVES, WE HAVE NO ONE TO BLAME BUT OUR-SELVES.
YOU DON'T HOLD GRUDGES AGAINST ANYBODY, AND THERE'S NO CAUSE FOR REGRET.

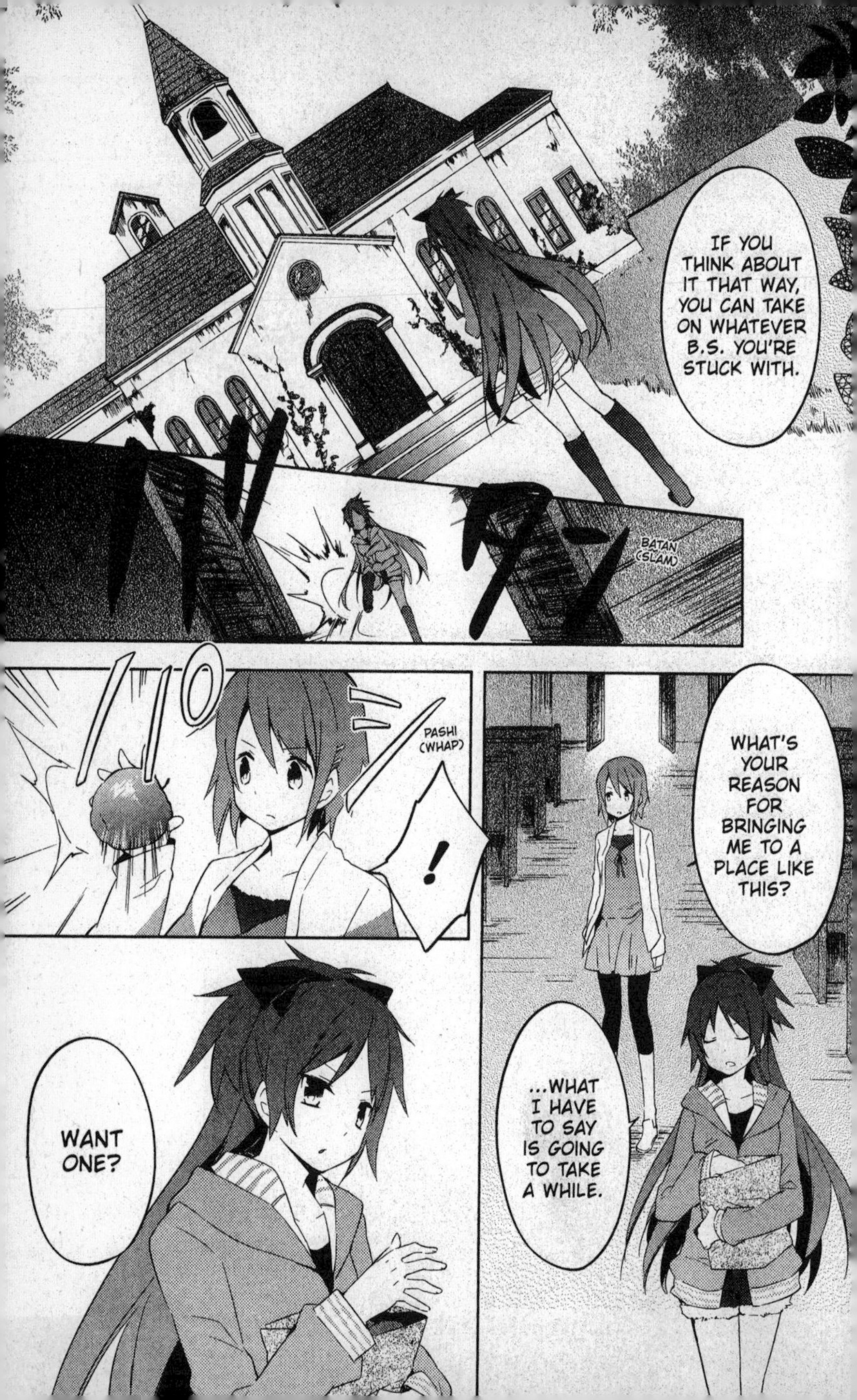
IF YOU THINK ABOUT IT THAT WAY, YOU CAN TAKE ON WHATEVER B.S. YOU'RE STUCK WITH.
BATAN (SLAM)
WHAT'S YOUR REASON FOR BRINGING ME TO A PLACE LIKE THIS?
...WHAT I HAVE TO SAY IS GOING TO TAKE A WHILE.
PASHI (WHAP)
!
WANT ONE?

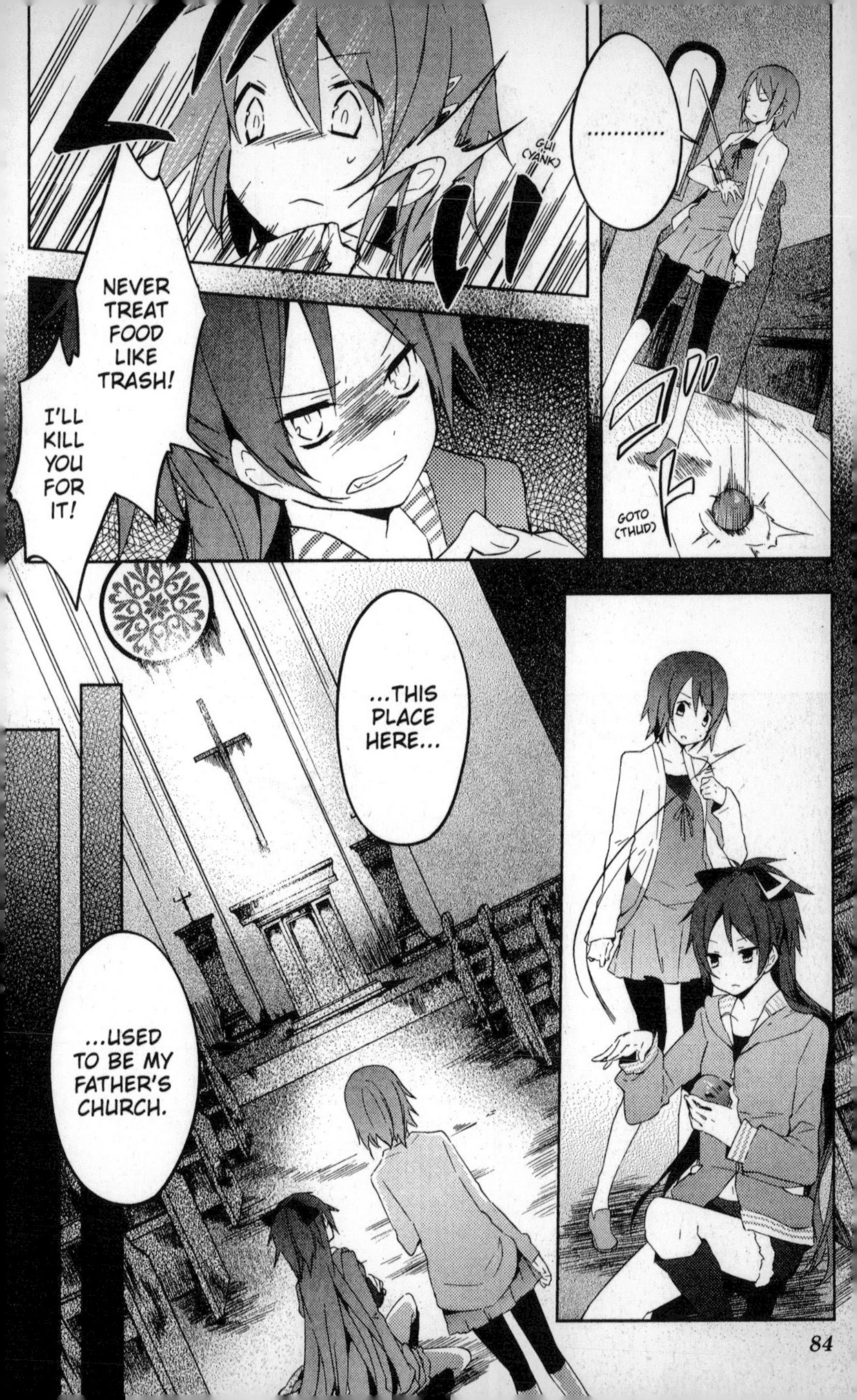
....
GUI (YANK)
GOTO (THUD)
NEVER TREAT FOOD LIKE TRASH!
I'LL KILL YOU FOR IT!
...THIS PLACE HERE...
...USED TO BE MY FATHER'S CHURCH.

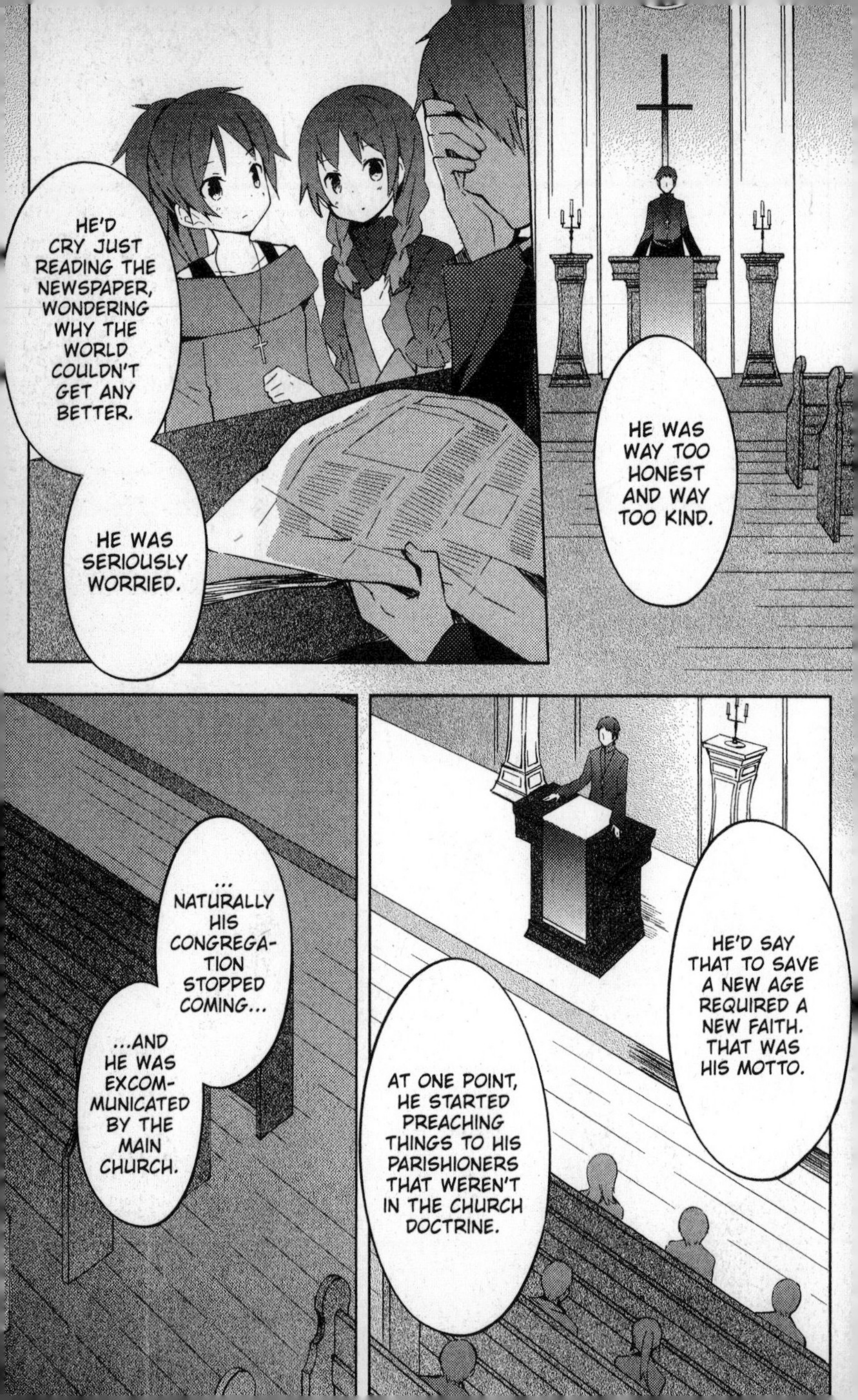
HE WAS WAY TOO HONEST AND WAY TOO KIND.
HE'D CRY JUST READING THE NEWSPAPER, WONDERING WHY THE WORLD COULDN'T GET ANY BETTER.
HE WAS SERIOUSLY WORRIED.
HE'D SAY THAT TO SAVE A NEW AGE REQUIRED A NEW FAITH. THAT WAS HIS MOTTO.
AT ONE POINT, HE STARTED PREACHING THINGS TO HIS PARISHIONERS THAT WEREN'T IN THE CHURCH DOCTRINE.
... NATURALLY HIS CONGREGATION STOPPED COMING...
...AND HE WAS EXCOMMUNICATED BY THE MAIN CHURCH.

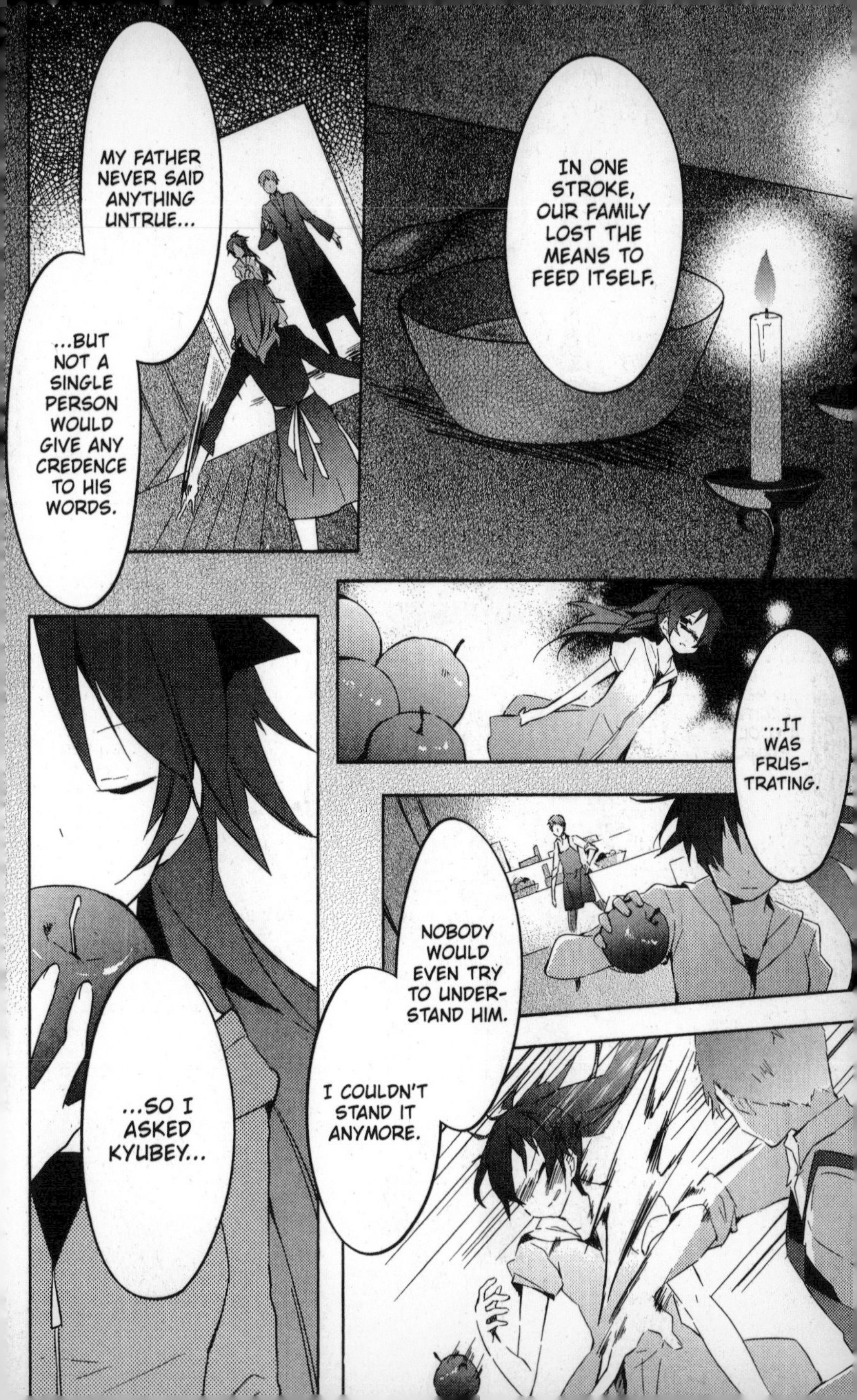
IN ONE STROKE, OUR FAMILY LOST THE MEANS TO FEED ITSELF.
MY FATHER NEVER SAID ANYTHING UNTRUE...
...BUT NOT A SINGLE PERSON WOULD GIVE ANY CREDENCE TO HIS WORDS.
...IT WAS FRUS-TRATING.
NOBODY WOULD EVEN TRY TO UNDER-STAND HIM.
I COULDN'T STAND IT ANYMORE.
...SO I ASKED KYUBEY...

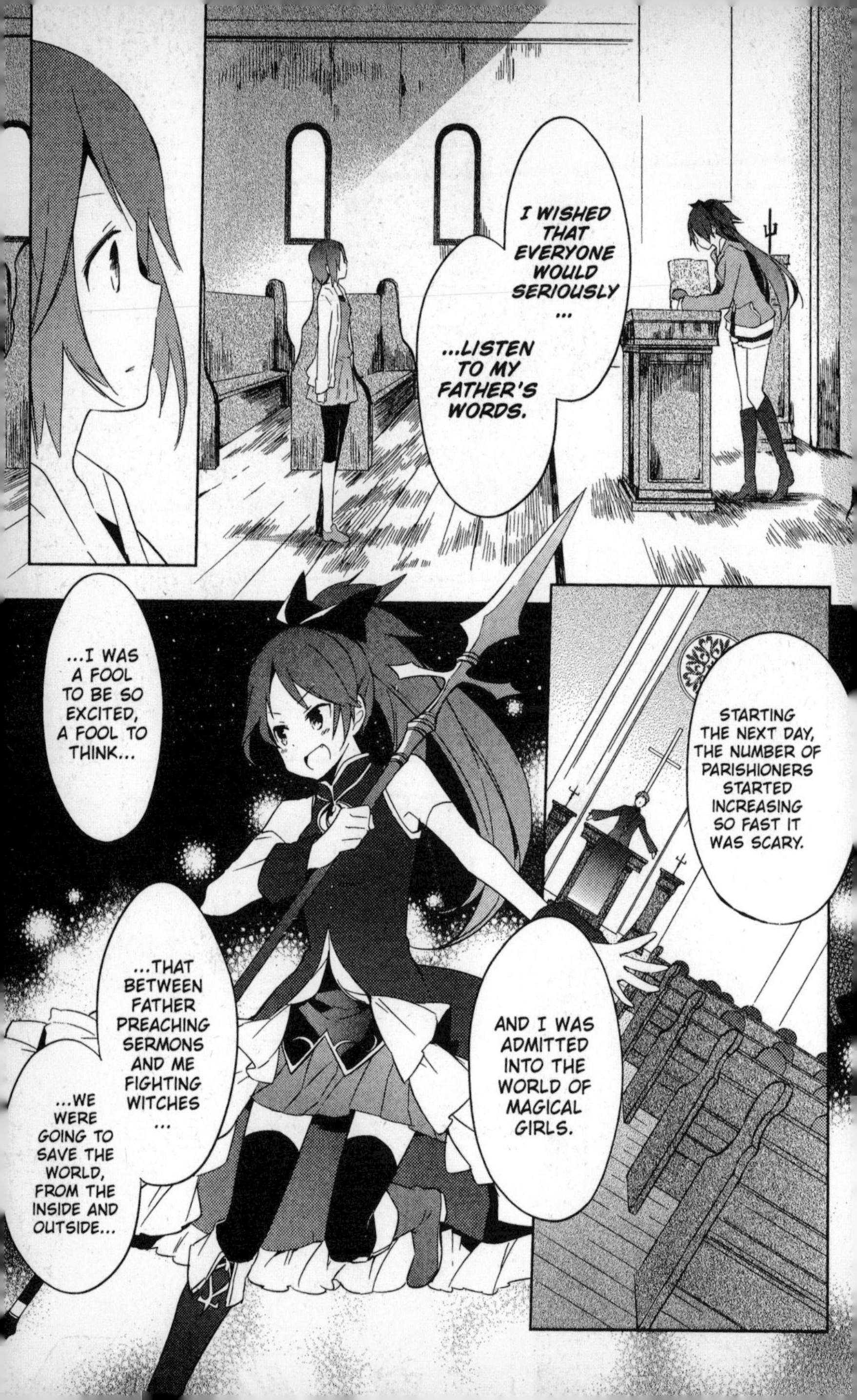
I WISHED THAT EVERYONE WOULD SERIOUSLY ...
...LISTEN TO MY FATHER'S WORDS.
STARTING THE NEXT DAY, THE NUMBER OF PARISHIONERS STARTED INCREASING SO FAST IT WAS SCARY.
AND I WAS ADMITTED INTO THE WORLD OF MAGICAL GIRLS.
...I WAS A FOOL TO BE SO EXCITED, A FOOL TO THINK...
...THAT BETWEEN FATHER PREACHING SERMONS AND ME FIGHTING WITCHES ...
...WE WERE GOING TO SAVE THE WORLD, FROM THE INSIDE AND OUTSIDE...

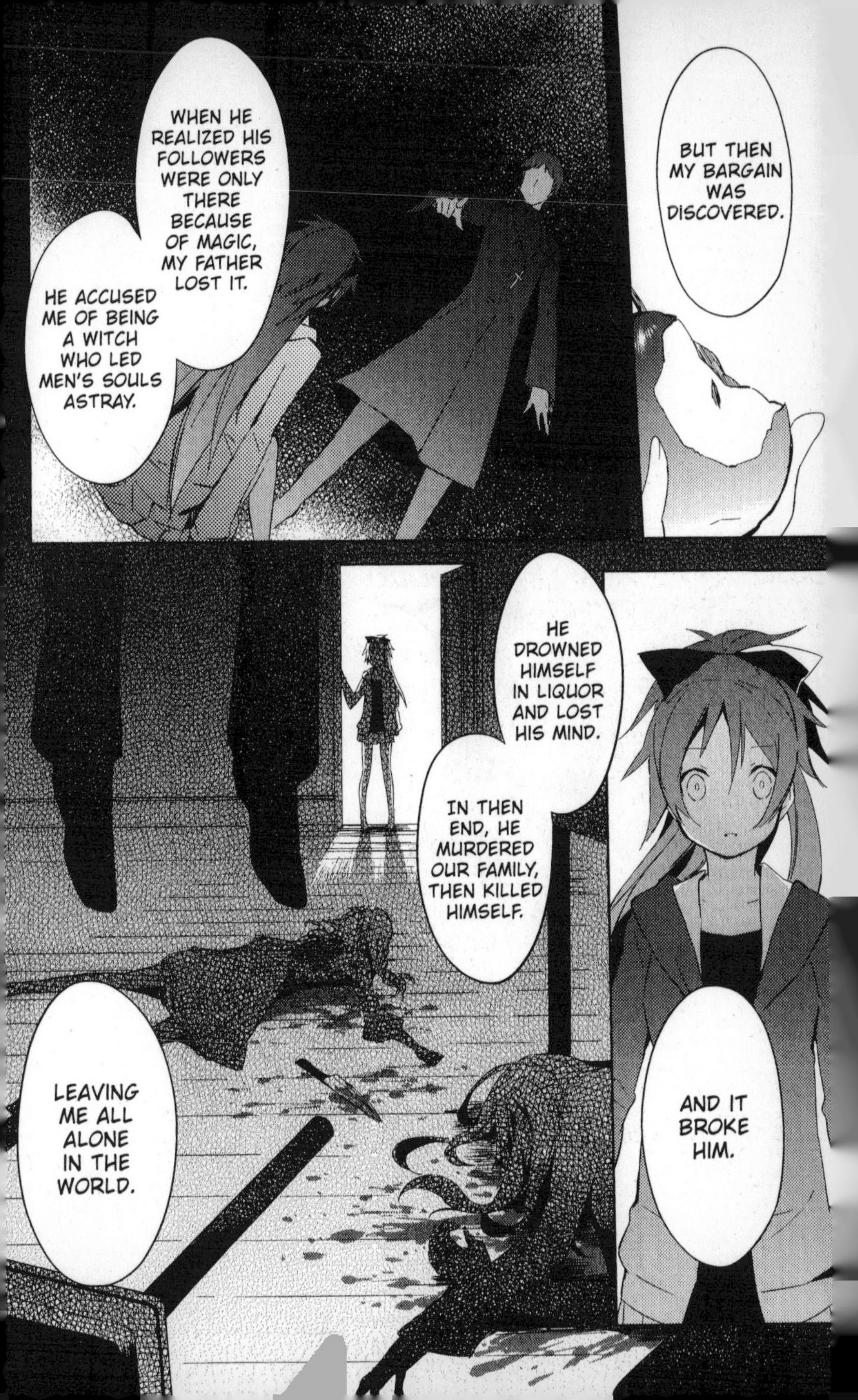
BUT THEN MY BARGAIN WAS DISCOVERED.
WHEN HE REALIZED HIS FOLLOWERS WERE ONLY THERE BECAUSE OF MAGIC, MY FATHER LOST IT.
HE ACCUSED ME OF BEING A WITCH WHO LED MEN'S SOULS ASTRAY.
AND IT BROKE HIM.
HE DROWNED HIMSELF IN LIQUOR AND LOST HIS MIND.
IN THEN END, HE MURDERED OUR FAMILY, THEN KILLED HIMSELF.
LEAVING ME ALL ALONE IN THE WORLD.

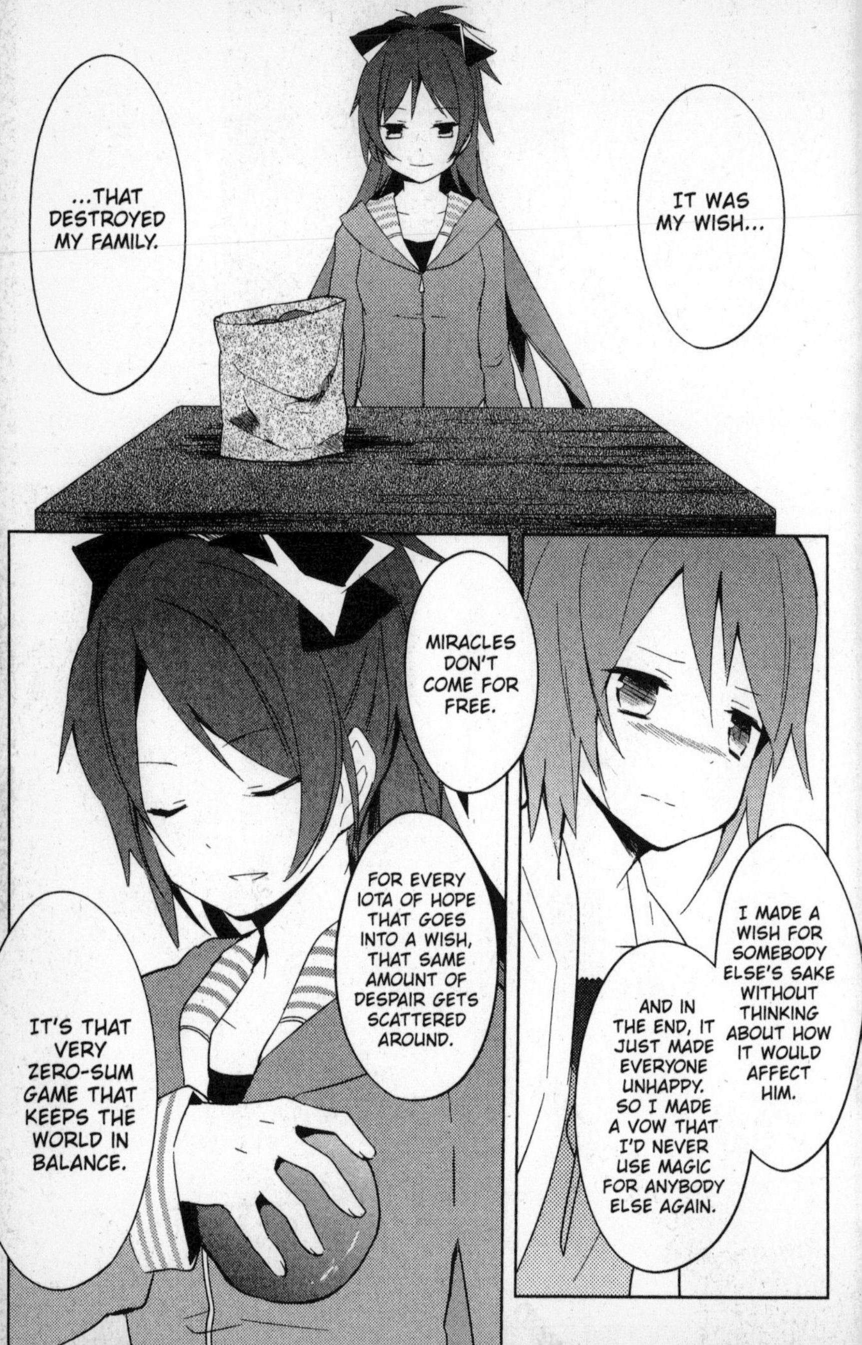
IT WAS MY WISH...
...THAT DESTROYED MY FAMILY.
I MADE A WISH FOR SOMEBODY ELSE'S SAKE WITHOUT THINKING ABOUT HOW IT WOULD AFFECT HIM.
AND IN THE END, IT JUST MADE EVERYONE UNHAPPY. SO I MADE A VOW THAT I'D NEVER USE MAGIC FOR ANYBODY ELSE AGAIN.
MIRACLES DON'T COME FOR FREE.
FOR EVERY IOTA OF HOPE THAT GOES INTO A WISH, THAT SAME AMOUNT OF DESPAIR GETS SCATTERED AROUND.
IT'S THAT VERY ZERO-SUM GAME THAT KEEPS THE WORLD IN BALANCE.

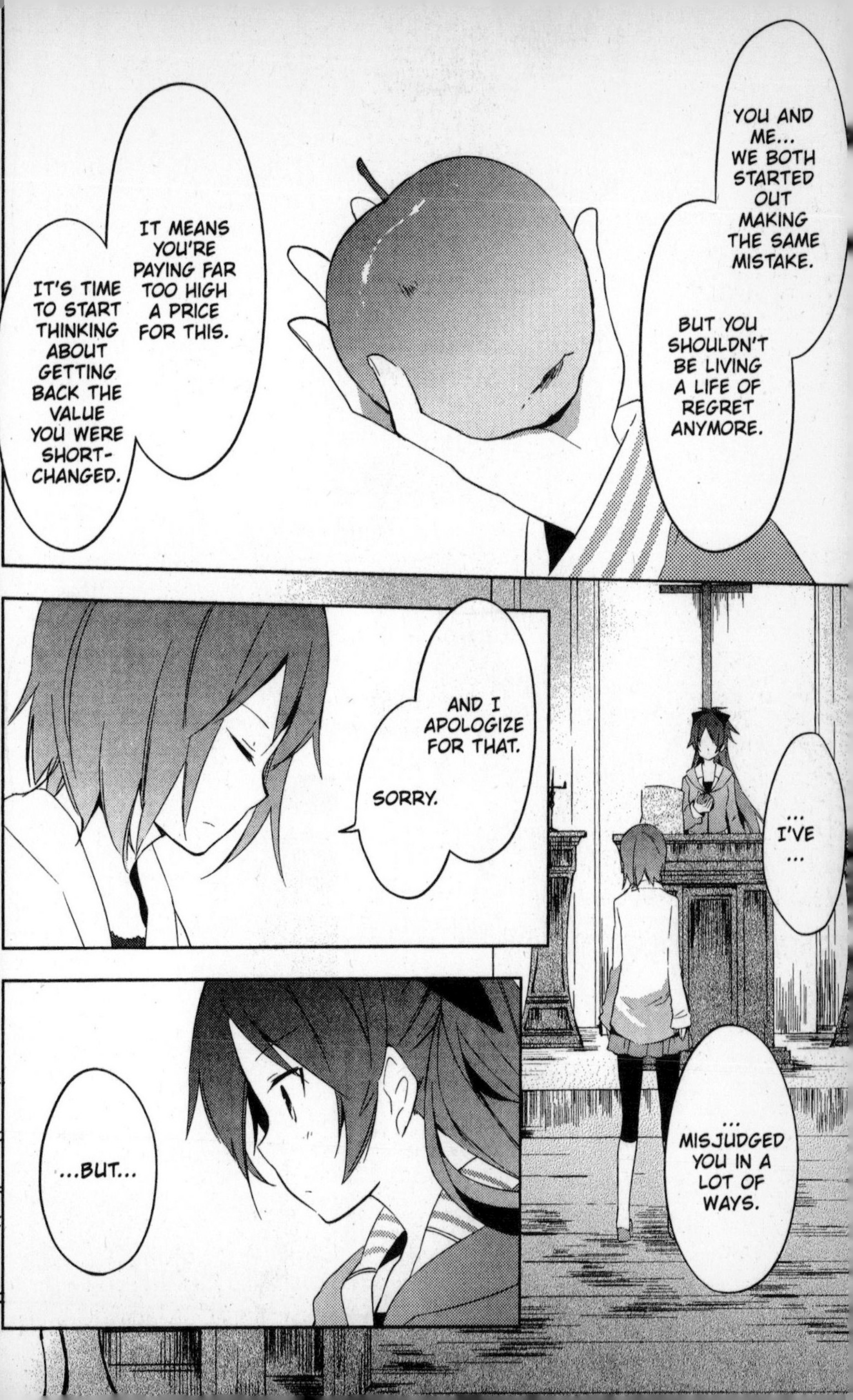
YOU AND ME... WE BOTH STARTED OUT MAKING THE SAME MISTAKE.
BUT YOU SHOULDN'T BE LIVING A LIFE OF REGRET ANYMORE.
IT MEANS YOU'RE PAYING FAR TOO HIGH A PRICE FOR THIS.
IT'S TIME TO START THINKING ABOUT GETTING BACK THE VALUE YOU WERE SHORT-CHANGED.
...I'VE...
...MISJUDGED YOU IN A LOT OF WAYS.
AND I APOLOGIZE FOR THAT.
SORRY.
...BUT...

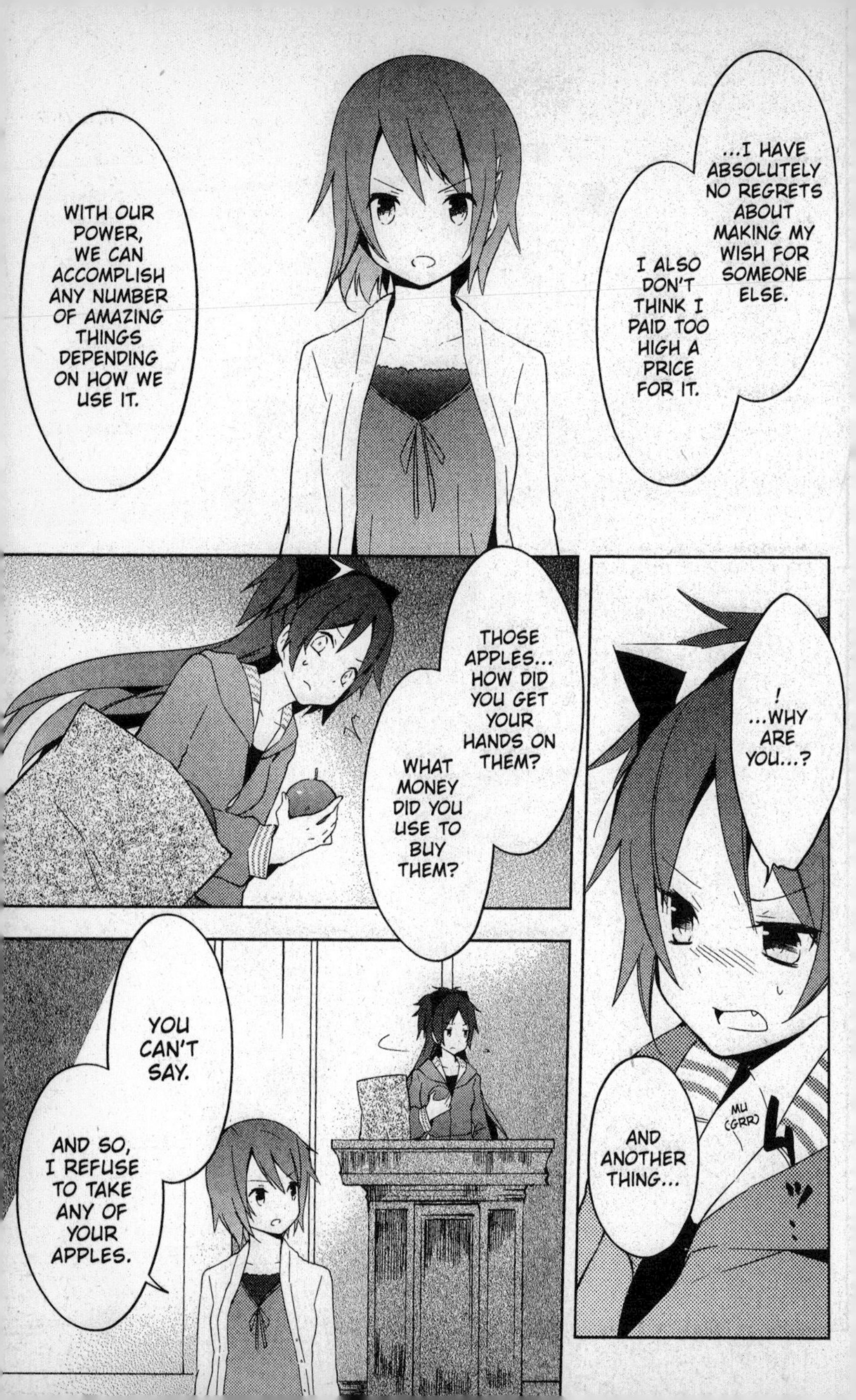
...I HAVE ABSOLUTELY NO REGRETS ABOUT MAKING MY WISH FOR SOMEONE ELSE.
I ALSO DON'T THINK I PAID TOO HIGH A PRICE FOR IT.
WITH OUR POWER, WE CAN ACCOMPLISH ANY NUMBER OF AMAZING THINGS DEPENDING ON HOW WE USE IT.
THOSE APPLES... HOW DID YOU GET YOUR HANDS ON THEM?
WHAT MONEY DID YOU USE TO BUY THEM?
! ...WHY ARE YOU...?
MU (GRR)
AND ANOTHER THING...
YOU CAN'T SAY.
AND SO, I REFUSE TO TAKE ANY OF YOUR APPLES.

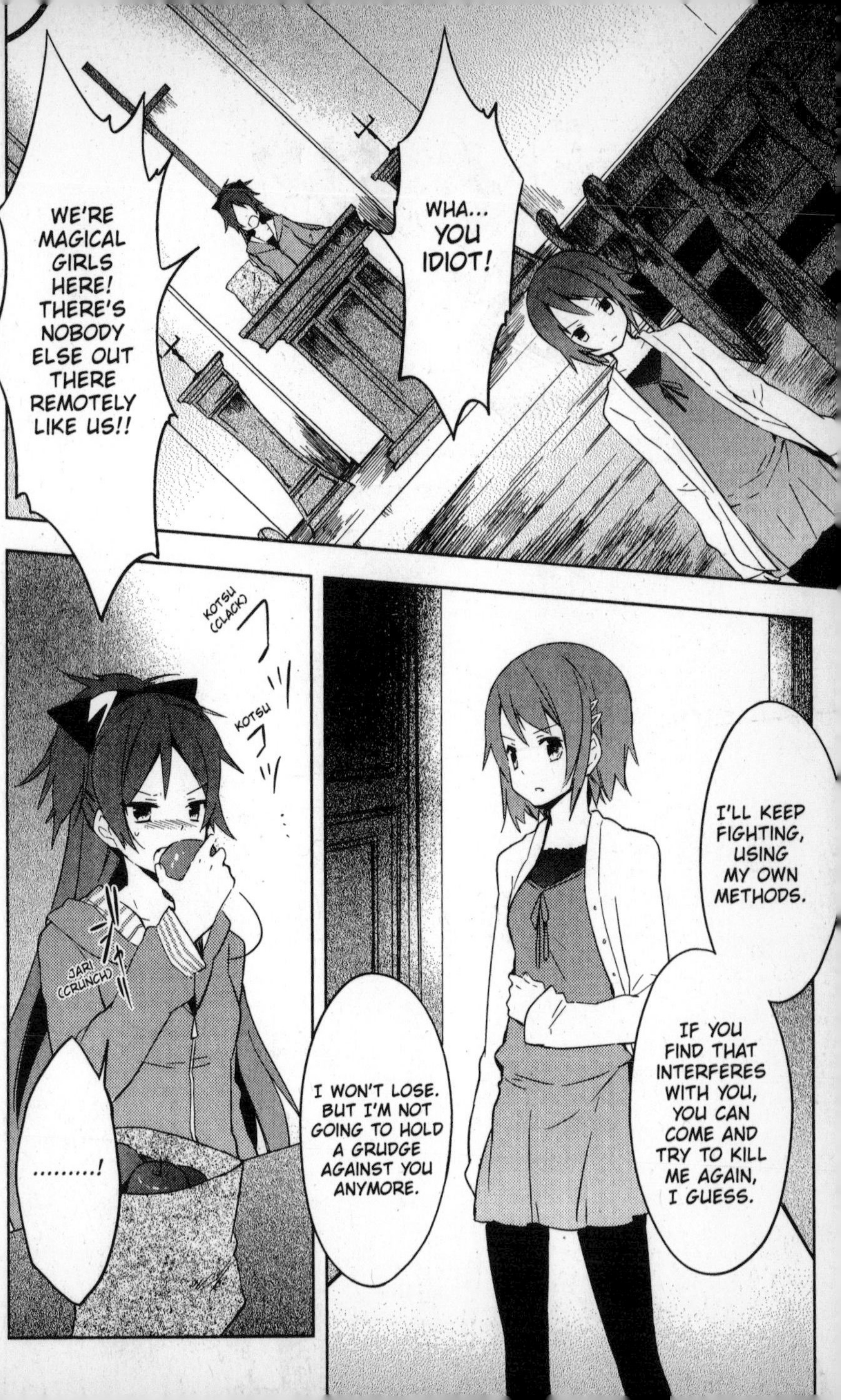
WHA... YOU IDIOT!
WE'RE MAGICAL GIRLS HERE! THERE'S NOBODY ELSE OUT THERE REMOTELY LIKE US!!
I'LL KEEP FIGHTING, USING MY OWN METHODS.
IF YOU FIND THAT INTERFERES WITH YOU, YOU CAN COME AND TRY TO KILL ME AGAIN, I GUESS.
I WON'T LOSE. BUT I'M NOT GOING TO HOLD A GRUDGE AGAINST YOU ANYMORE.
KOTSU (CLACK)
KOTSU
JARI (CRUNCH)
.........!

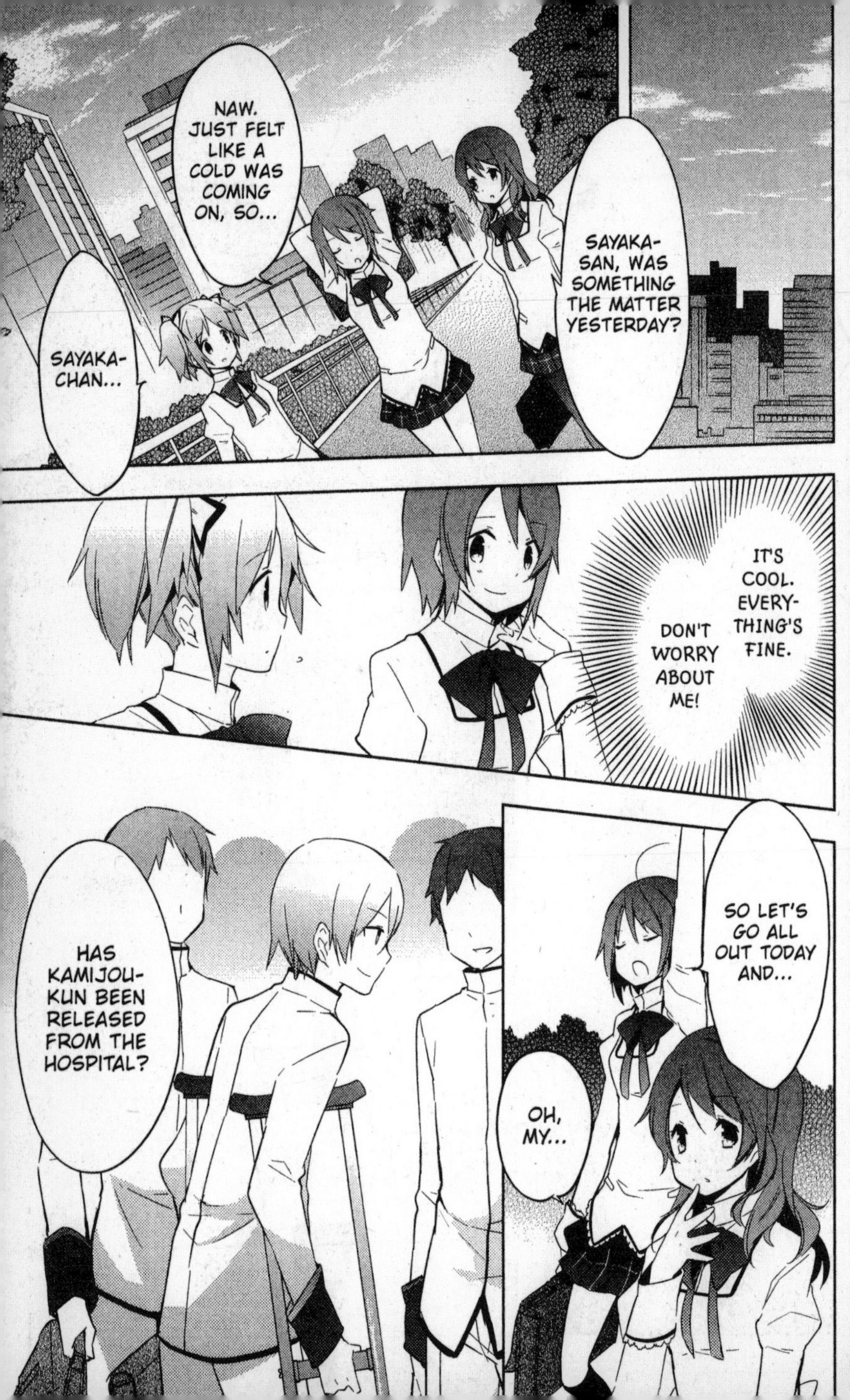
SAYAKA-SAN, WAS SOMETHING THE MATTER YESTERDAY?
NAW. JUST FELT LIKE A COLD WAS COMING ON, SO...
SAYAKA-CHAN...
IT'S COOL. EVERY-THING'S FINE.
DON'T WORRY ABOUT ME!
SO LET'S GO ALL OUT TODAY AND...
OH, MY...
HAS KAMIJOU-KUN BEEN RELEASED FROM THE HOSPITAL?

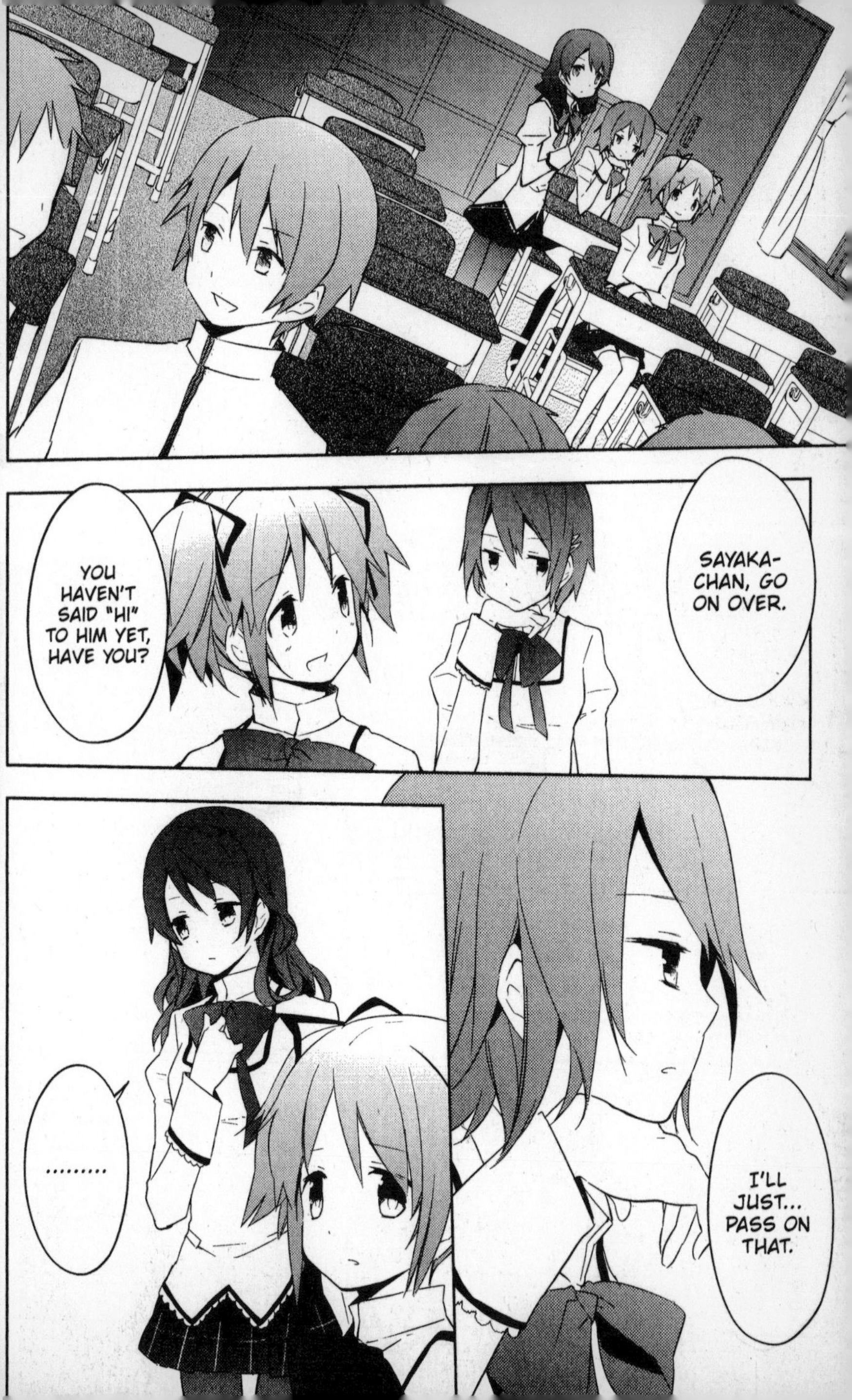
SAYAKA-CHAN, GO ON OVER.
YOU HAVEN'T SAID "HI" TO HIM YET, HAVE YOU?
I'LL JUST... PASS ON THAT.
....

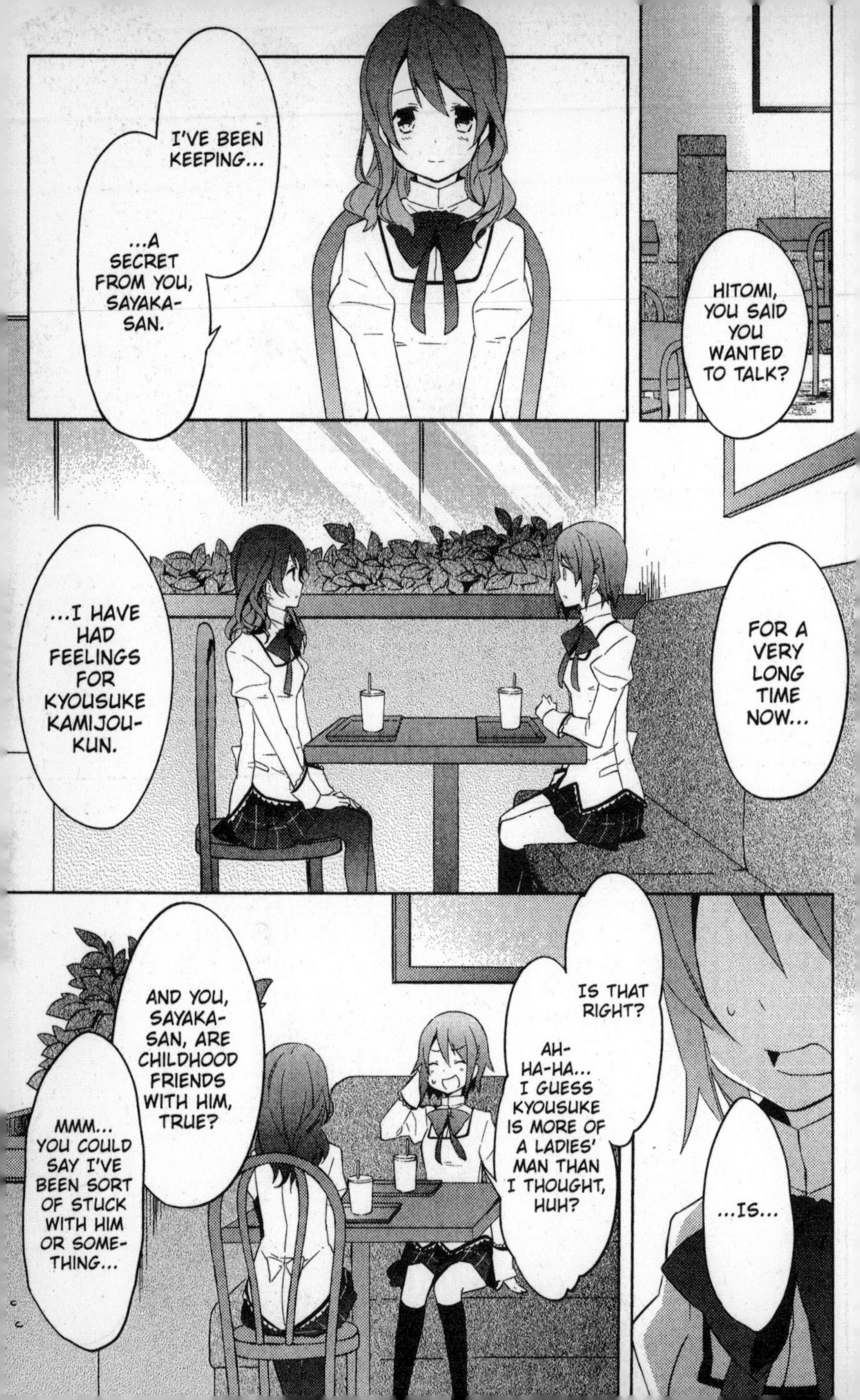
HITOMI, YOU SAID YOU WANTED TO TALK?
I'VE BEEN KEEPING...
...A SECRET FROM YOU, SAYAKA-SAN.
FOR A VERY LONG TIME NOW...
...I HAVE HAD FEELINGS FOR KYOUSUKE KAMIJOU-KUN.
...IS...
IS THAT RIGHT?
AH-HA-HA... I GUESS KYOUSUKE IS MORE OF A LADIES' MAN THAN I THOUGHT, HUH?
AND YOU, SAYAKA-SAN, ARE CHILDHOOD FRIENDS WITH HIM, TRUE?
MMM... YOU COULD SAY I'VE BEEN SORT OF STUCK WITH HIM OR SOME-THING...

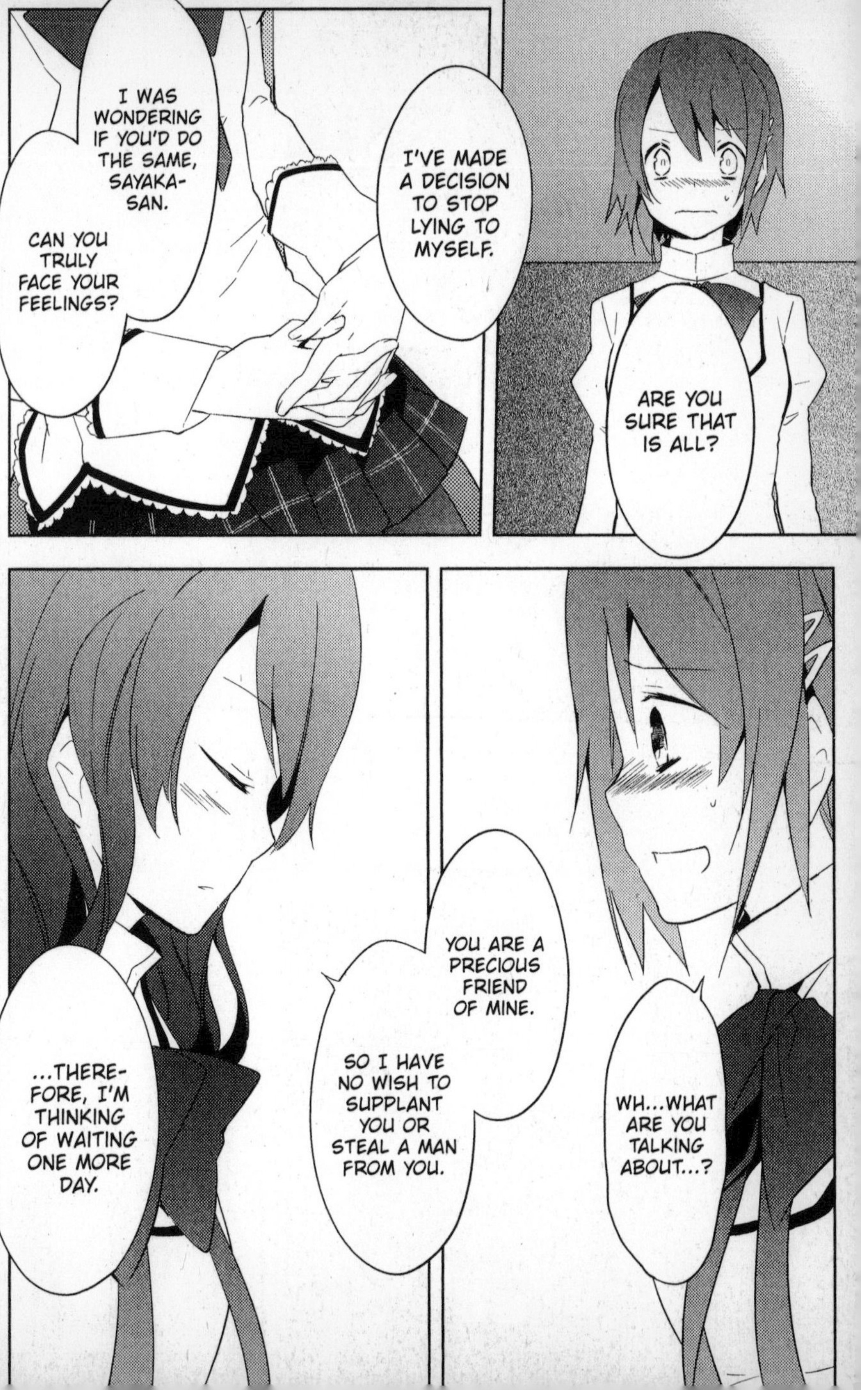
ARE YOU SURE THAT IS ALL?
I'VE MADE A DECISION TO STOP LYING TO MYSELF.
I WAS WONDERING IF YOU'D DO THE SAME, SAYAKA-SAN.
CAN YOU TRULY FACE YOUR FEELINGS?
WH...WHAT ARE YOU TALKING ABOUT...?
YOU ARE A PRECIOUS FRIEND OF MINE.
SO I HAVE NO WISH TO SUPPLANT YOU OR STEAL A MAN FROM YOU.
...THERE-FORE, I'M THINKING OF WAITING ONE MORE DAY.

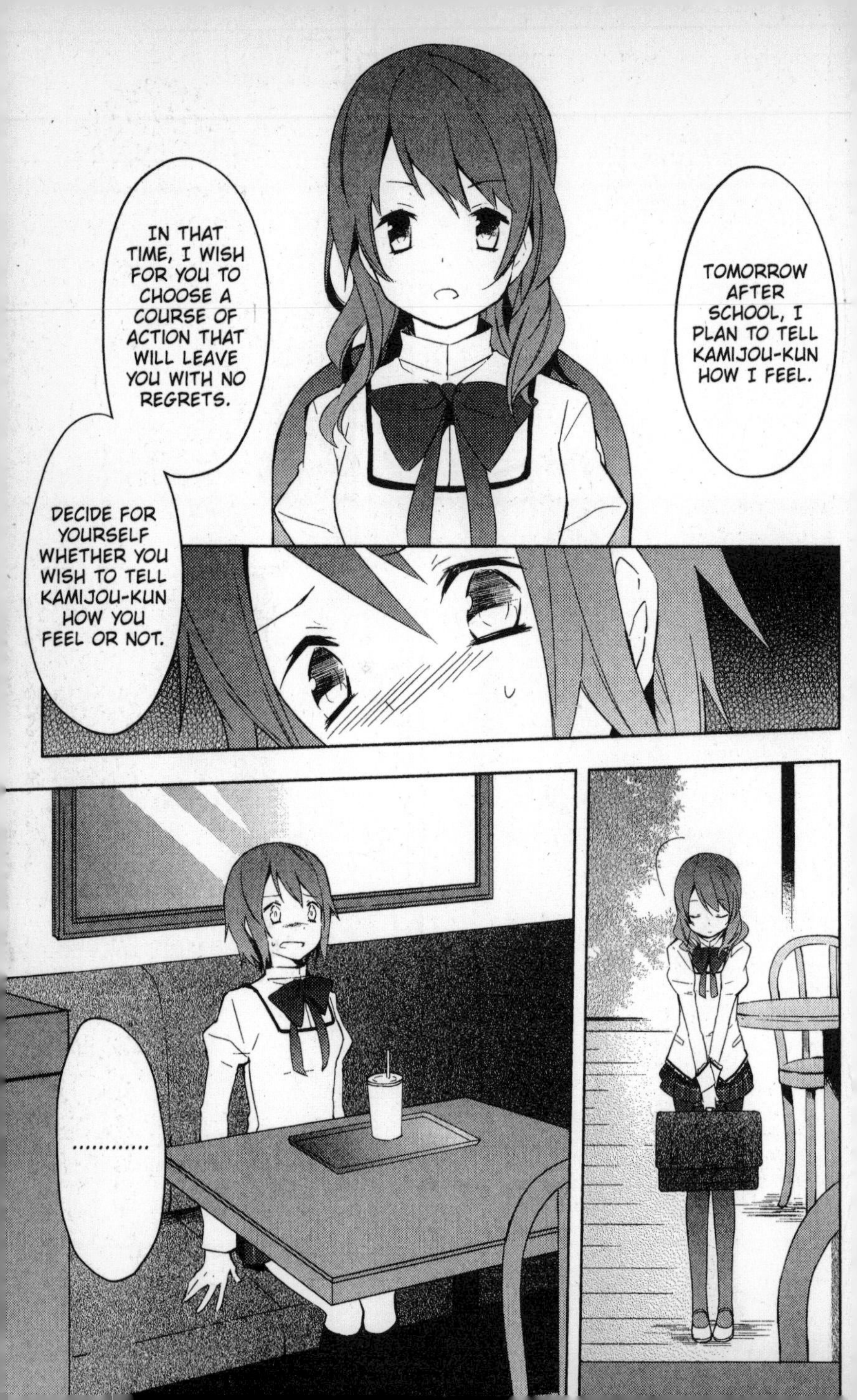
TOMORROW AFTER SCHOOL, I PLAN TO TELL KAMIJOU-KUN HOW I FEEL.
IN THAT TIME, I WISH FOR YOU TO CHOOSE A COURSE OF ACTION THAT WILL LEAVE YOU WITH NO REGRETS.
DECIDE FOR YOURSELF WHETHER YOU WISH TO TELL KAMIJOU-KUN HOW YOU FEEL OR NOT.
....

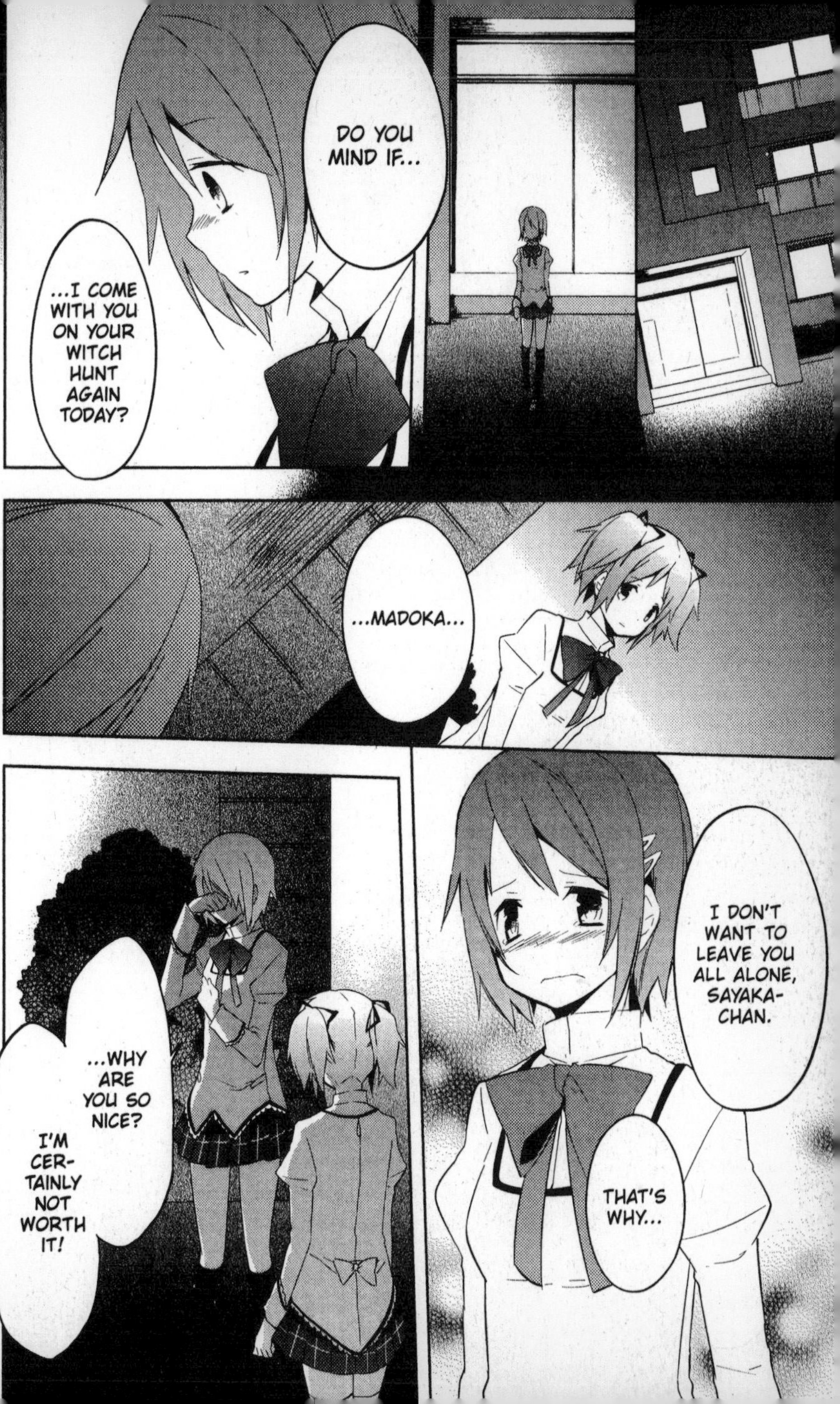
DO YOU MIND IF...
...I COME WITH YOU ON YOUR WITCH HUNT AGAIN TODAY?
...MADOKA...
I DON'T WANT TO LEAVE YOU ALL ALONE, SAYAKA-CHAN.
THAT'S WHY...
...WHY ARE YOU SO NICE?
I'M CER-TAINLY NOT WORTH IT!

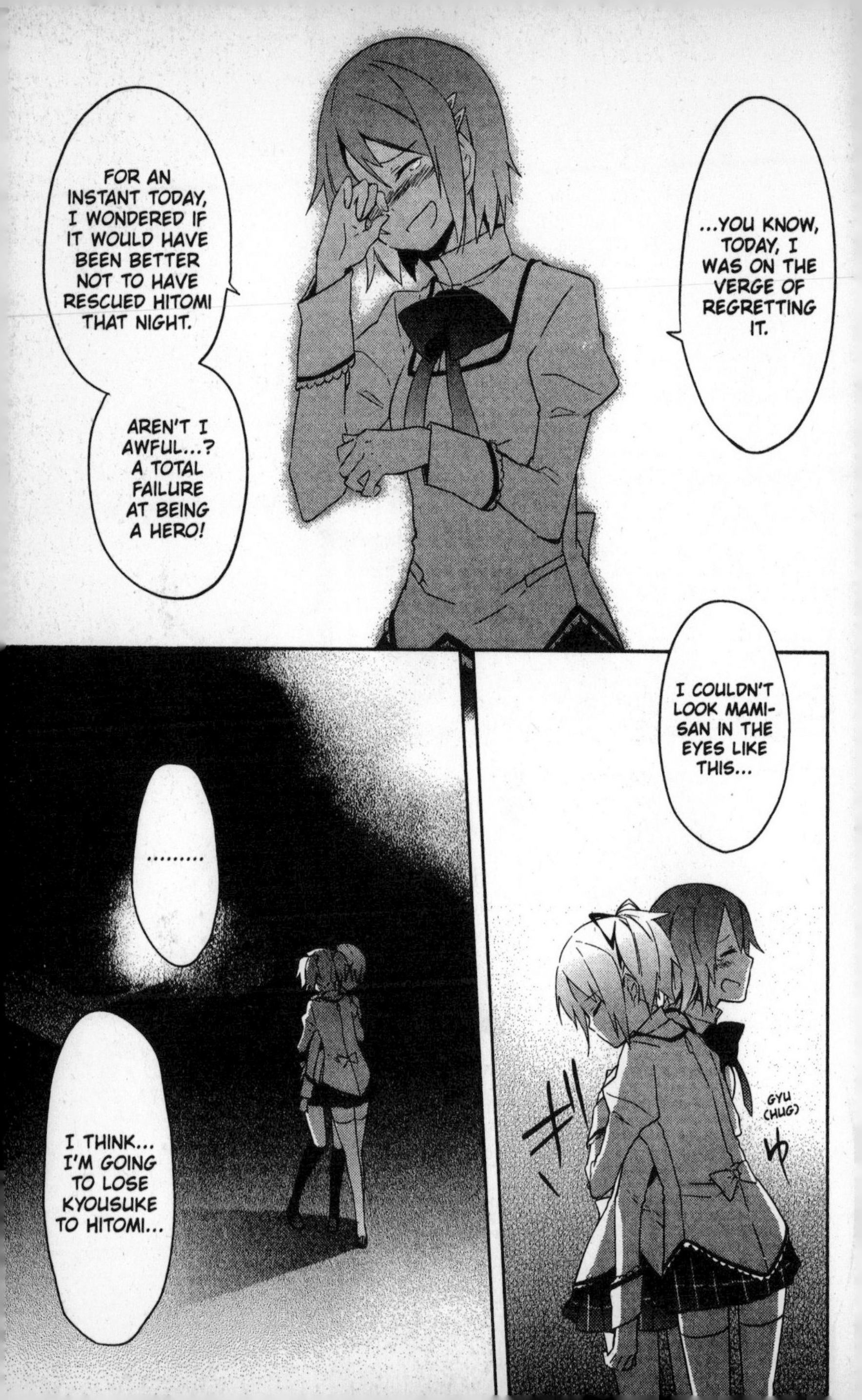
...YOU KNOW, TODAY, I WAS ON THE VERGE OF REGRETTING IT.
FOR AN INSTANT TODAY, I WONDERED IF IT WOULD HAVE BEEN BETTER NOT TO HAVE RESCUED HITOMI THAT NIGHT.
AREN'T I AWFUL...? A TOTAL FAILURE AT BEING A HERO!
I COULDN'T LOOK MAMI-SAN IN THE EYES LIKE THIS...
GYU (HUG)
....
I THINK... I'M GOING TO LOSE KYOUSUKE TO HITOMI...

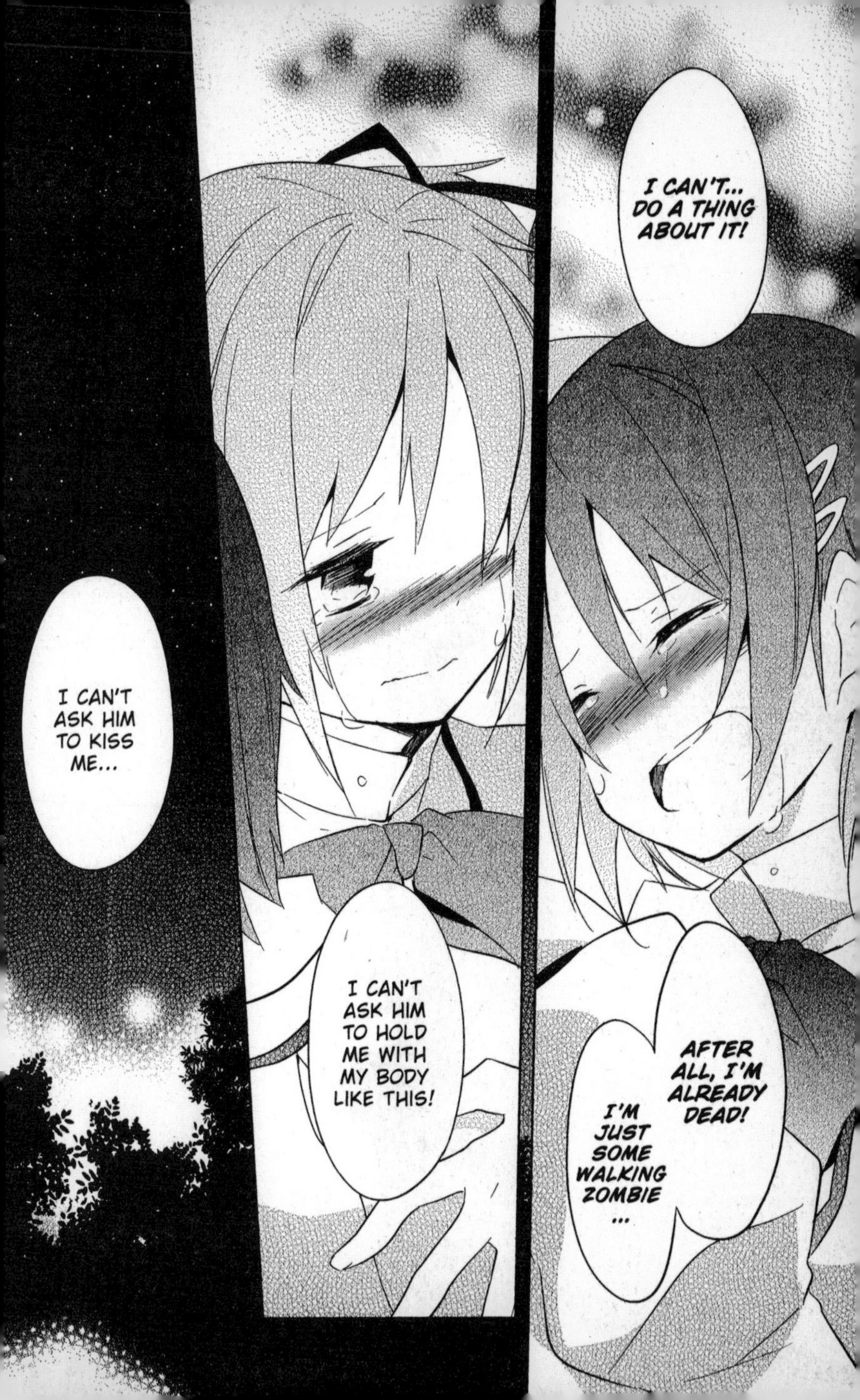
I CAN'T... DO A THING ABOUT IT!
AFTER ALL, I'M ALREADY DEAD!
I'M JUST SOME WALKING ZOMBIE...
I CAN'T ASK HIM TO HOLD ME WITH MY BODY LIKE THIS!
I CAN'T ASK HIM TO KISS ME...

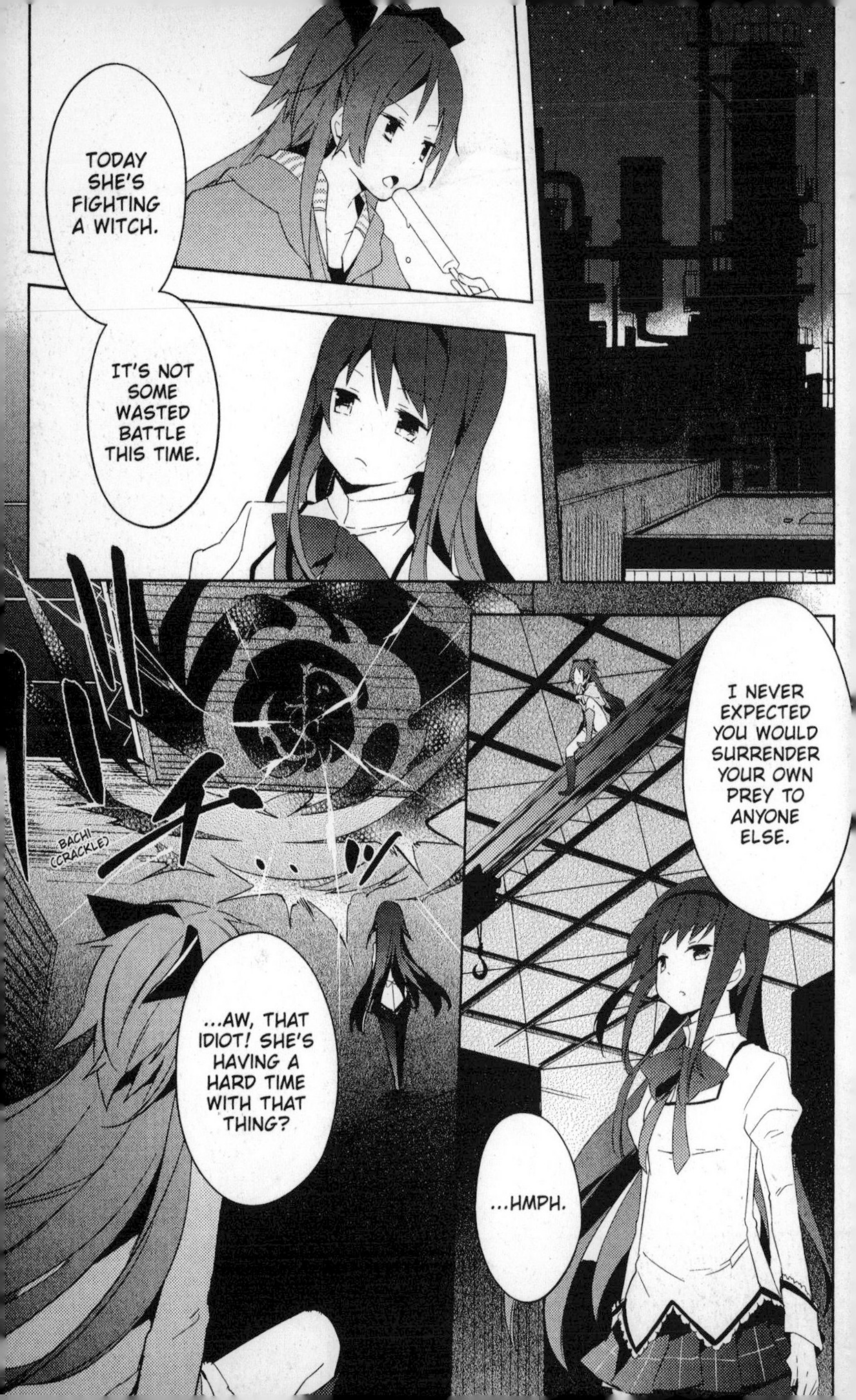
TODAY SHE'S FIGHTING A WITCH.
IT'S NOT SOME WASTED BATTLE THIS TIME.
I NEVER EXPECTED YOU WOULD SURRENDER YOUR OWN PREY TO ANYONE ELSE.
...HMPH.
BACHI (CRACKLE)
...AW, THAT IDIOT! SHE'S HAVING A HARD TIME WITH THAT THING?

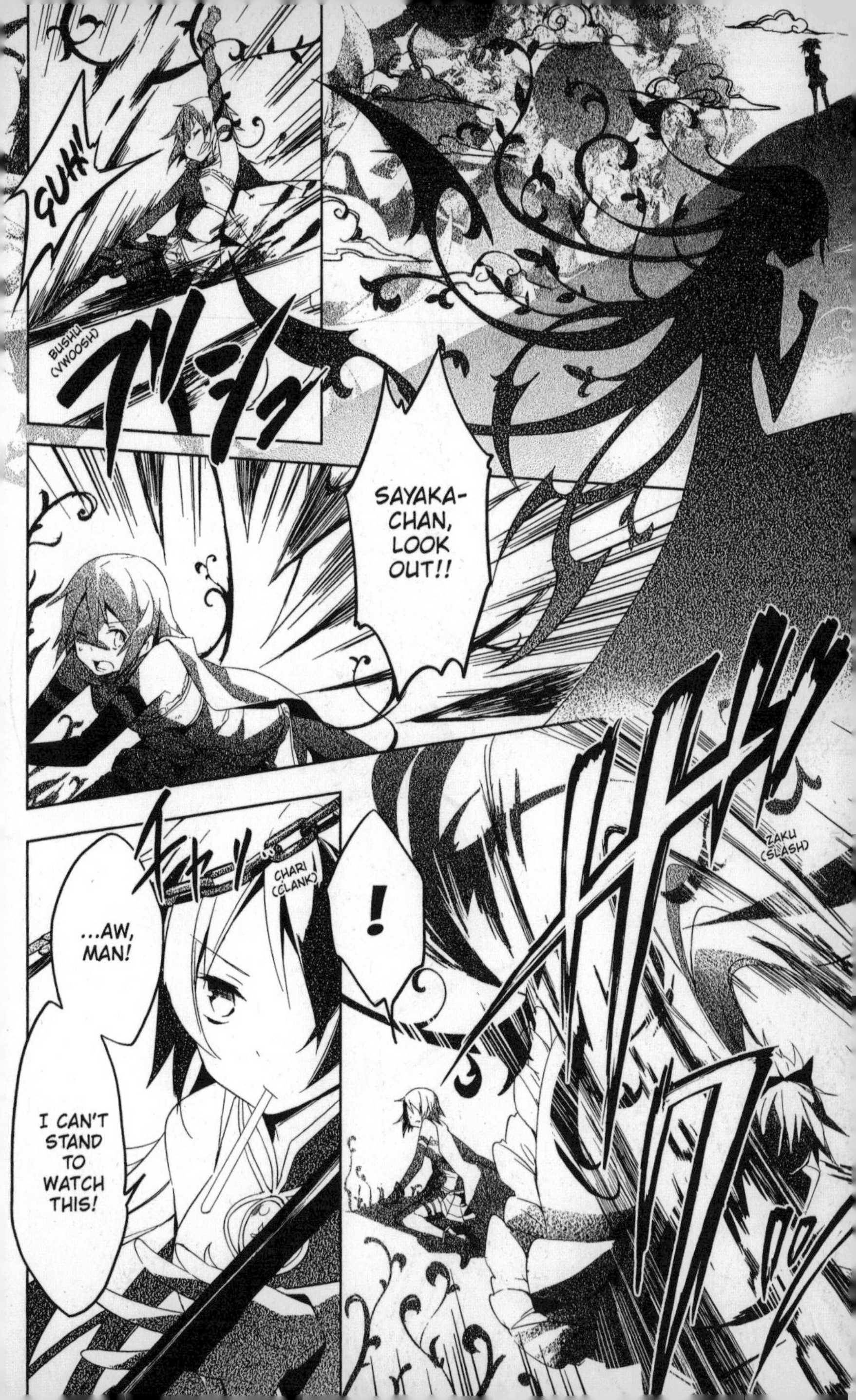
GUH!!
BUSHU (VWOOSH)
SAYAKA-CHAN, LOOK OUT!!
ZAKU (SLASH)
!
CHARI (CLANK)
...AW, MAN!
I CAN'T STAND TO WATCH THIS!

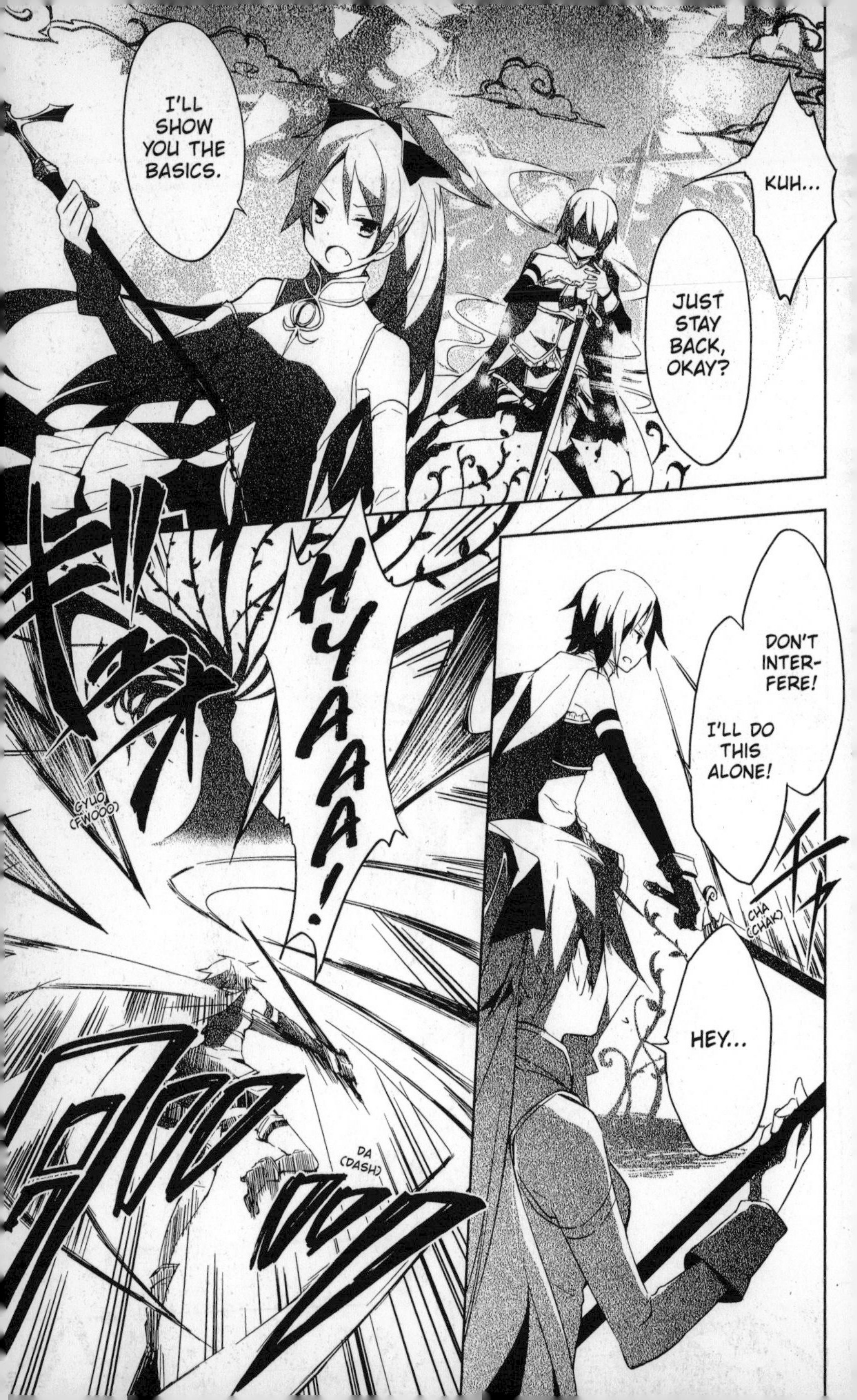
KUH...
JUST STAY BACK, OKAY?
I'LL SHOW YOU THE BASICS.
DON'T INTER-FERE!
I'LL DO THIS ALONE!
CHA (CHAK)
HEY...
HYAAAA!!
GYUO (FWOOO)
DA (DASH)

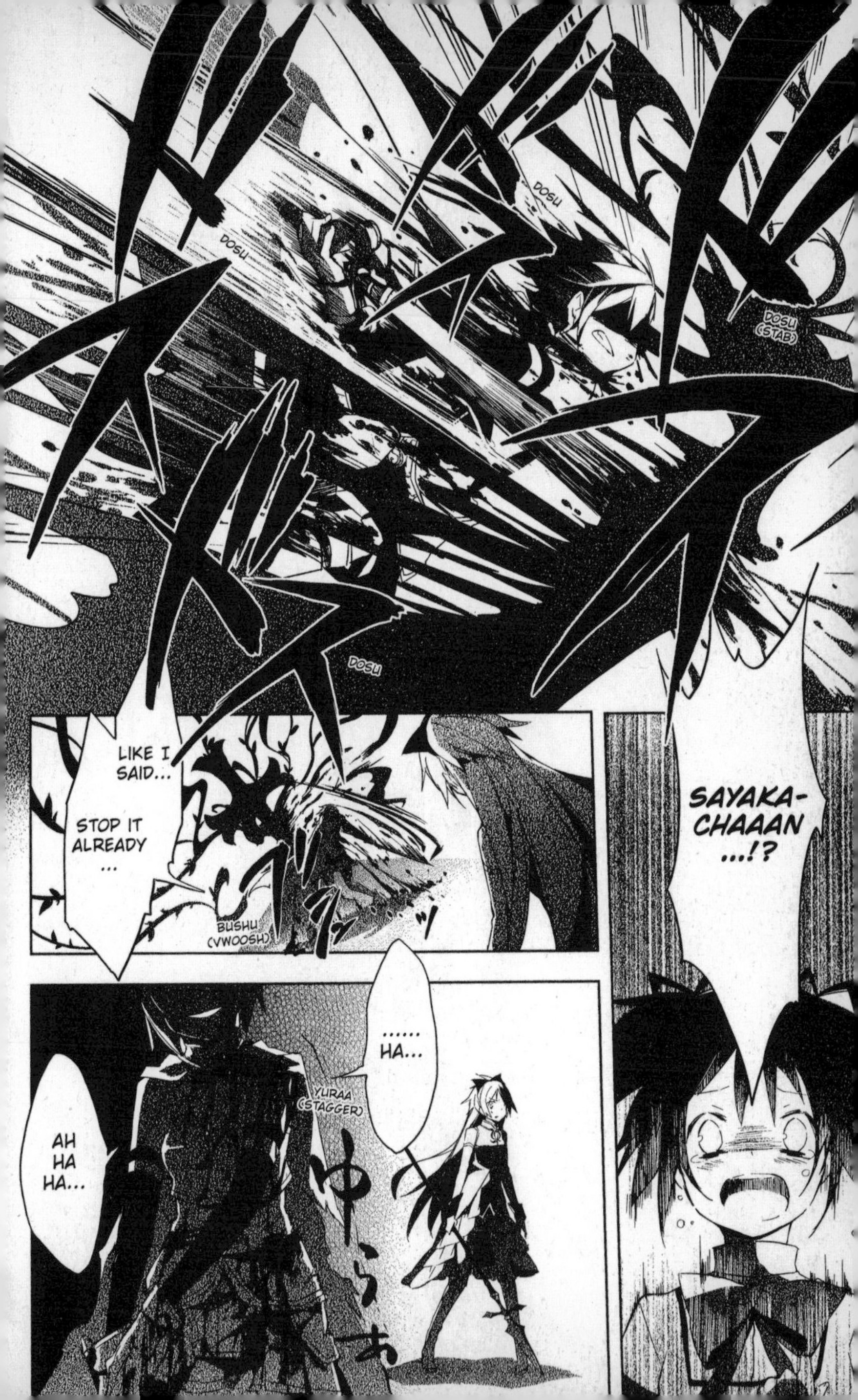
DOSU
DOSU (STAB)
DOSU
DOSU
SAYAKA-CHAAAN...!?
LIKE I SAID...
STOP IT ALREADY...
BUSHU (VWOOSH)
......HA...
YURAA (STAGGER)
AH HA HA...

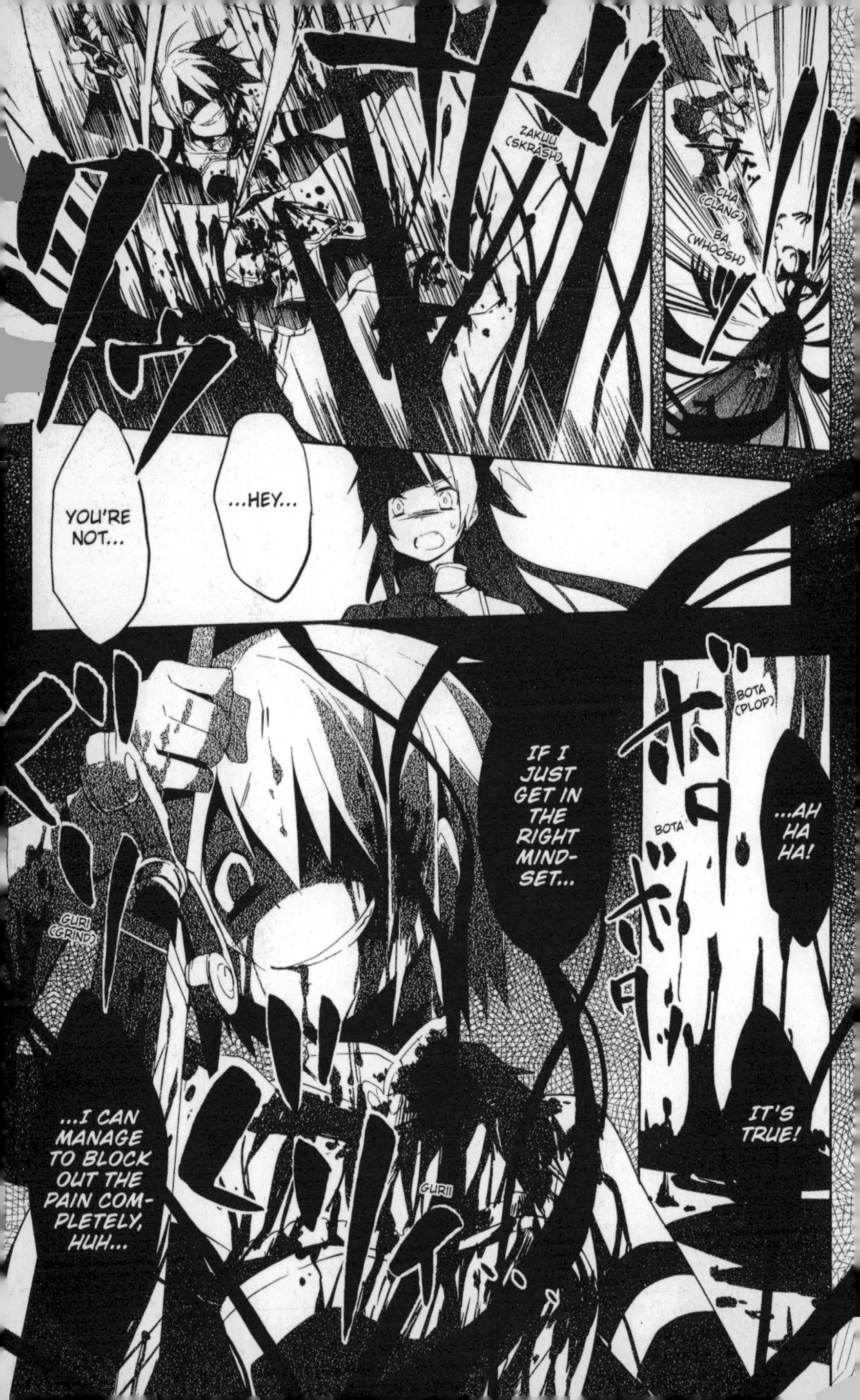
CHA (CLANG)
BA (WHOOSH)
ZAKUU (SKRASH)
...HEY...
YOU'RE NOT...
BOTA (PLOP)
BOTA
...AH HA HA!
IT'S TRUE!
IF I JUST GET IN THE RIGHT MIND-SET...
GURI (GRIND)
GURII
...I CAN MANAGE TO BLOCK OUT THE PAIN COM-PLETELY, HUH...

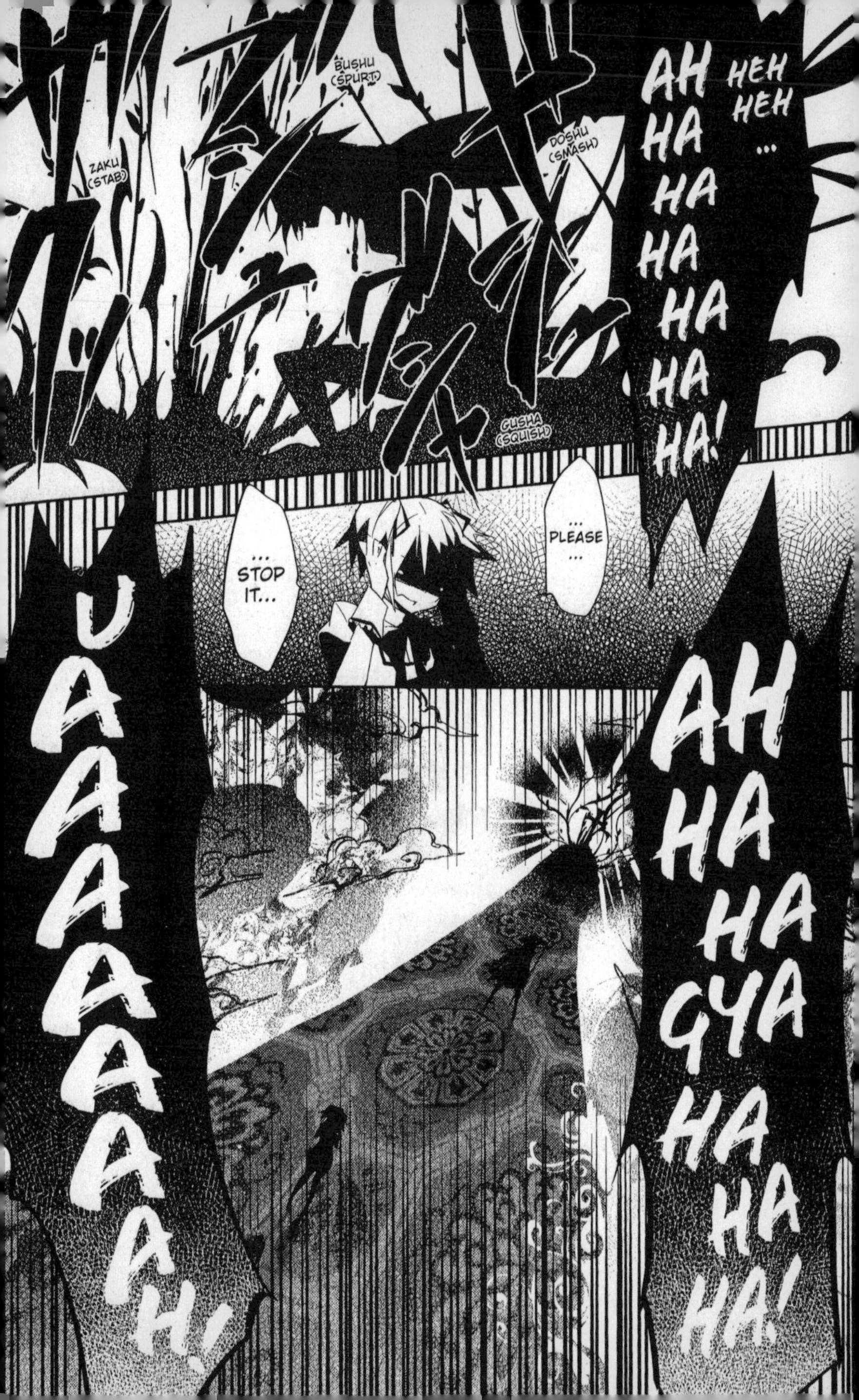
AH HA HA HA HA HA HA HA!
HEH HEH ...
DOSHU (SMASH)
BUSHU (SPURT)
ZAKU (STAB)
GUSHA (SQUISH)
... PLEASE ...
... STOP IT...
AH HA HA HA HA GYA HA HA HA HA!
UAAAAAAAH!

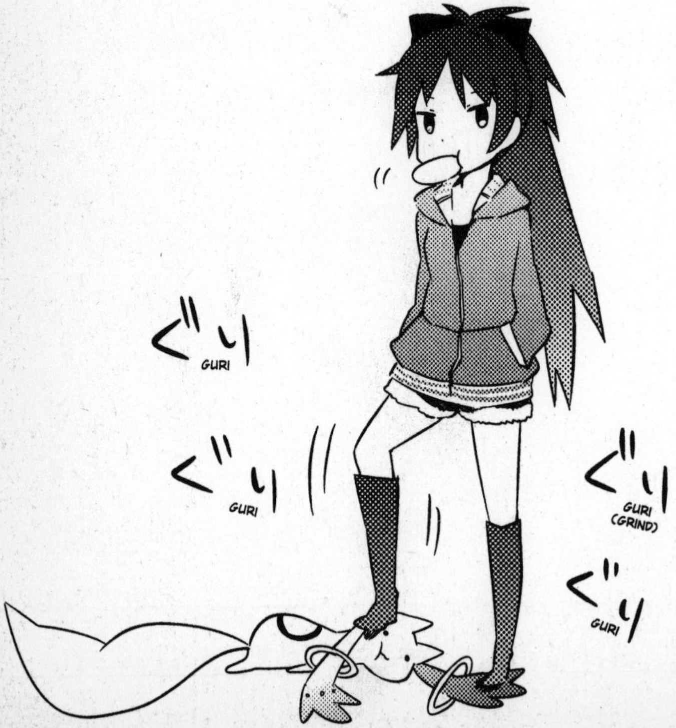
ぐり
GURI
(GRIND)
ぐり
GURI
ぐり
GURI
ぐり
GURI

PUELLA MAGI
MADOKA★MAGICA

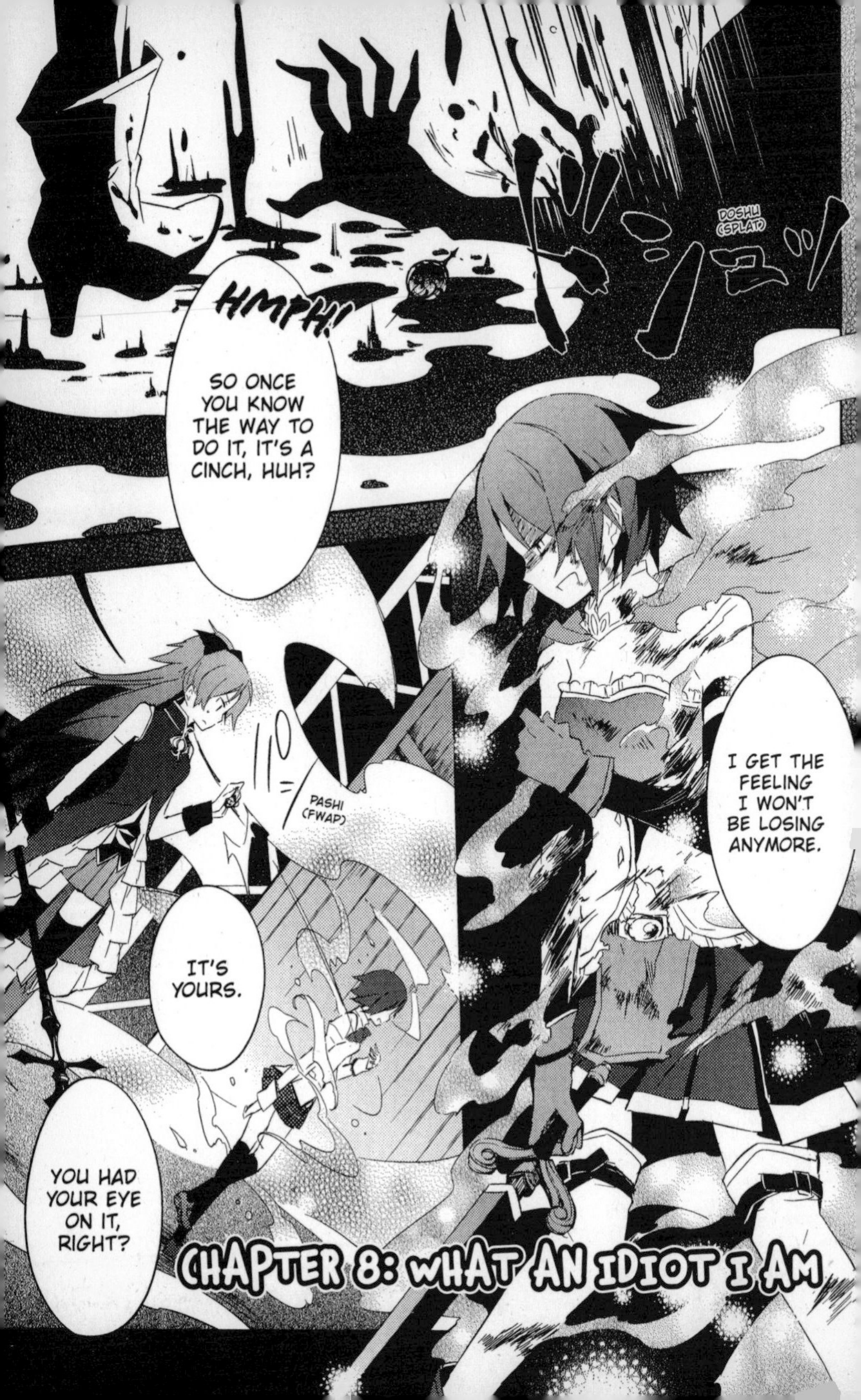
DOSHU (SPLAT)
HMPH!
SO ONCE YOU KNOW THE WAY TO DO IT, IT'S A CINCH, HUH?
I GET THE FEELING I WON'T BE LOSING ANYMORE.
PASHI (FWAP)
IT'S YOURS.
YOU HAD YOUR EYE ON IT, RIGHT?
CHAPTER 8: WHAT AN IDIOT I AM

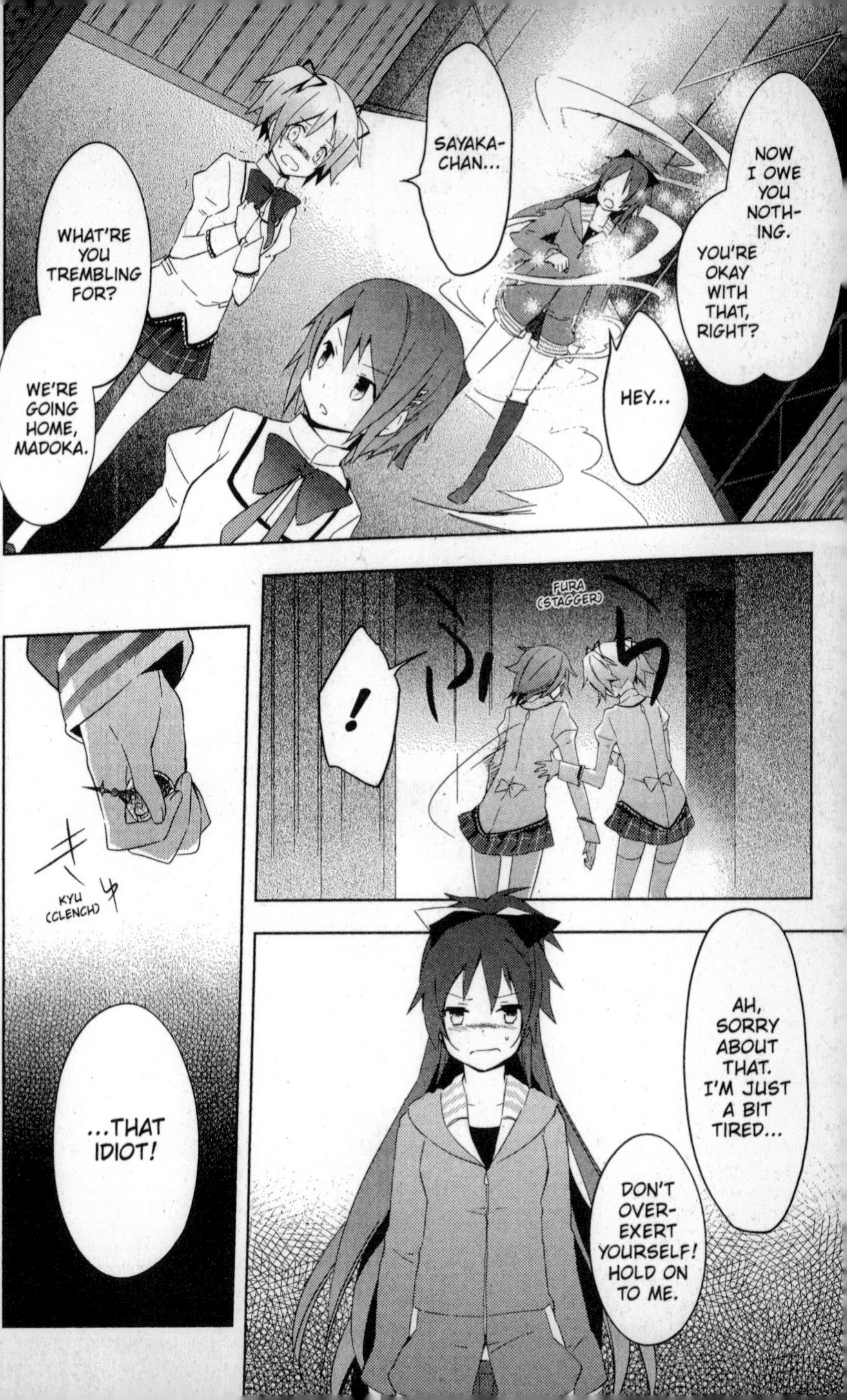
NOW I OWE YOU NOTHING. YOU'RE OKAY WITH THAT, RIGHT?
SAYAKA-CHAN...
HEY...
WHAT'RE YOU TREMBLING FOR?
WE'RE GOING HOME, MADOKA.
FURA (STAGGER)
!
AH, SORRY ABOUT THAT. I'M JUST A BIT TIRED...
DON'T OVER-EXERT YOURSELF! HOLD ON TO ME.
KYU (CLENCH)
...THAT IDIOT!

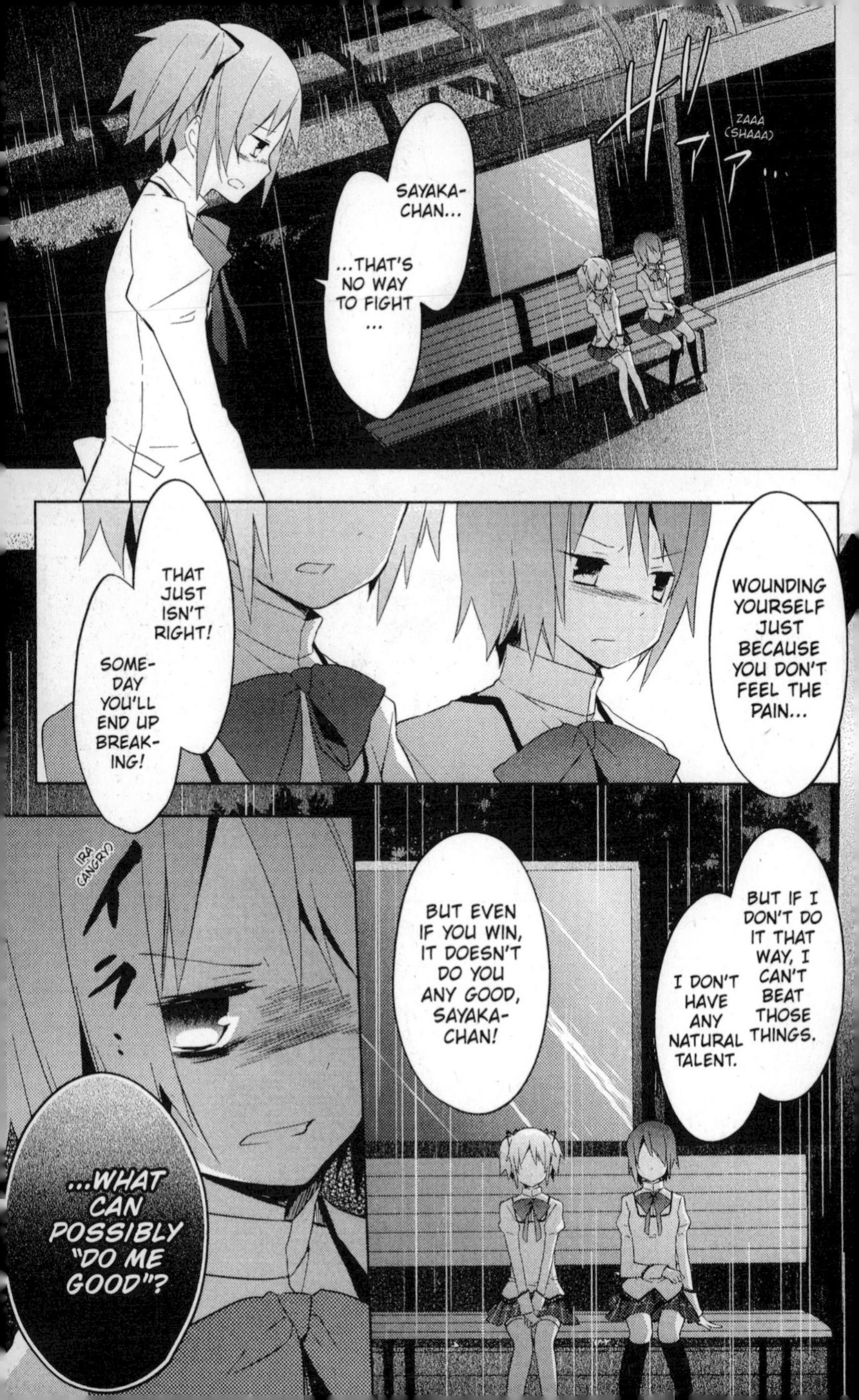
ZAAA (SHAAA)
SAYAKA-CHAN... ...THAT'S NO WAY TO FIGHT...
WOUNDING YOURSELF JUST BECAUSE YOU DON'T FEEL THE PAIN...
THAT JUST ISN'T RIGHT! SOME-DAY YOU'LL END UP BREAK-ING!
BUT IF I DON'T DO IT THAT WAY, I CAN'T BEAT THOSE THINGS.
I DON'T HAVE ANY NATURAL TALENT.
BUT EVEN IF YOU WIN, IT DOESN'T DO YOU ANY GOOD, SAYAKA-CHAN!
IRA (ANGRY)
...WHAT CAN POSSIBLY "DO ME GOOD"?

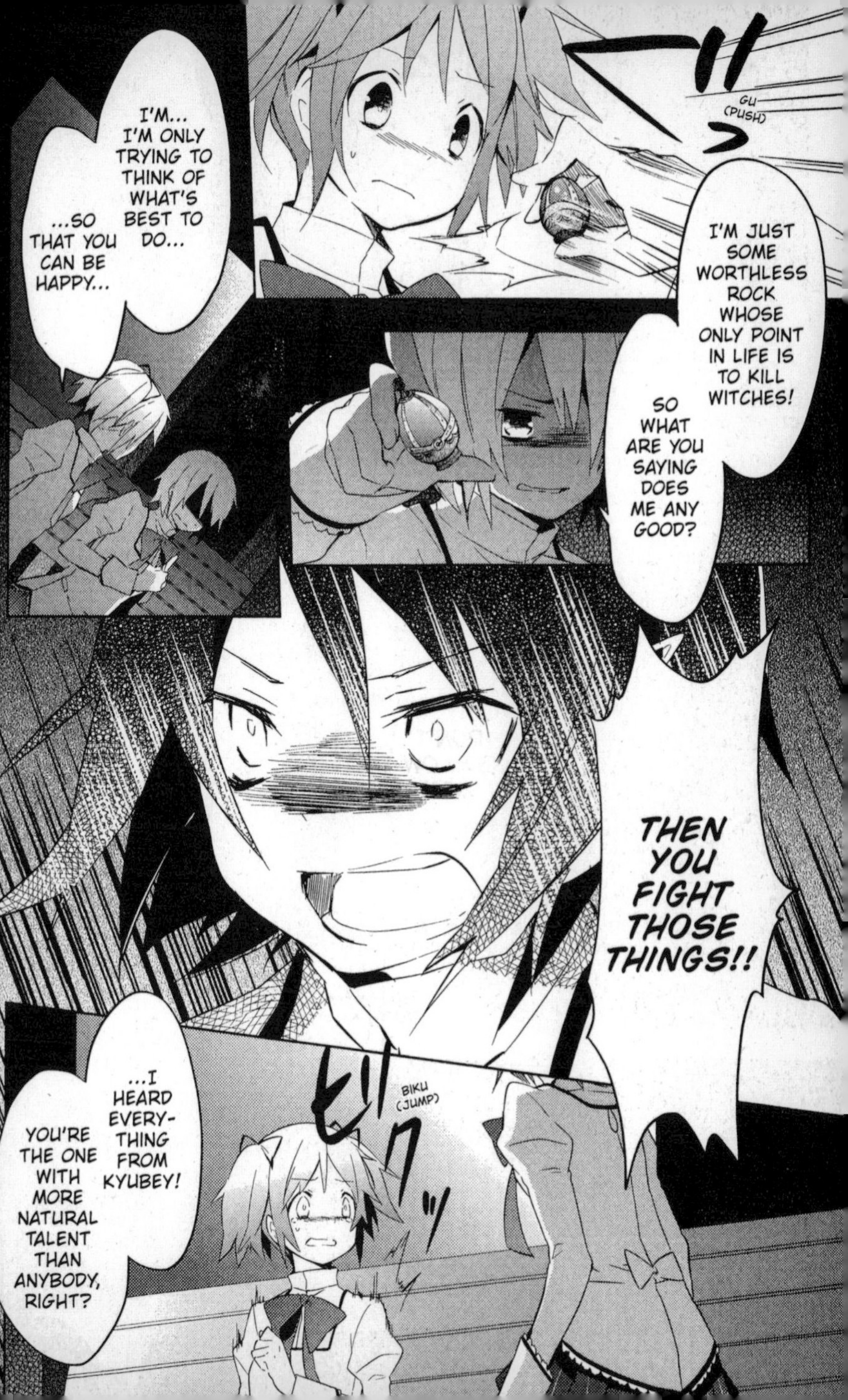
GU (PUSH)
I'M JUST SOME WORTHLESS ROCK WHOSE ONLY POINT IN LIFE IS TO KILL WITCHES!
SO WHAT ARE YOU SAYING DOES ME ANY GOOD?
I'M... I'M ONLY TRYING TO THINK OF WHAT'S BEST TO DO...
...SO THAT YOU CAN BE HAPPY...
THEN YOU FIGHT THOSE THINGS!!
BIKU (JUMP)
...I HEARD EVERY-THING FROM KYUBEY!
YOU'RE THE ONE WITH MORE NATURAL TALENT THAN ANYBODY, RIGHT?

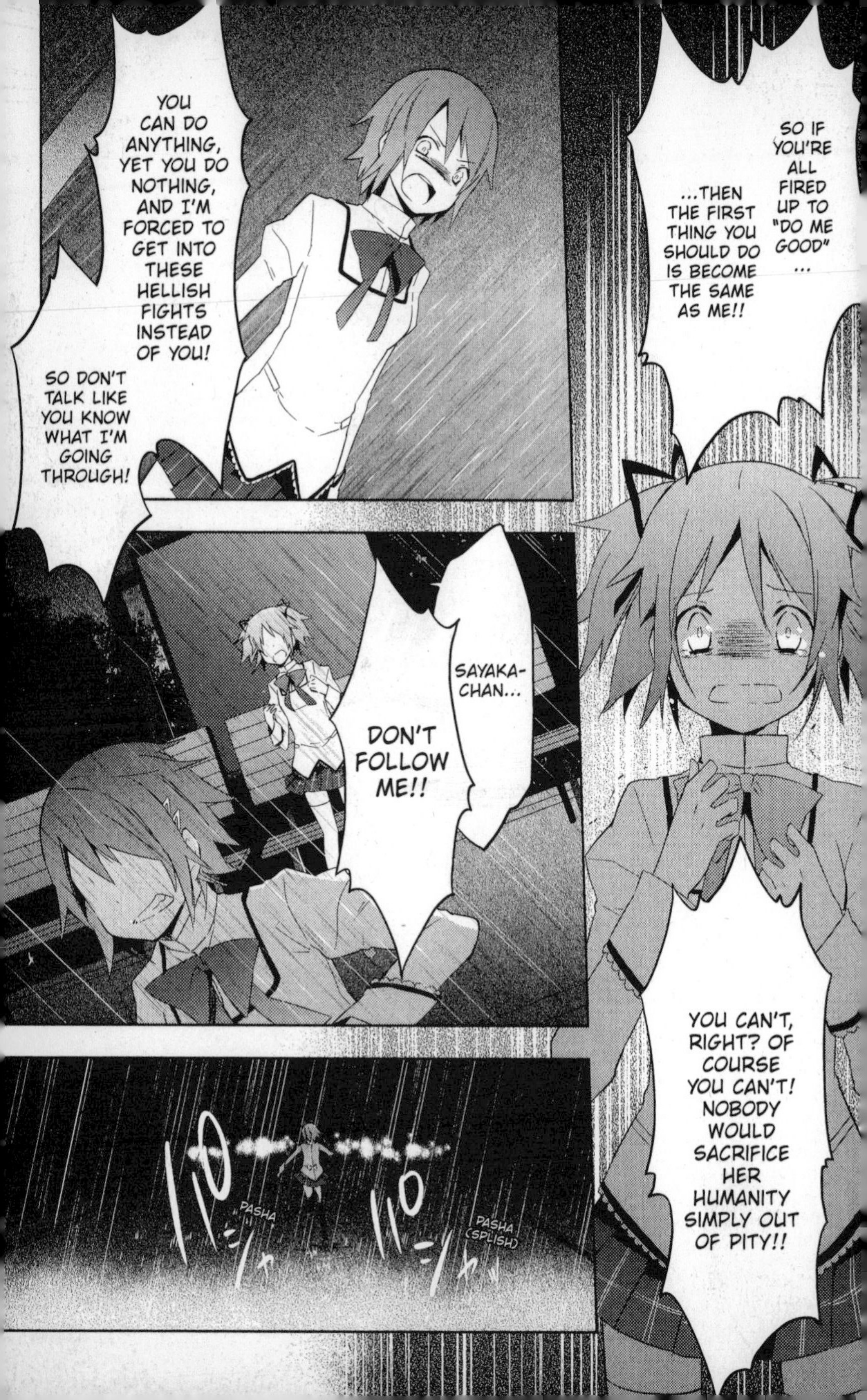
SO IF YOU'RE ALL FIRED UP TO "DO ME GOOD"...
...THEN THE FIRST THING YOU SHOULD DO IS BECOME THE SAME AS ME!!
YOU CAN'T, RIGHT? OF COURSE YOU CAN'T! NOBODY WOULD SACRIFICE HER HUMANITY SIMPLY OUT OF PITY!!
YOU CAN DO ANYTHING, YET YOU DO NOTHING, AND I'M FORCED TO GET INTO THESE HELLISH FIGHTS INSTEAD OF YOU!
SO DON'T TALK LIKE YOU KNOW WHAT I'M GOING THROUGH!
SAYAKA-CHAN...
DON'T FOLLOW ME!!
PASHA
PASHA (SPLISH)

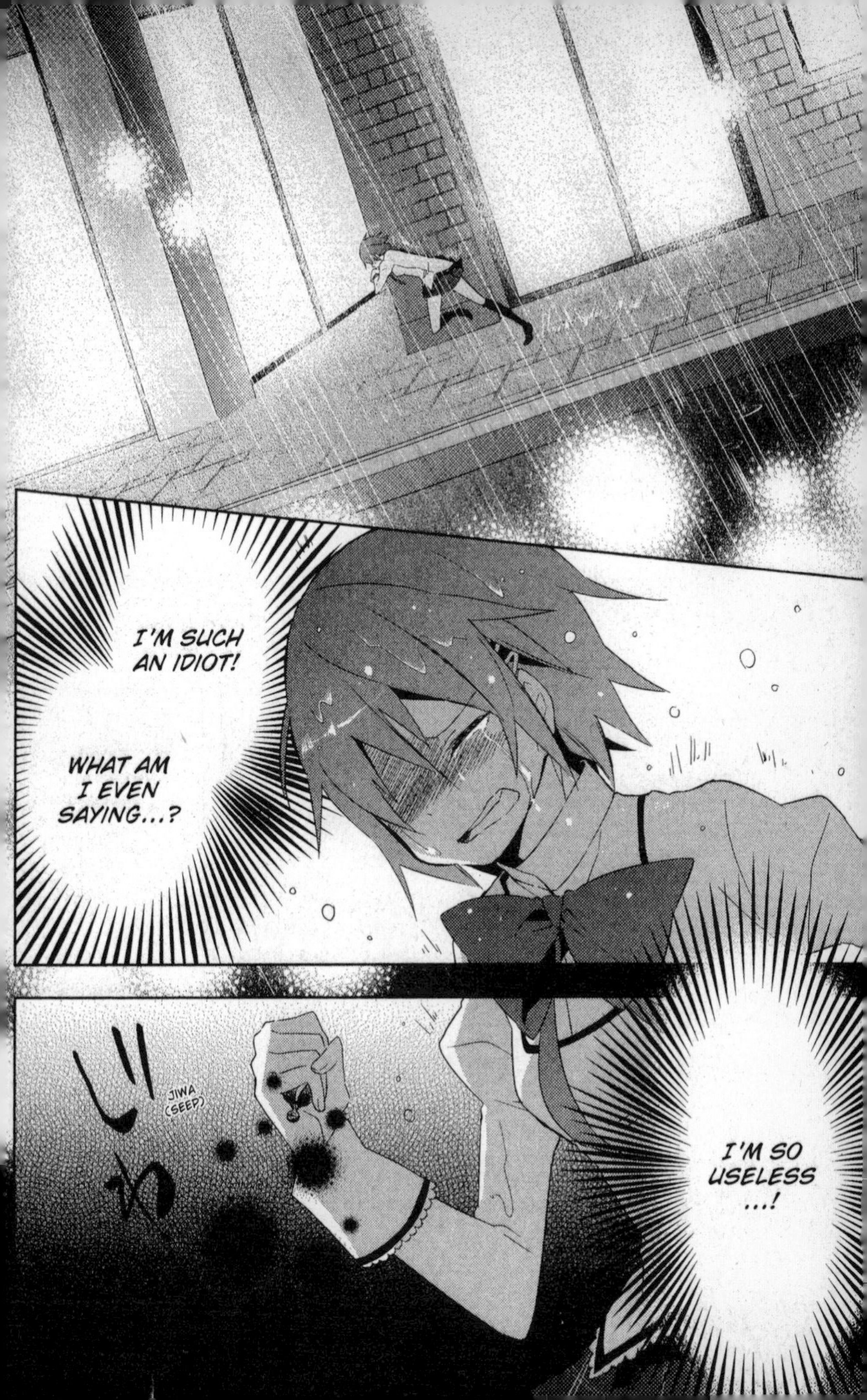
I'M SUCH AN IDIOT!
WHAT AM I EVEN SAYING...?
I'M SO USELESS ...!
JIWA (SEEP)

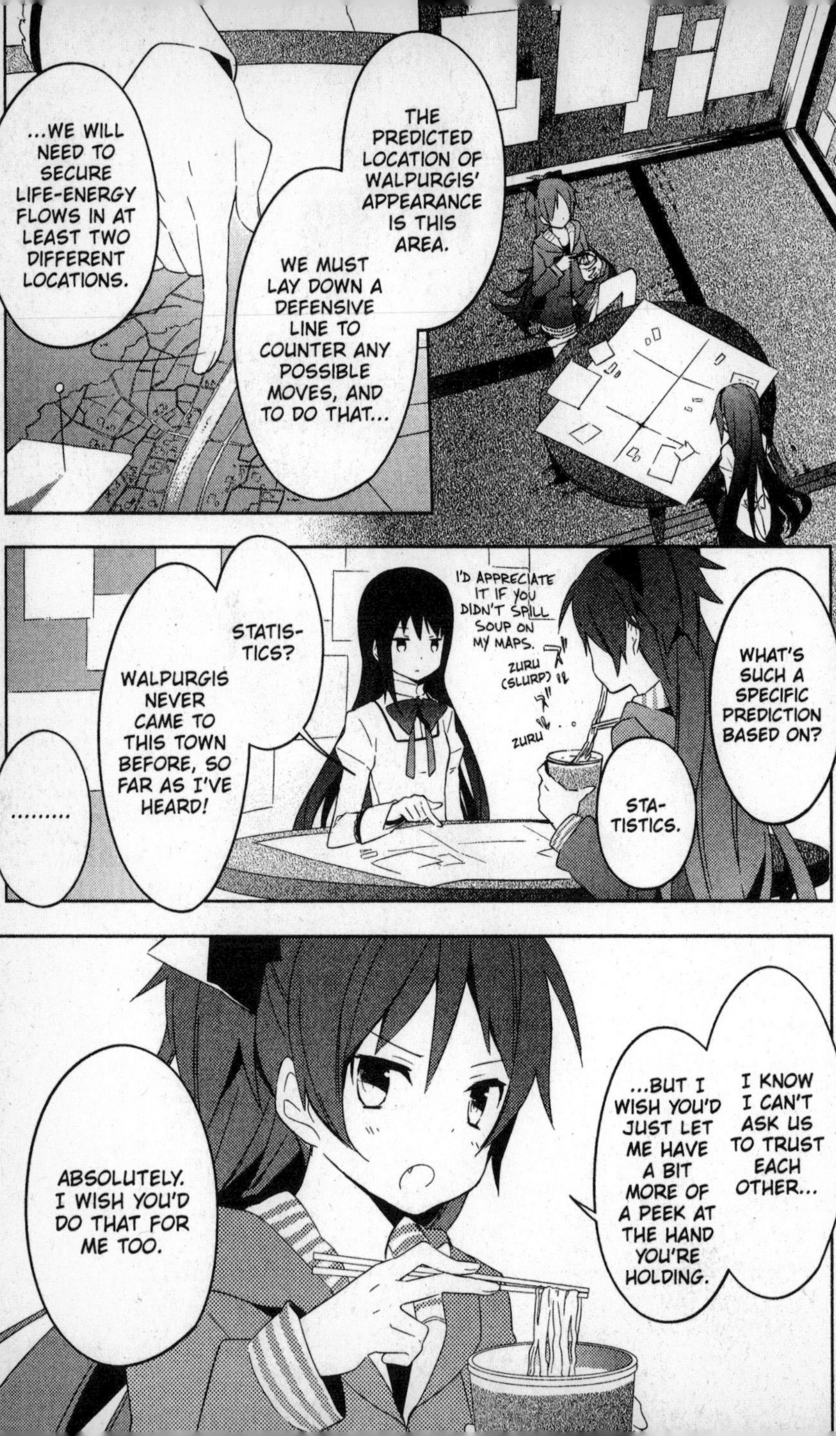
THE PREDICTED LOCATION OF WALPURGIS' APPEARANCE IS THIS AREA.
WE MUST LAY DOWN A DEFENSIVE LINE TO COUNTER ANY POSSIBLE MOVES, AND TO DO THAT...
...WE WILL NEED TO SECURE LIFE-ENERGY FLOWS IN AT LEAST TWO DIFFERENT LOCATIONS.
WHAT'S SUCH A SPECIFIC PREDICTION BASED ON?
STA-TISTICS.
I'D APPRECIATE IT IF YOU DIDN'T SPILL SOUP ON MY MAPS.
ZURU (SLURP)
ZURU
STATIS-TICS?
WALPURGIS NEVER CAME TO THIS TOWN BEFORE, SO FAR AS I'VE HEARD!
....
I KNOW I CAN'T ASK US TO TRUST EACH OTHER...
...BUT I WISH YOU'D JUST LET ME HAVE A BIT MORE OF A PEEK AT THE HAND YOU'RE HOLDING.
ABSOLUTELY. I WISH YOU'D DO THAT FOR ME TOO.

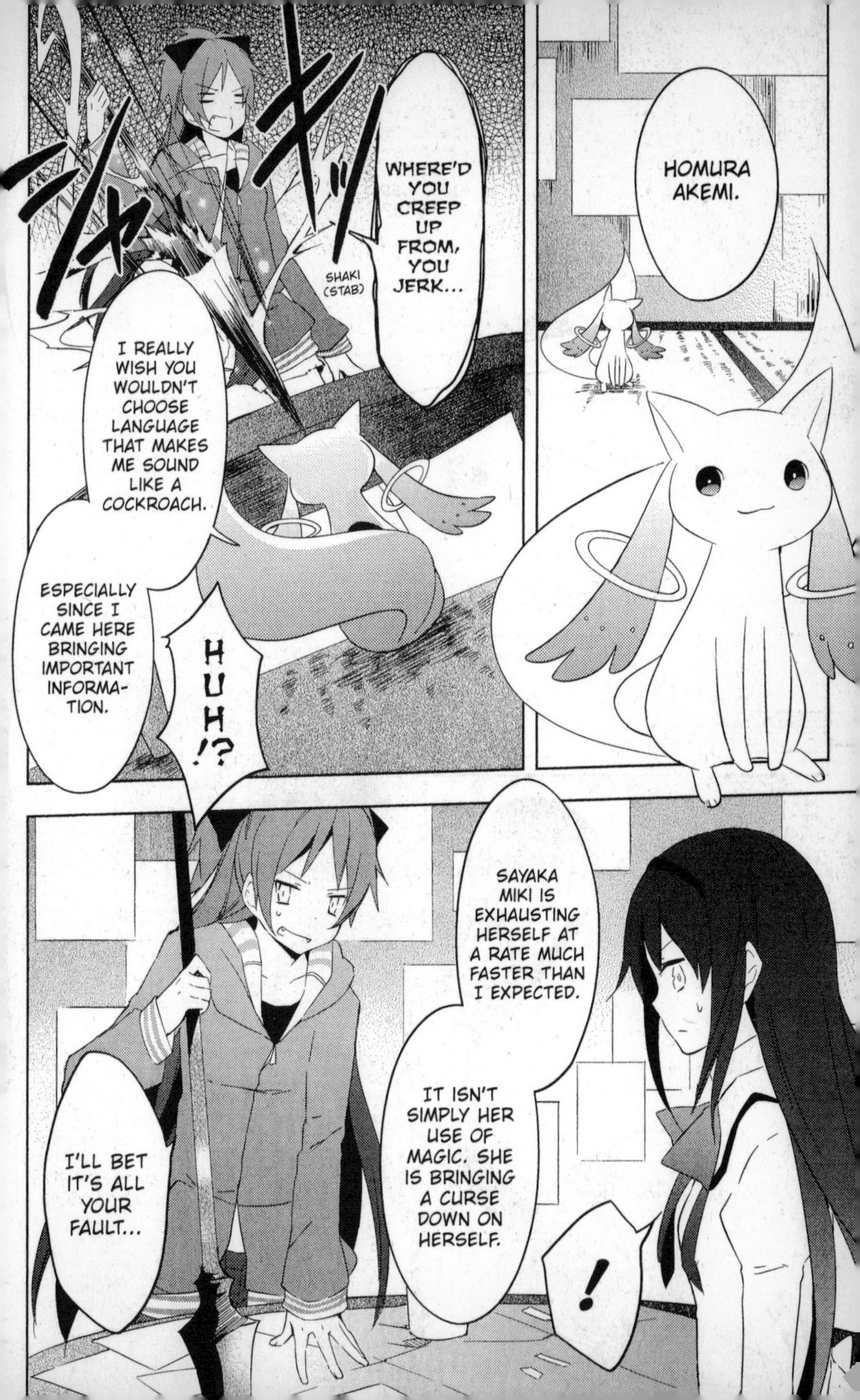
HOMURA AKEMI.
WHERE'D YOU CREEP UP FROM, YOU JERK...
SHAKI (STAB)
I REALLY WISH YOU WOULDN'T CHOOSE LANGUAGE THAT MAKES ME SOUND LIKE A COCKROACH.
ESPECIALLY SINCE I CAME HERE BRINGING IMPORTANT INFORMATION.
HUH!?
!
SAYAKA MIKI IS EXHAUSTING HERSELF AT A RATE MUCH FASTER THAN I EXPECTED.
IT ISN'T SIMPLY HER USE OF MAGIC. SHE IS BRINGING A CURSE DOWN ON HERSELF.
I'LL BET IT'S ALL YOUR FAULT...

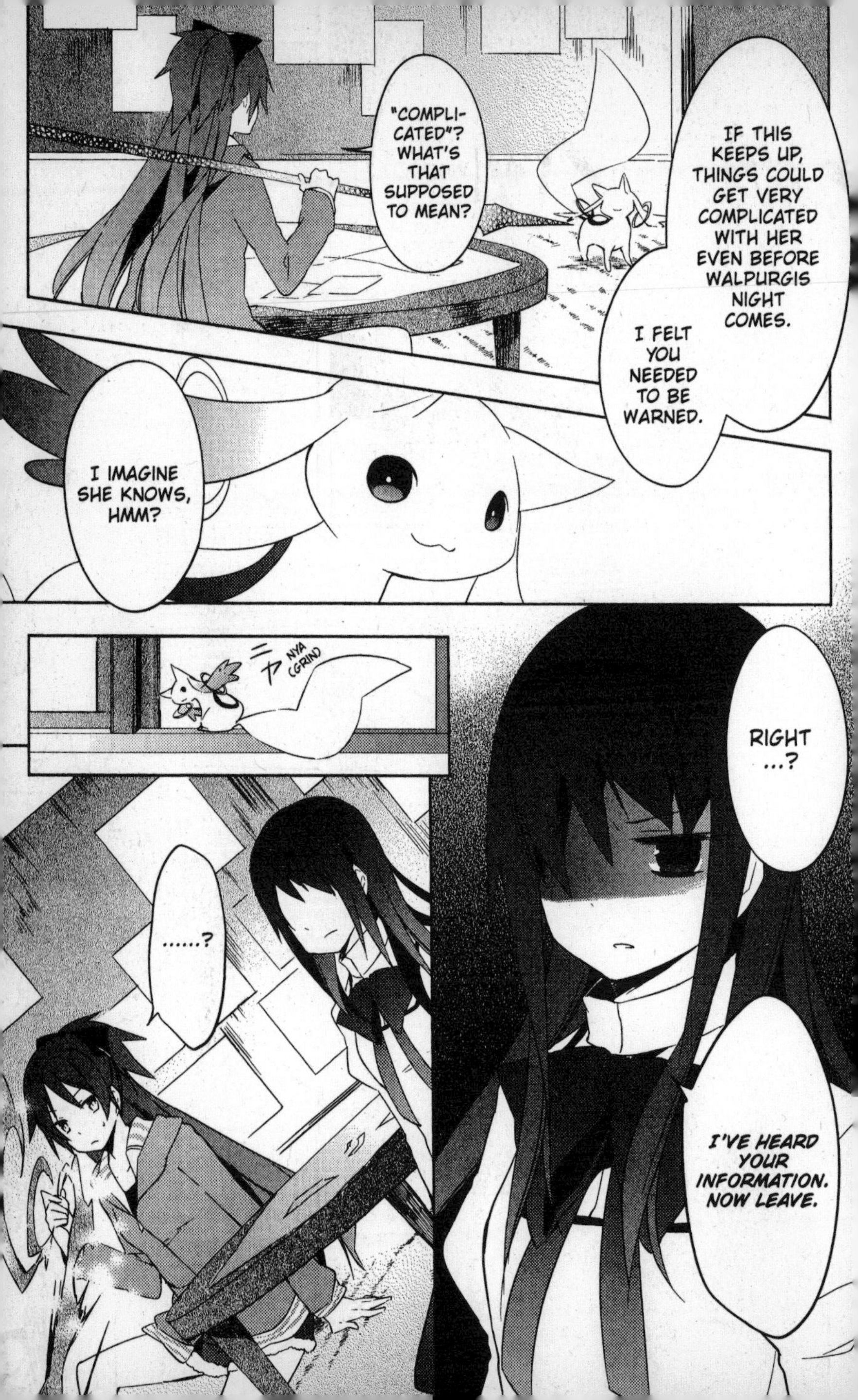
IF THIS KEEPS UP, THINGS COULD GET VERY COMPLICATED WITH HER EVEN BEFORE WALPURGIS NIGHT COMES.
I FELT YOU NEEDED TO BE WARNED.
"COMPLI-CATED"? WHAT'S THAT SUPPOSED TO MEAN?
I IMAGINE SHE KNOWS, HMM?
RIGHT ...?
I'VE HEARD YOUR INFORMATION. NOW LEAVE.
NYA (GRIN)
......?

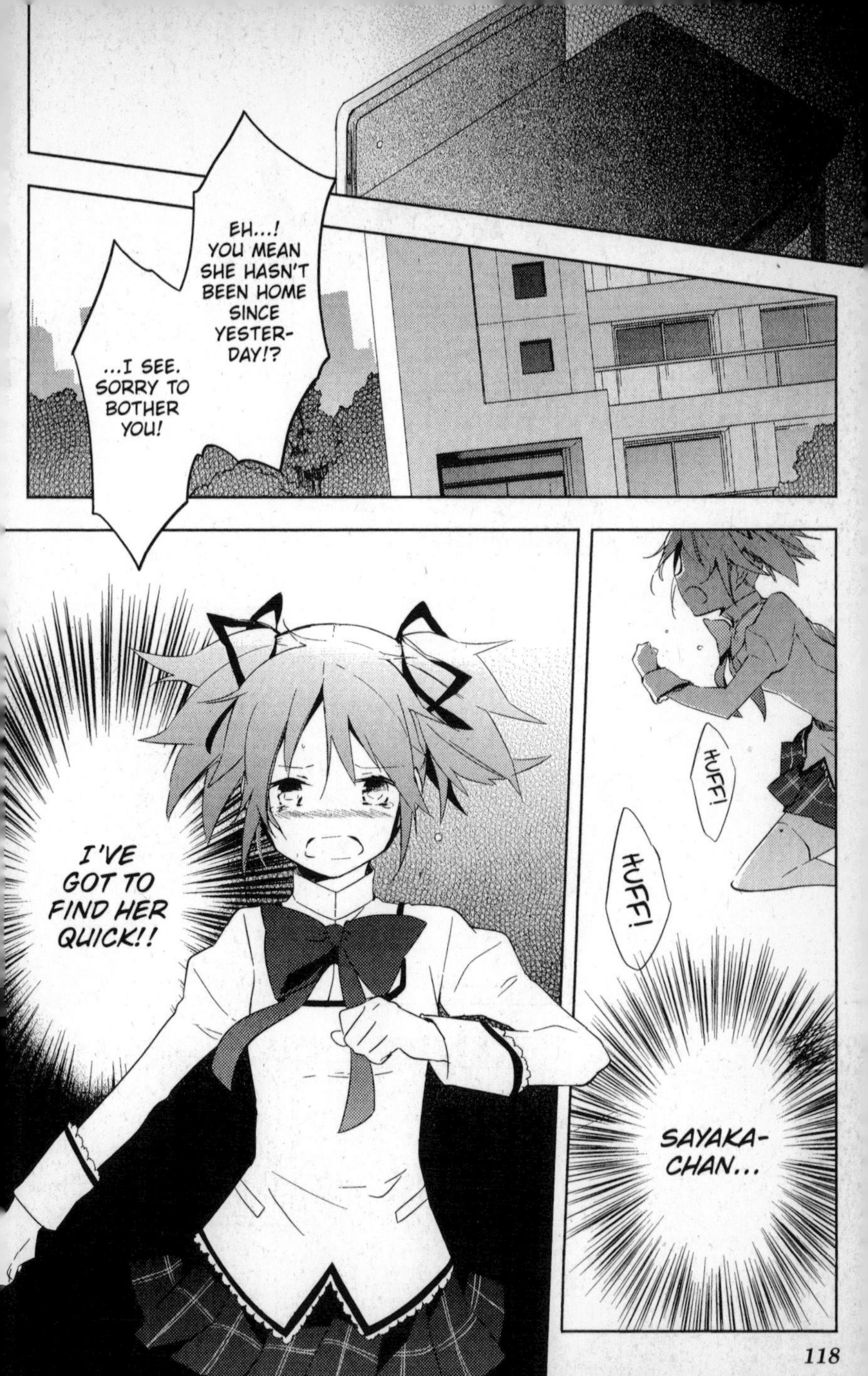
EH...! YOU MEAN SHE HASN'T BEEN HOME SINCE YESTER-DAY!?
...I SEE. SORRY TO BOTHER YOU!
HUFF!
HUFF!
SAYAKA-CHAN...
I'VE GOT TO FIND HER QUICK!!

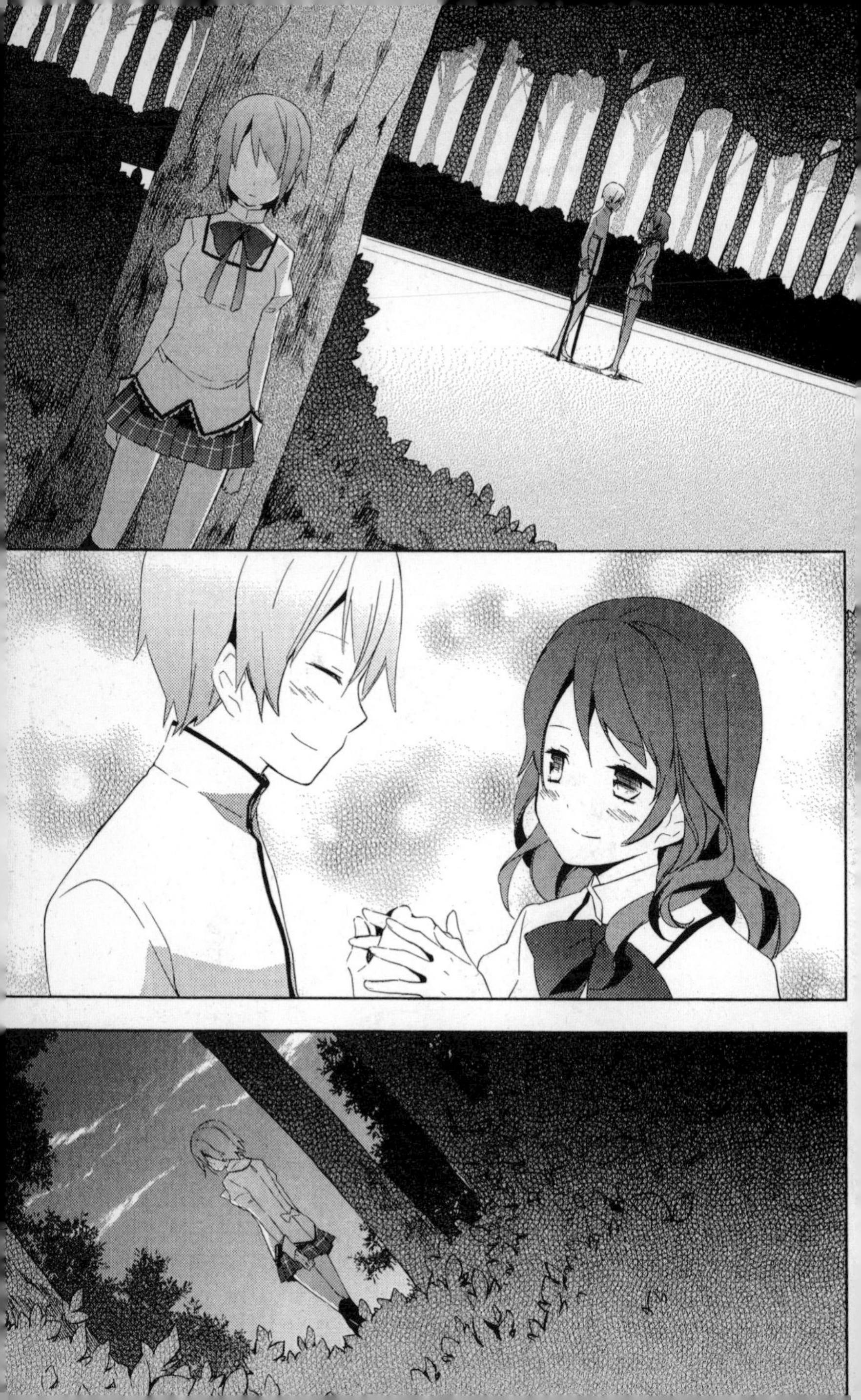

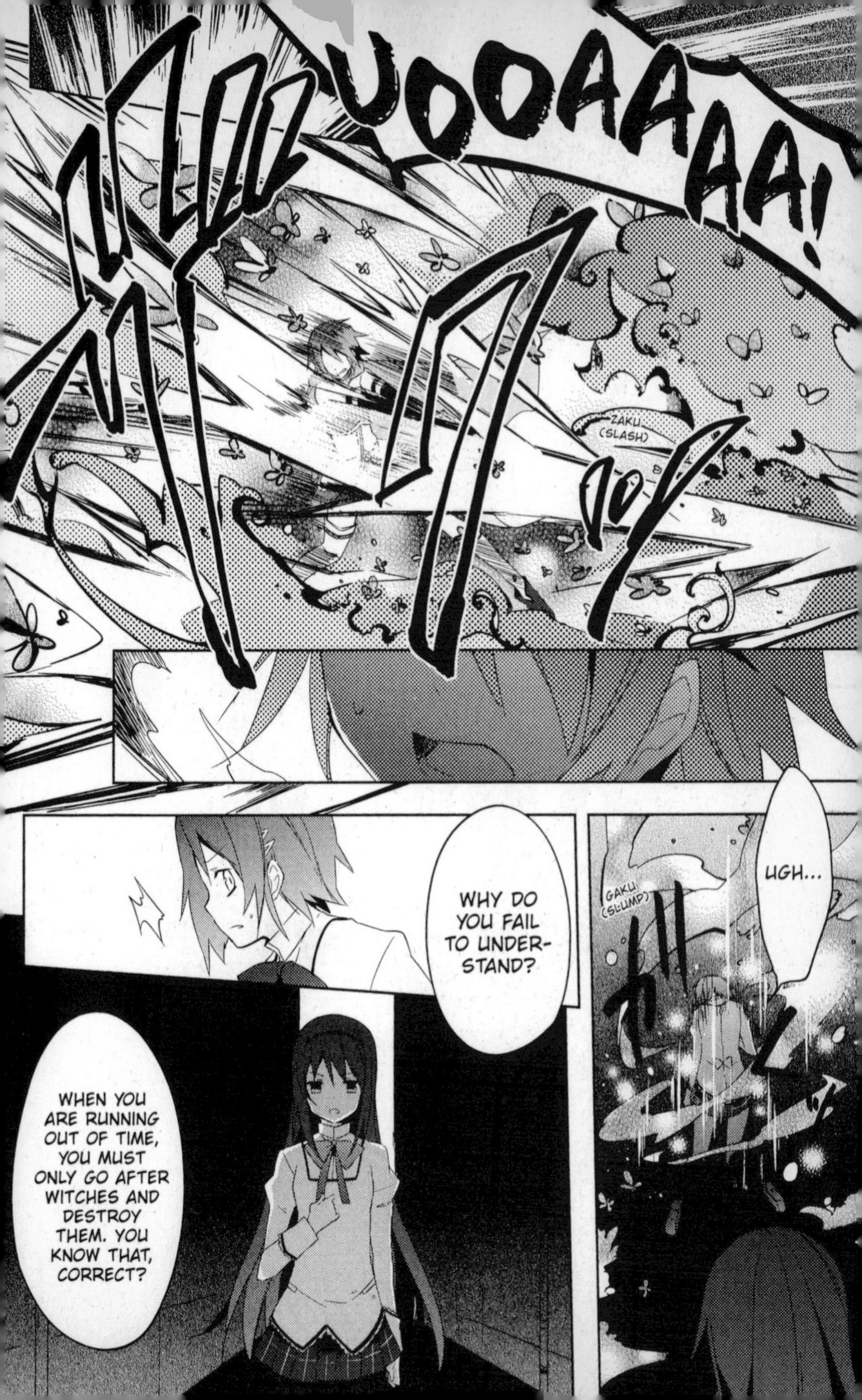
UOOAAAAAA!
ZAKU (SLASH)
UGH...
GAKU (SLUMP)
WHY DO YOU FAIL TO UNDER-STAND?
WHEN YOU ARE RUNNING OUT OF TIME, YOU MUST ONLY GO AFTER WITCHES AND DESTROY THEM. YOU KNOW THAT, CORRECT?

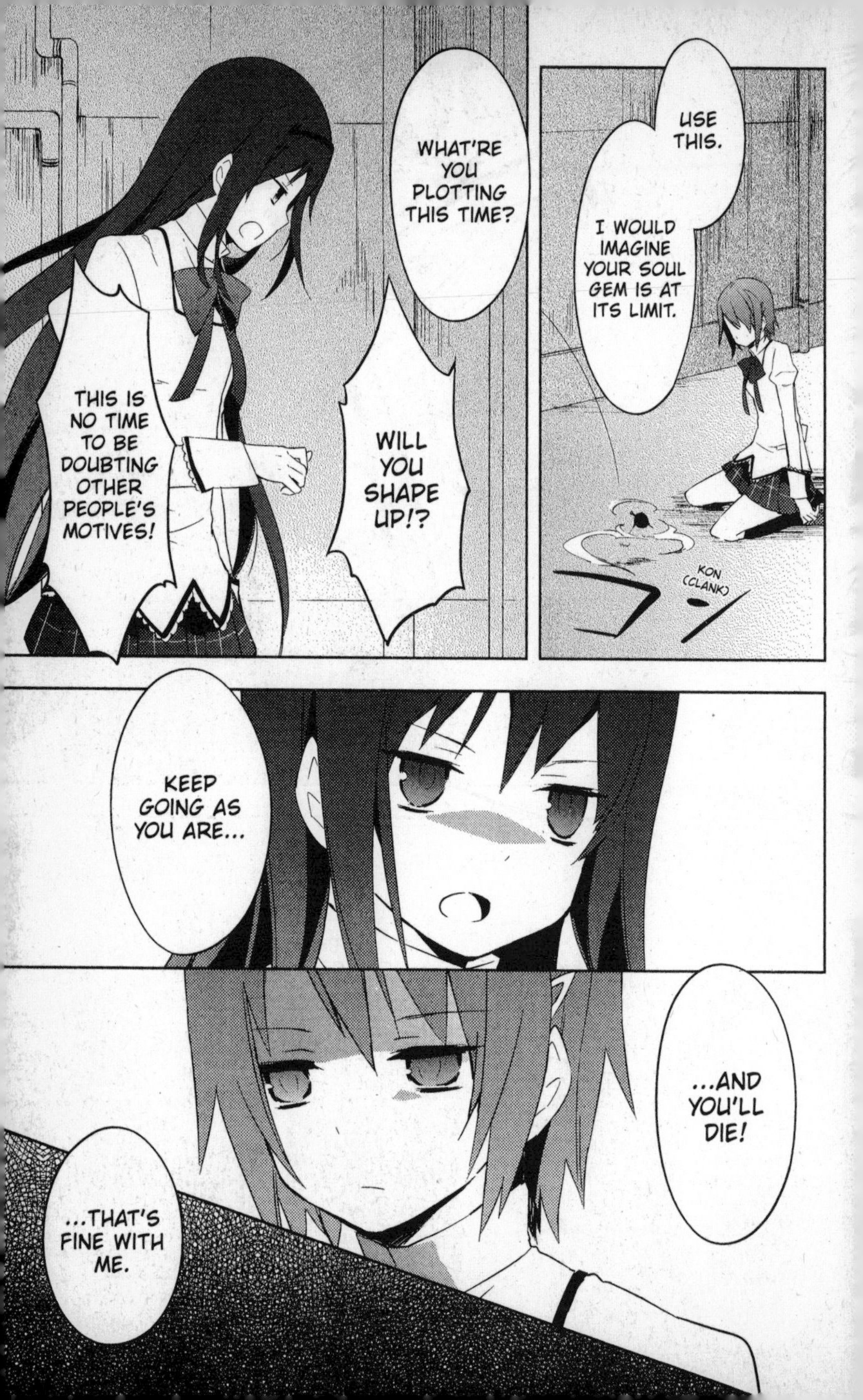
USE THIS.
I WOULD IMAGINE YOUR SOUL GEM IS AT ITS LIMIT.
KON (CLANK)
WHAT'RE YOU PLOTTING THIS TIME?
WILL YOU SHAPE UP!?
THIS IS NO TIME TO BE DOUBTING OTHER PEOPLE'S MOTIVES!
KEEP GOING AS YOU ARE...
...AND YOU'LL DIE!
...THAT'S FINE WITH ME.

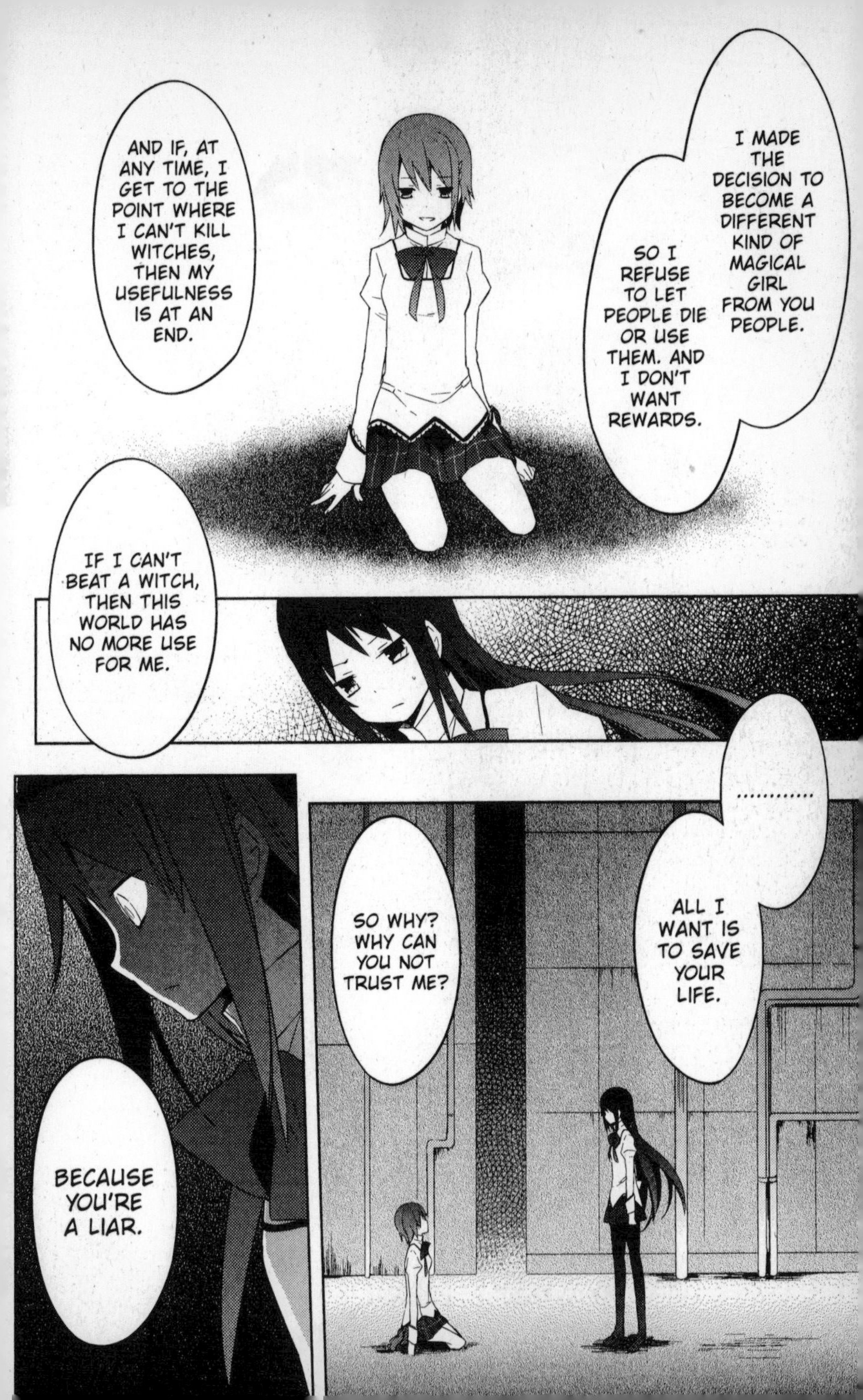
I MADE THE DECISION TO BECOME A DIFFERENT KIND OF MAGICAL GIRL FROM YOU PEOPLE.
SO I REFUSE TO LET PEOPLE DIE OR USE THEM. AND I DON'T WANT REWARDS.
AND IF, AT ANY TIME, I GET TO THE POINT WHERE I CAN'T KILL WITCHES, THEN MY USEFULNESS IS AT AN END.
IF I CAN'T BEAT A WITCH, THEN THIS WORLD HAS NO MORE USE FOR ME.
....
ALL I WANT IS TO SAVE YOUR LIFE.
SO WHY? WHY CAN YOU NOT TRUST ME?
BECAUSE YOU'RE A LIAR.

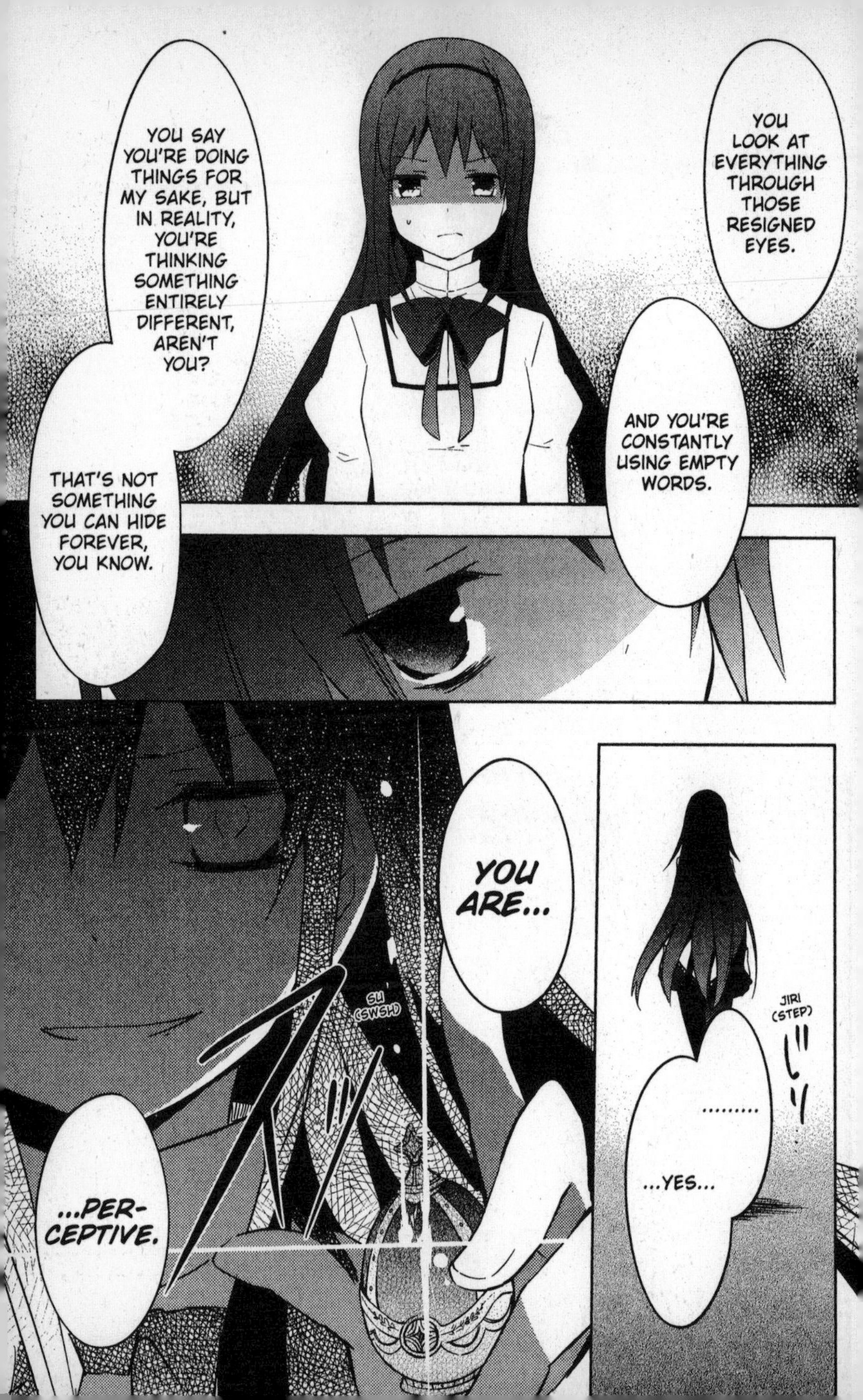
YOU LOOK AT EVERYTHING THROUGH THOSE RESIGNED EYES.
AND YOU'RE CONSTANTLY USING EMPTY WORDS.
YOU SAY YOU'RE DOING THINGS FOR MY SAKE, BUT IN REALITY, YOU'RE THINKING SOMETHING ENTIRELY DIFFERENT, AREN'T YOU?
THAT'S NOT SOMETHING YOU CAN HIDE FOREVER, YOU KNOW.
JIRI (STEP)
....
...YES...
YOU ARE...
SU (SWSH)
...PER-CEPTIVE.

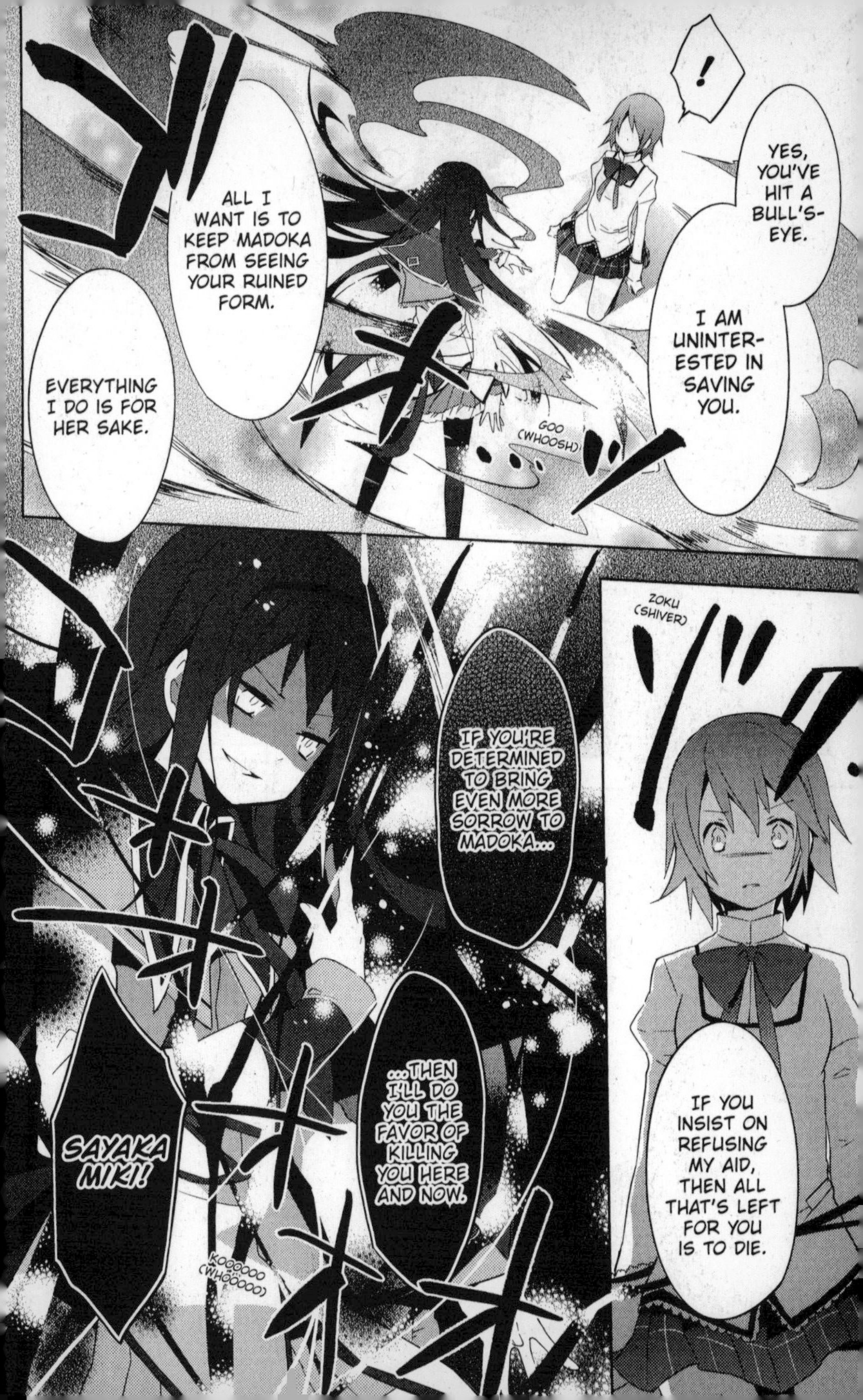
!
YES, YOU'VE HIT A BULL'S-EYE.
I AM UNINTER-ESTED IN SAVING YOU.
GOO (WHOOSH)
ALL I WANT IS TO KEEP MADOKA FROM SEEING YOUR RUINED FORM.
EVERYTHING I DO IS FOR HER SAKE.
ZOKU (SHIVER)
IF YOU INSIST ON REFUSING MY AID, THEN ALL THAT'S LEFT FOR YOU IS TO DIE.
IF YOU'RE DETERMINED TO BRING EVEN MORE SORROW TO MADOKA...
...THEN I'LL DO YOU THE FAVOR OF KILLING YOU HERE AND NOW.
SAYAKA MIKI!
KOOOOOO (WHOOOOO)

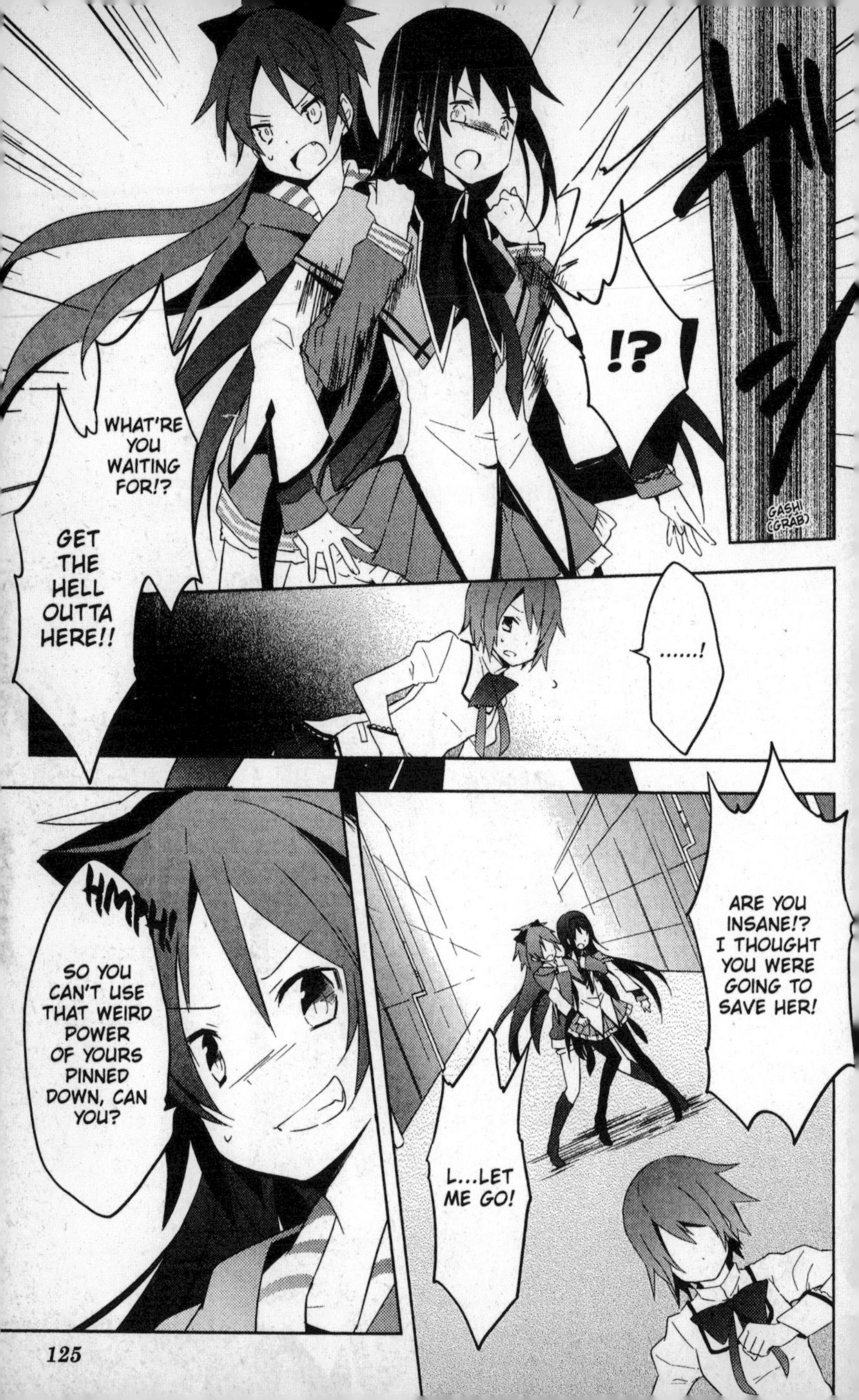
GASHI (GRAB)
!?
WHAT'RE YOU WAITING FOR!?
GET THE HELL OUTTA HERE!!
......!
ARE YOU INSANE!? I THOUGHT YOU WERE GOING TO SAVE HER!
L...LET ME GO!
HMPH!
SO YOU CAN'T USE THAT WEIRD POWER OF YOURS PINNED DOWN, CAN YOU?

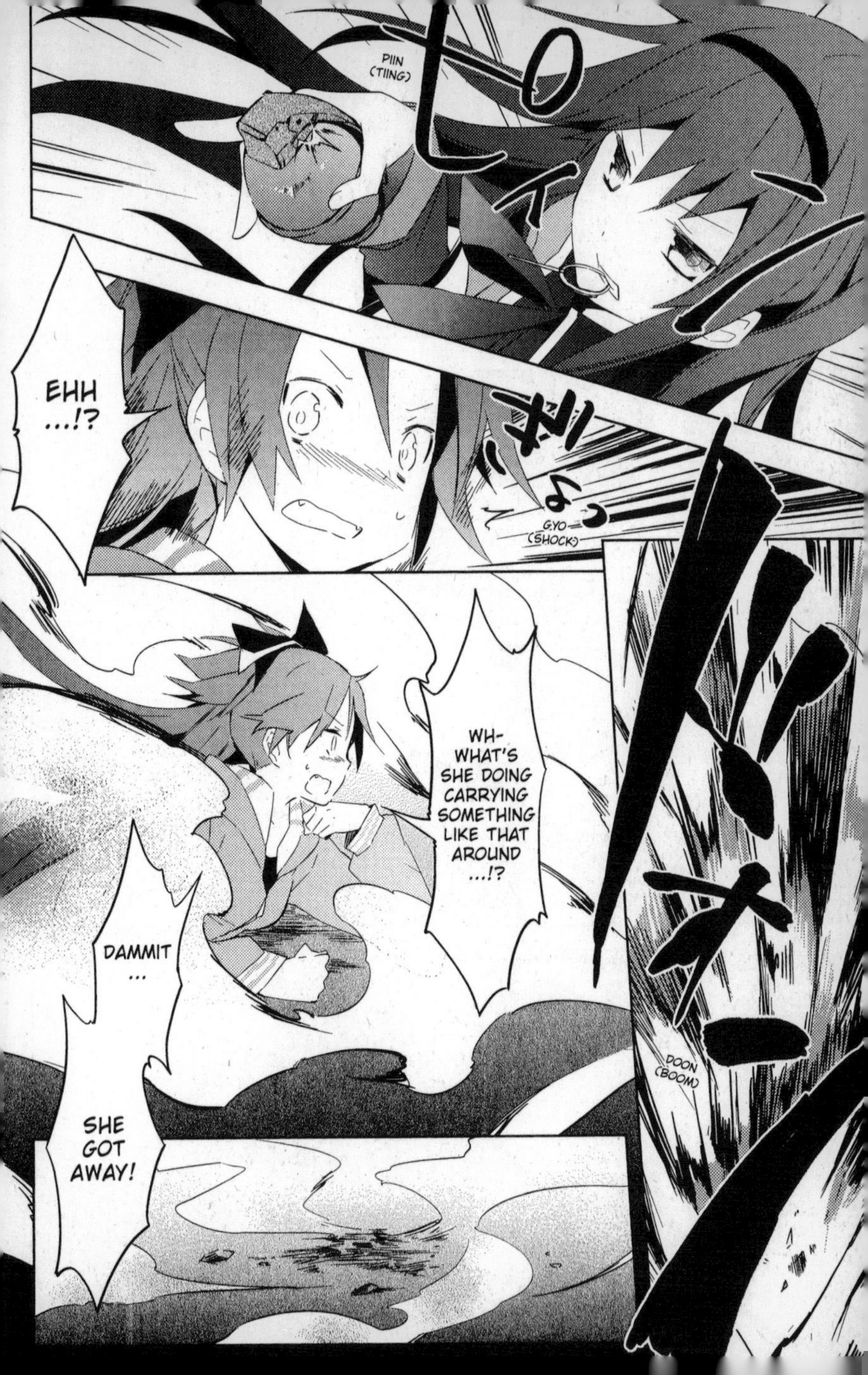
PIIN (TIING)
EHH ...!?
GYO (SHOCK)
DOON (BOOM)
WH-WHAT'S SHE DOING CARRYING SOMETHING LIKE THAT AROUND ...!?
DAMMIT ...
SHE GOT AWAY!

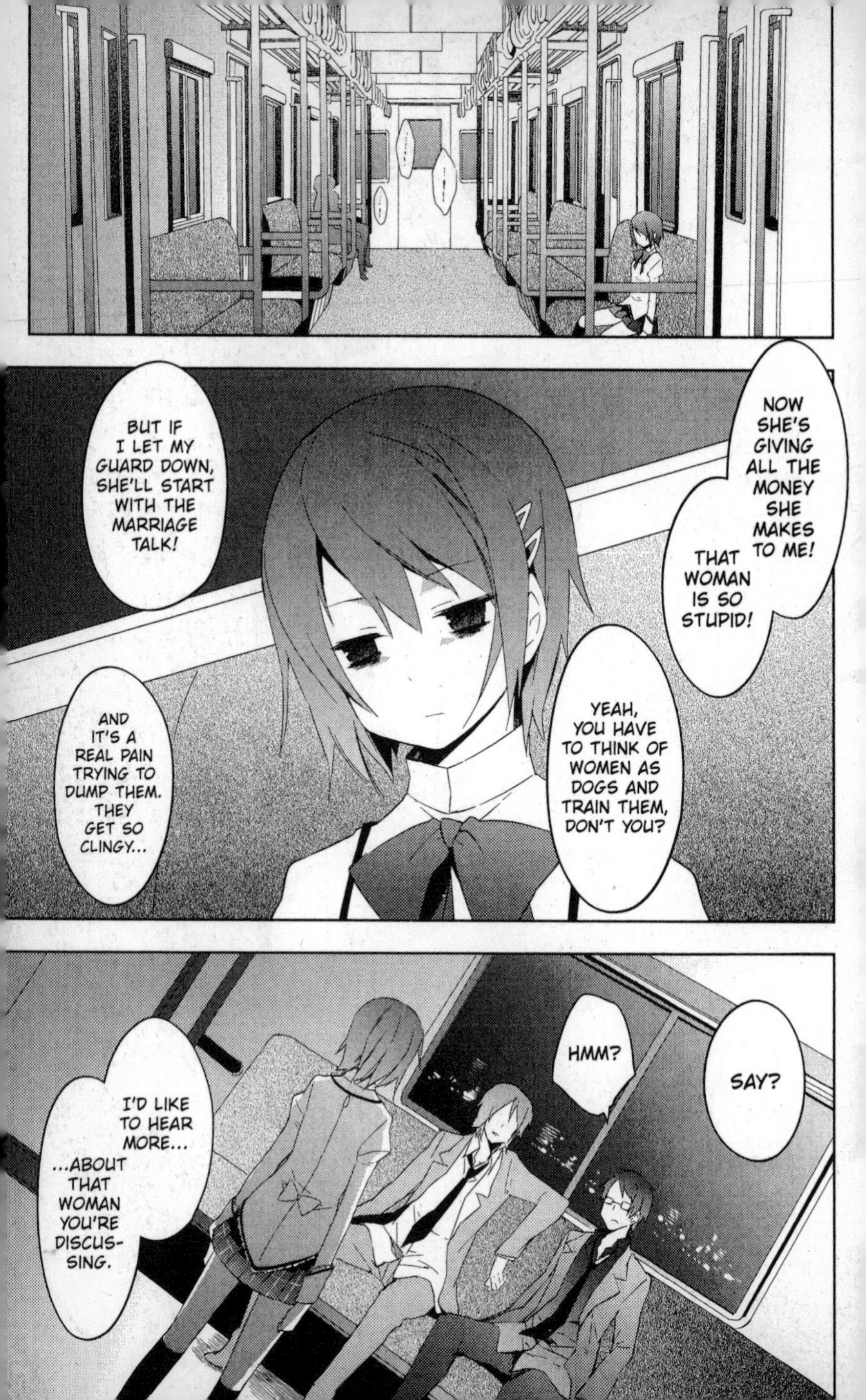
NOW SHE'S GIVING ALL THE MONEY SHE MAKES TO ME!
THAT WOMAN IS SO STUPID!
BUT IF I LET MY GUARD DOWN, SHE'LL START WITH THE MARRIAGE TALK!
YEAH, YOU HAVE TO THINK OF WOMEN AS DOGS AND TRAIN THEM, DON'T YOU?
AND IT'S A REAL PAIN TRYING TO DUMP THEM. THEY GET SO CLINGY...
SAY?
HMM?
I'D LIKE TO HEAR MORE... ...ABOUT THAT WOMAN YOU'RE DISCUS-SING.

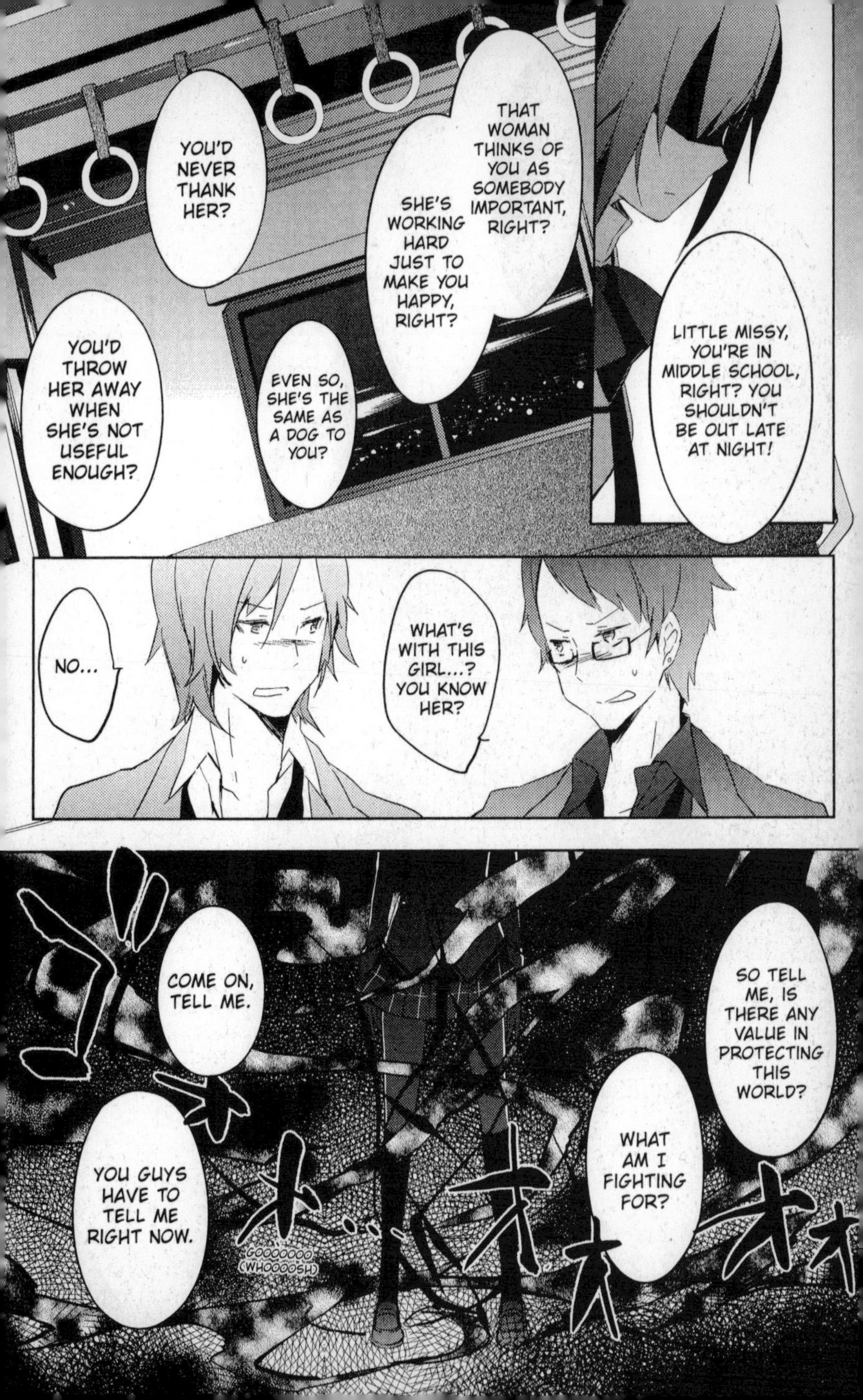
LITTLE MISSY, YOU'RE IN MIDDLE SCHOOL, RIGHT? YOU SHOULDN'T BE OUT LATE AT NIGHT!
THAT WOMAN THINKS OF YOU AS SOMEBODY IMPORTANT, RIGHT?
SHE'S WORKING HARD JUST TO MAKE YOU HAPPY, RIGHT?
YOU'D NEVER THANK HER?
EVEN SO, SHE'S THE SAME AS A DOG TO YOU?
YOU'D THROW HER AWAY WHEN SHE'S NOT USEFUL ENOUGH?
WHAT'S WITH THIS GIRL...? YOU KNOW HER?
NO...
SO TELL ME, IS THERE ANY VALUE IN PROTECTING THIS WORLD?
WHAT AM I FIGHTING FOR?
COME ON, TELL ME.
YOU GUYS HAVE TO TELL ME RIGHT NOW.
GOOOOOOO (WHOOOOSH)

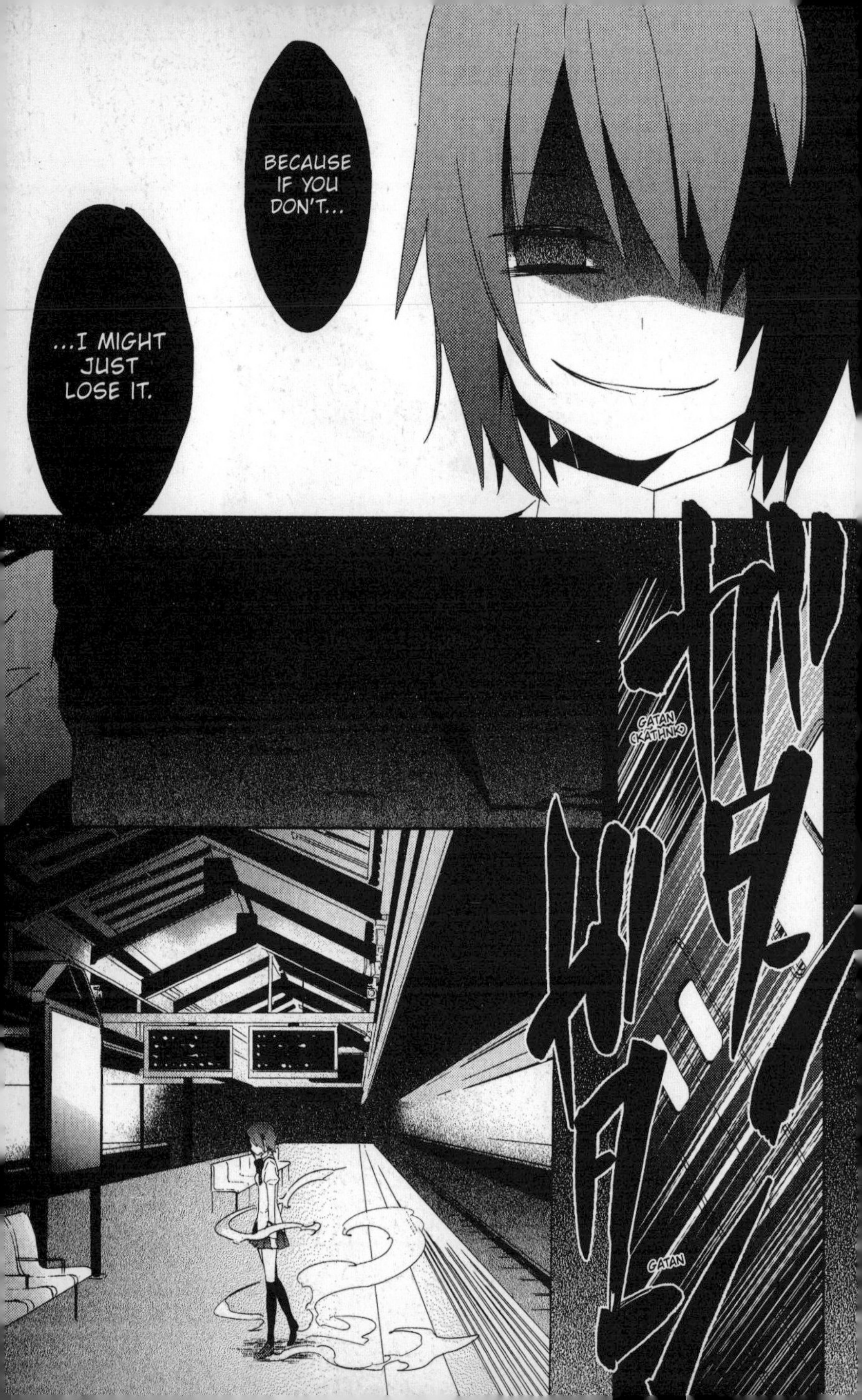
BECAUSE IF YOU DON'T...
...I MIGHT JUST LOSE IT.
GATAN (KATHNK)
GATAN

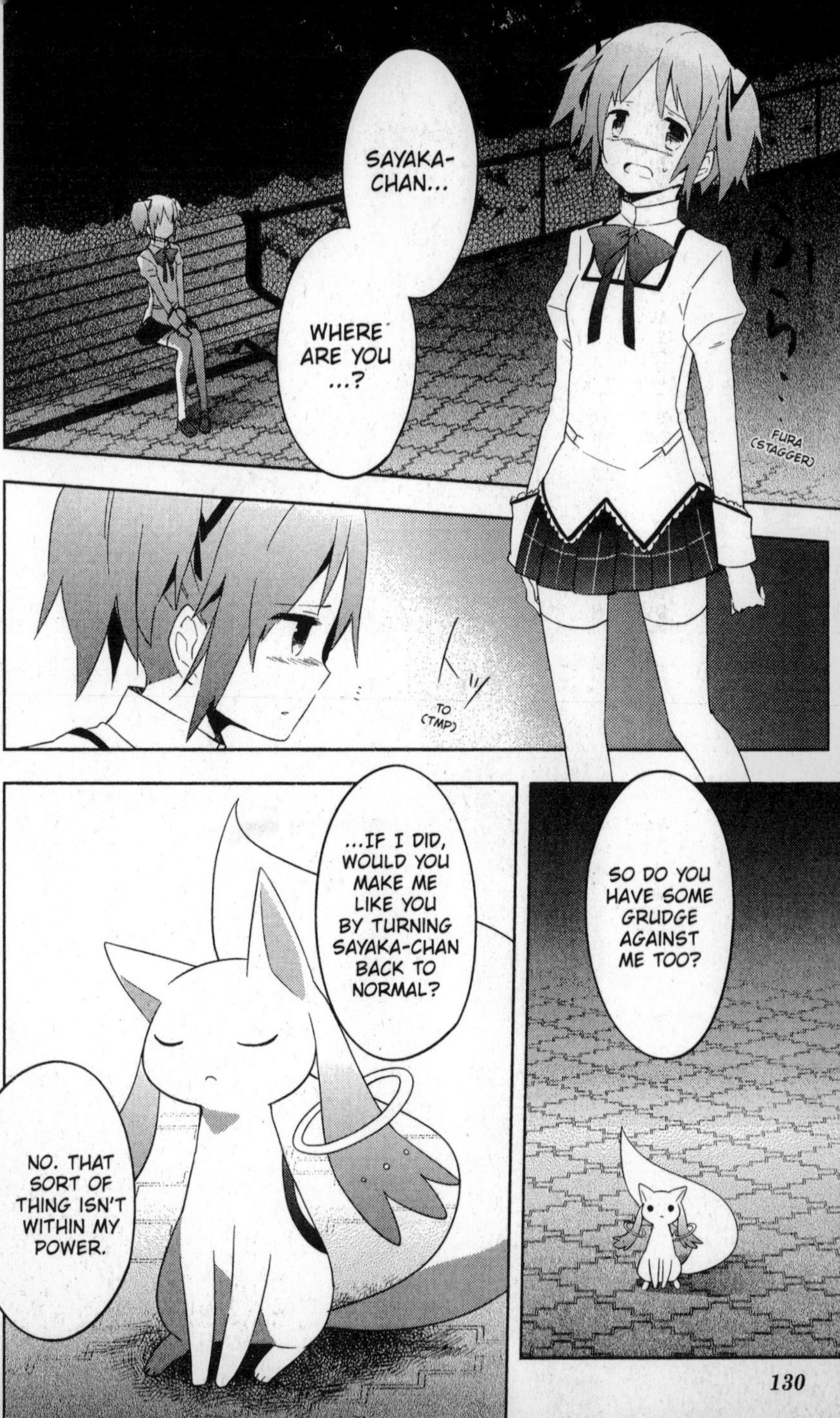
SAYAKA-CHAN...
WHERE ARE YOU ...?
FURA (STAGGER)
TO (TMP)
SO DO YOU HAVE SOME GRUDGE AGAINST ME TOO?
...IF I DID, WOULD YOU MAKE ME LIKE YOU BY TURNING SAYAKA-CHAN BACK TO NORMAL?
NO. THAT SORT OF THING ISN'T WITHIN MY POWER.

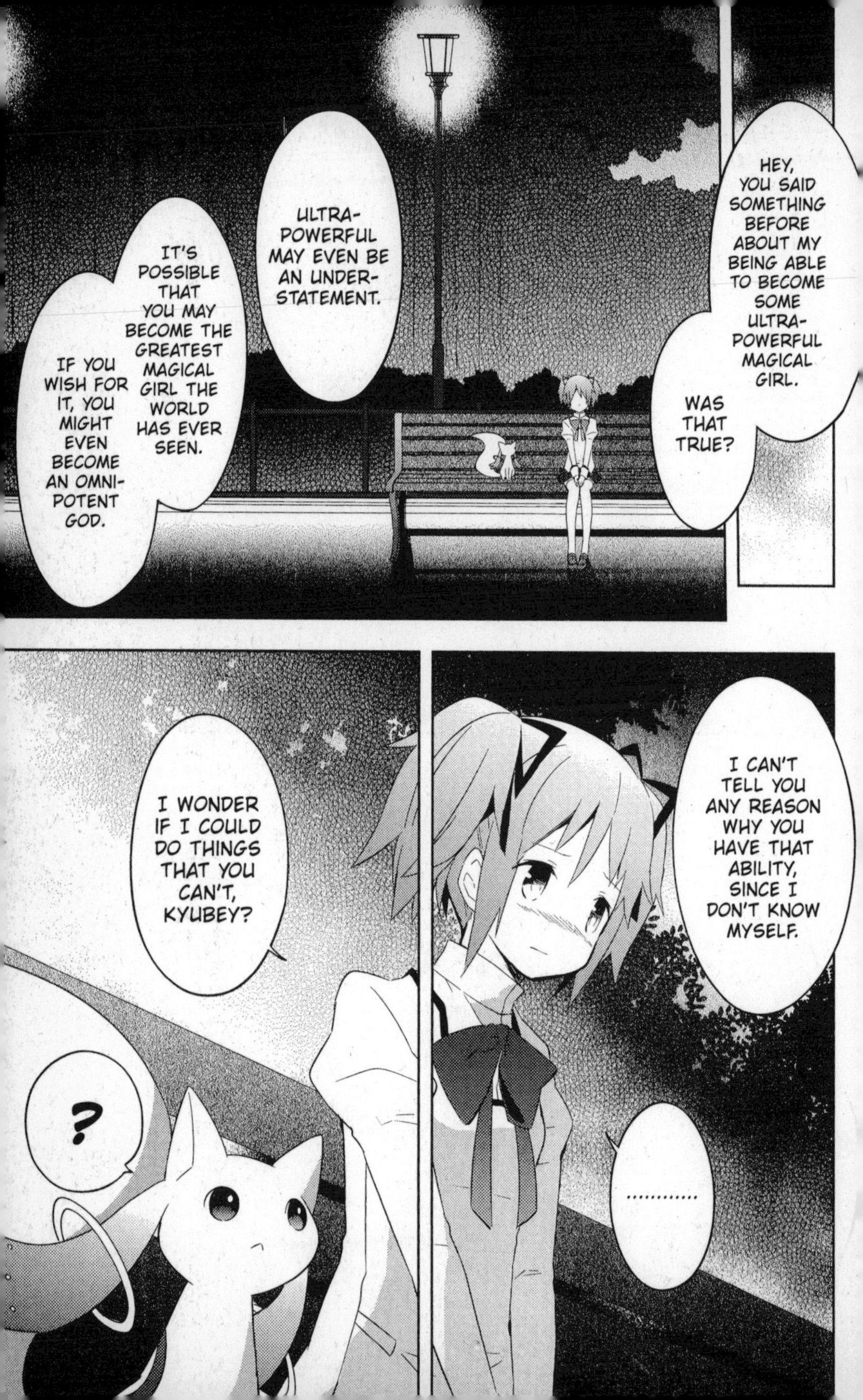
HEY, YOU SAID SOMETHING BEFORE ABOUT MY BEING ABLE TO BECOME SOME ULTRA-POWERFUL MAGICAL GIRL.
WAS THAT TRUE?
ULTRA-POWERFUL MAY EVEN BE AN UNDER-STATEMENT.
IT'S POSSIBLE THAT YOU MAY BECOME THE GREATEST MAGICAL GIRL THE WORLD HAS EVER SEEN.
IF YOU WISH FOR IT, YOU MIGHT EVEN BECOME AN OMNI-POTENT GOD.
I CAN'T TELL YOU ANY REASON WHY YOU HAVE THAT ABILITY, SINCE I DON'T KNOW MYSELF.
....
I WONDER IF I COULD DO THINGS THAT YOU CAN'T, KYUBEY?
?

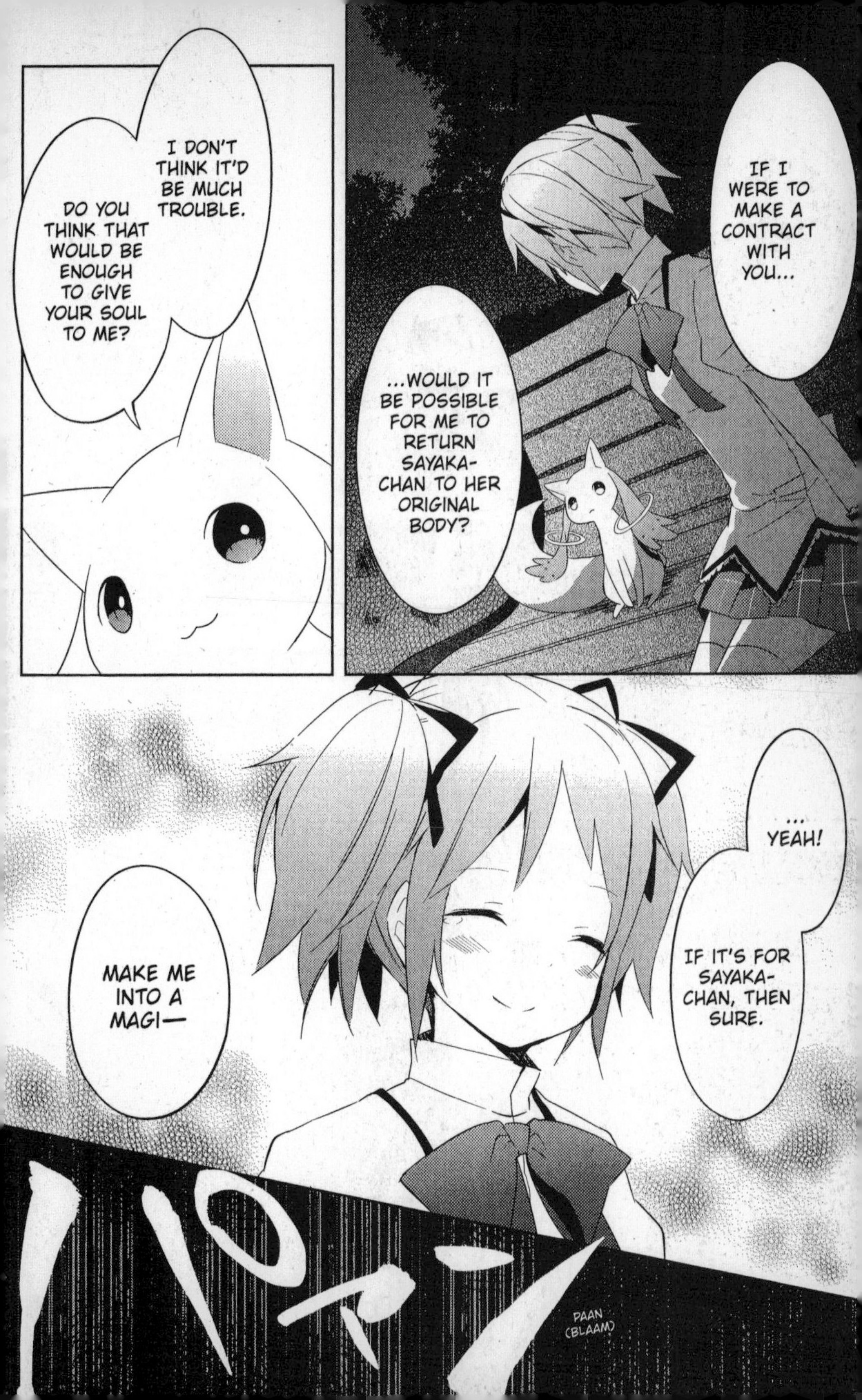
IF I WERE TO MAKE A CONTRACT WITH YOU...
...WOULD IT BE POSSIBLE FOR ME TO RETURN SAYAKA-CHAN TO HER ORIGINAL BODY?
I DON'T THINK IT'D BE MUCH TROUBLE.
DO YOU THINK THAT WOULD BE ENOUGH TO GIVE YOUR SOUL TO ME?
... YEAH!
IF IT'S FOR SAYAKA-CHAN, THEN SURE.
MAKE ME INTO A MAGI—
PAAN (BLAAM)

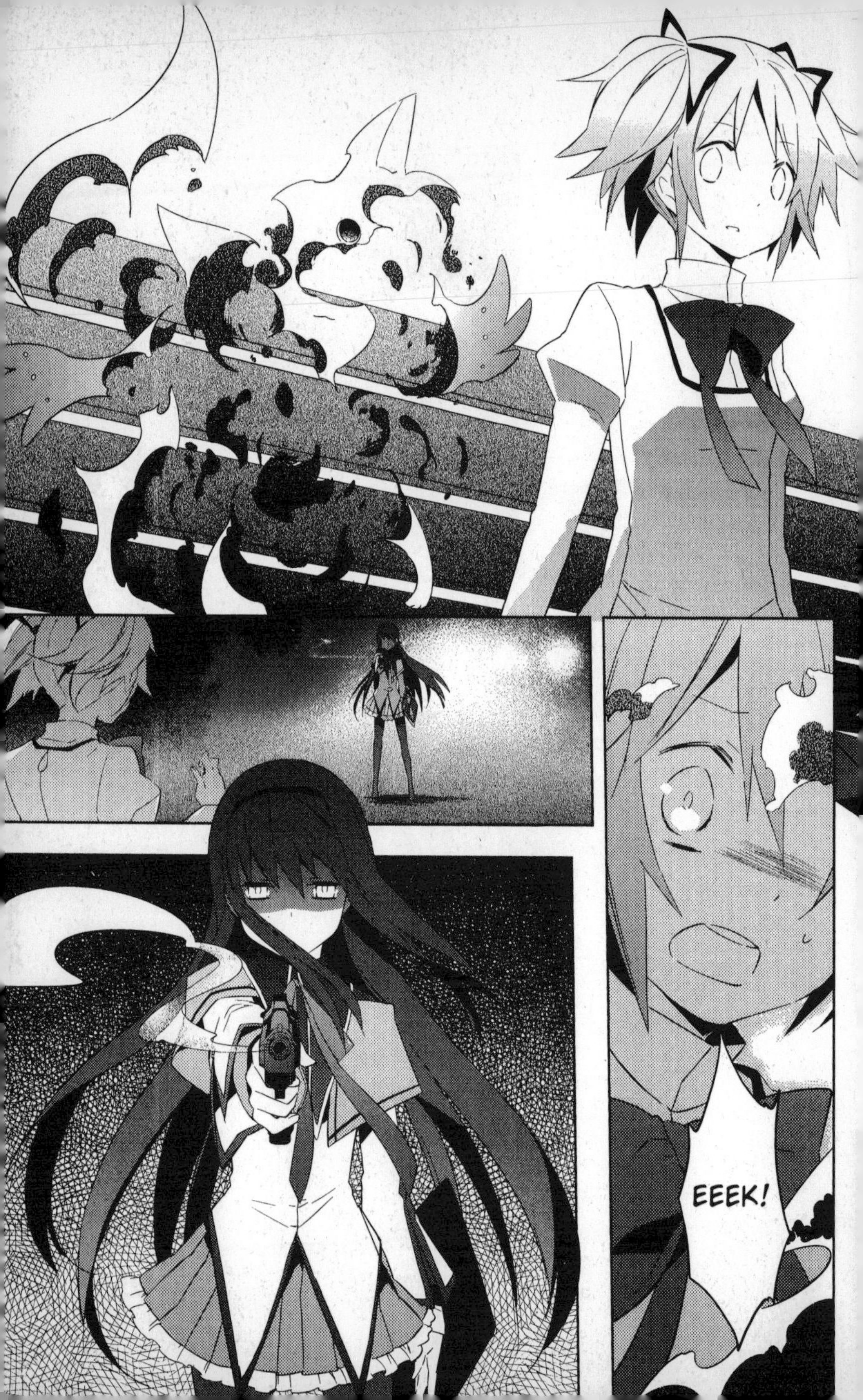
EEEK!

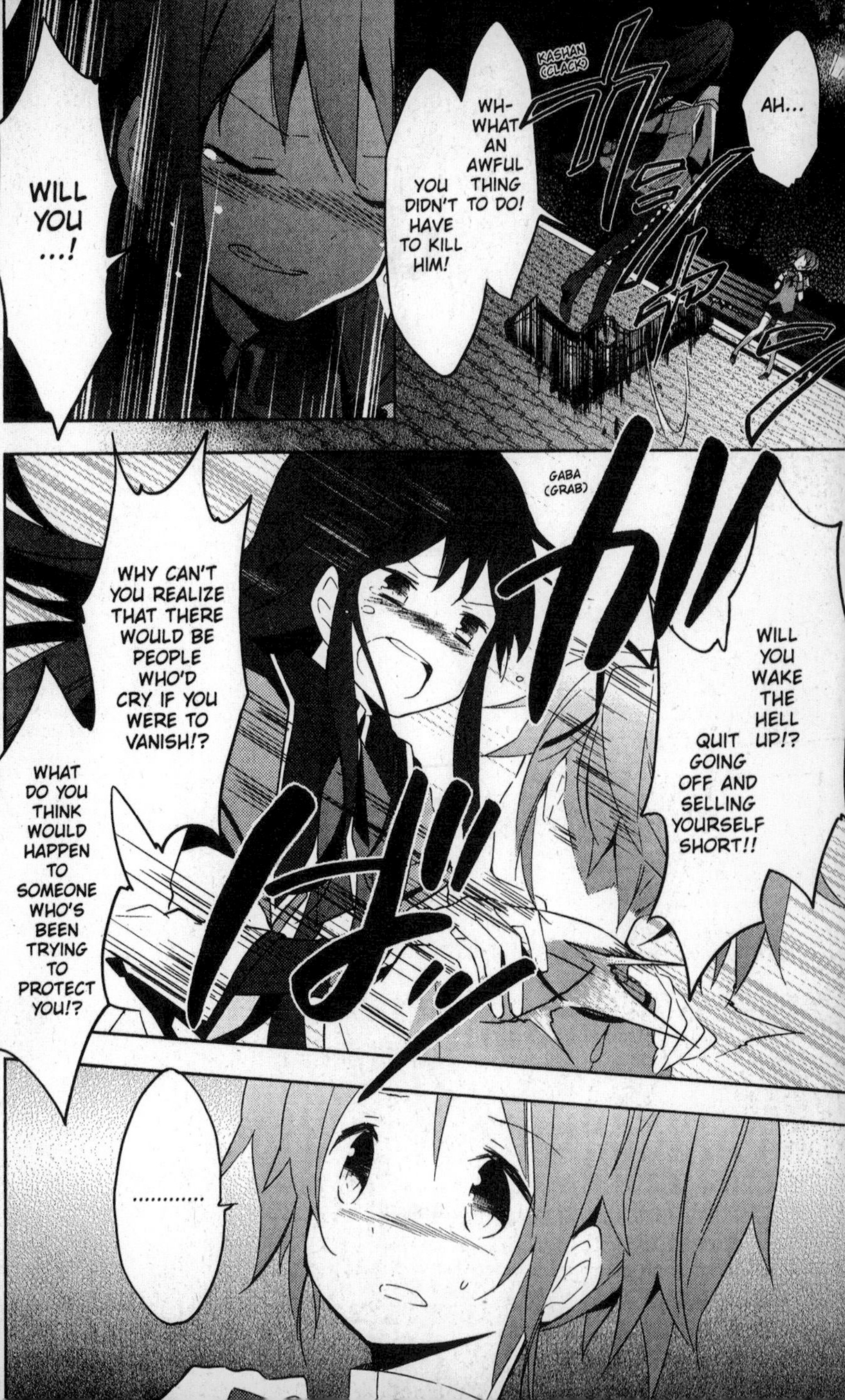
AH...
KASHAN (CLACK)
WH-WHAT AN AWFUL THING TO DO!
YOU DIDN'T HAVE TO KILL HIM!
WILL YOU ...!
GABA (GRAB)
WILL YOU WAKE THE HELL UP!?
QUIT GOING OFF AND SELLING YOURSELF SHORT!!
WHY CAN'T YOU REALIZE THAT THERE WOULD BE PEOPLE WHO'D CRY IF YOU WERE TO VANISH!?
WHAT DO YOU THINK WOULD HAPPEN TO SOMEONE WHO'S BEEN TRYING TO PROTECT YOU!?
....

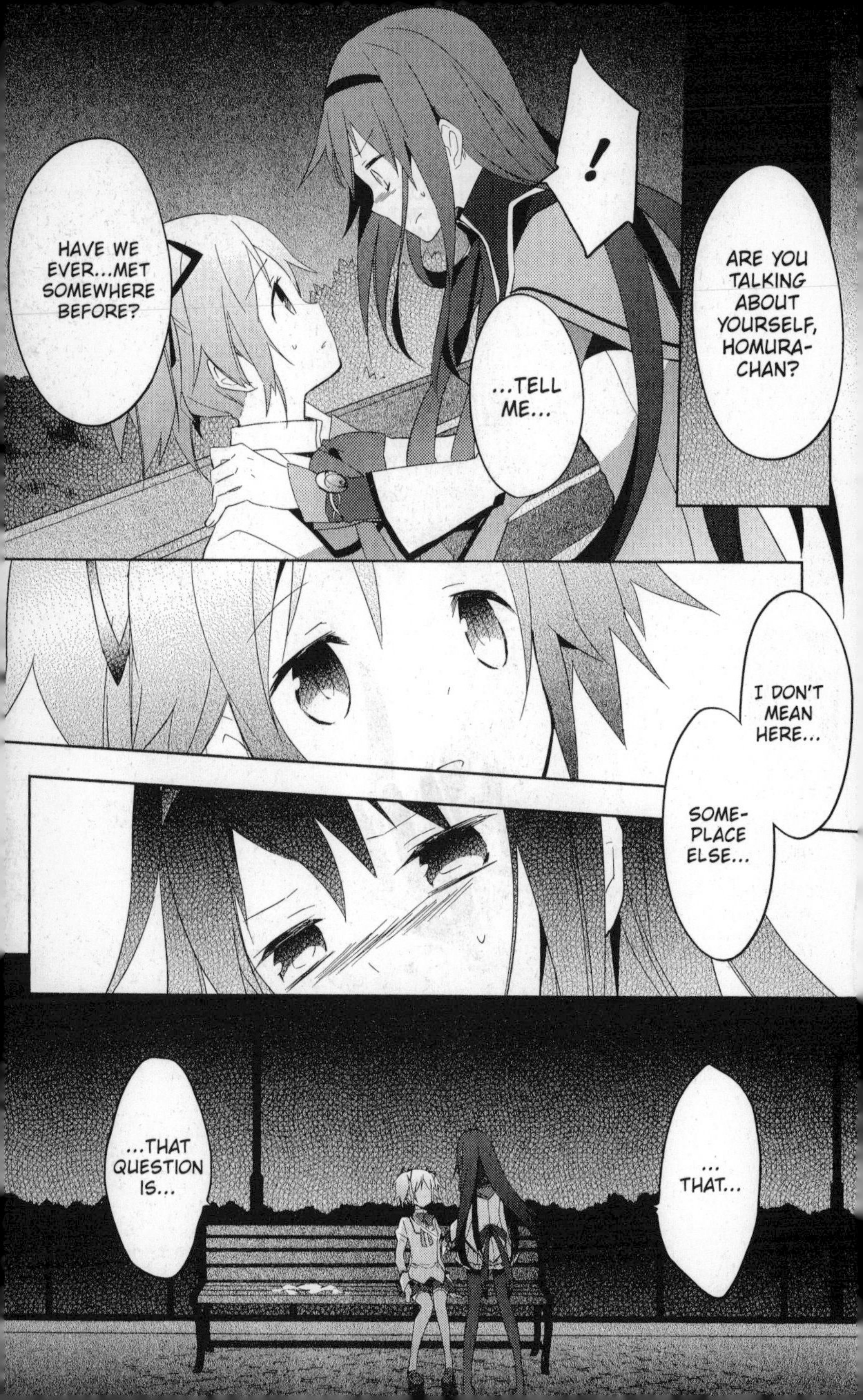
!
ARE YOU TALKING ABOUT YOURSELF, HOMURA-CHAN?
...TELL ME...
HAVE WE EVER...MET SOMEWHERE BEFORE?
I DON'T MEAN HERE...
SOME-PLACE ELSE...
... THAT...
...THAT QUESTION IS...

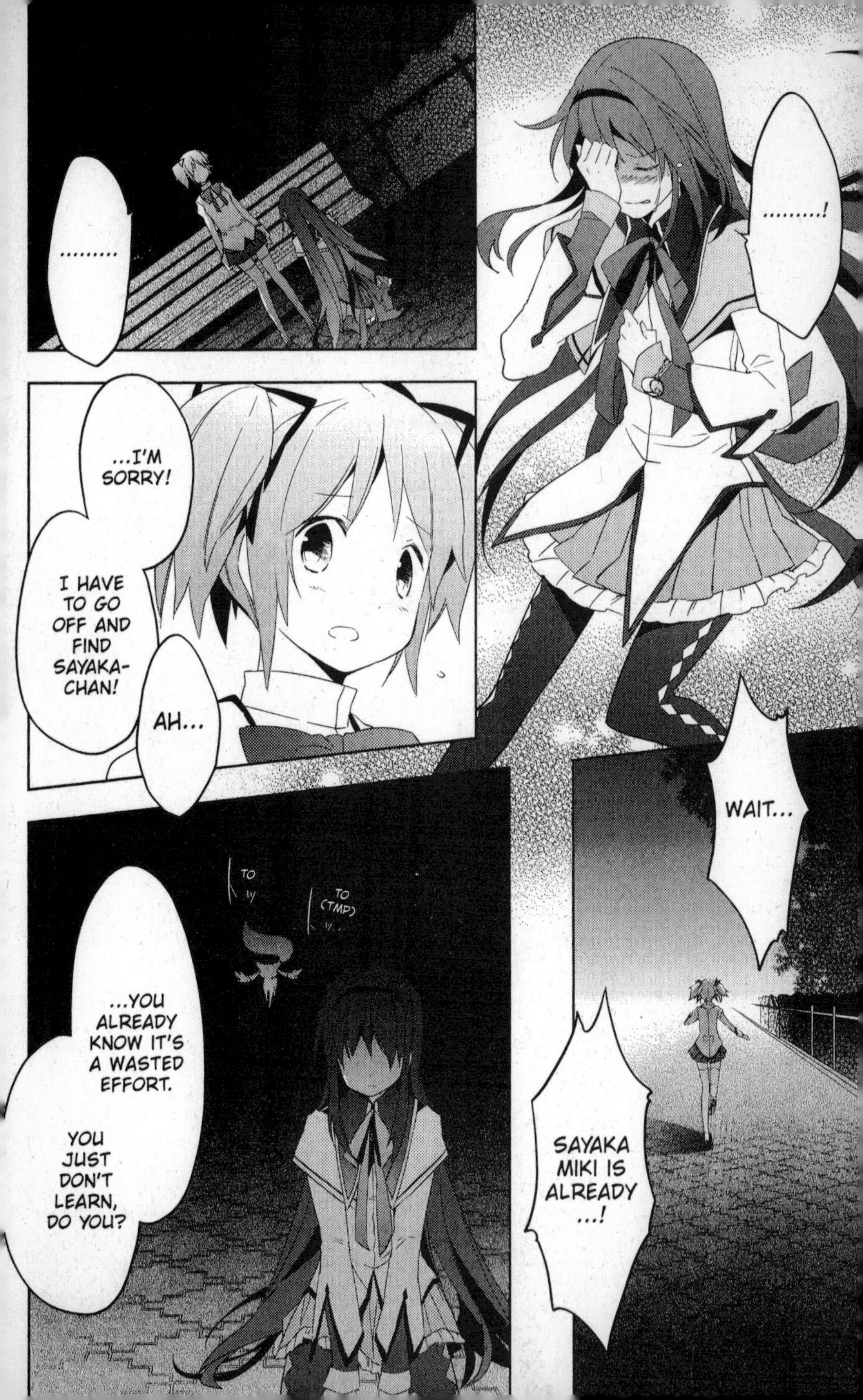
.........!
....
...I'M SORRY!
I HAVE TO GO OFF AND FIND SAYAKA-CHAN!
AH...
WAIT...
SAYAKA MIKI IS ALREADY ...!
TO
TO (TMP)
...YOU ALREADY KNOW IT'S A WASTED EFFORT.
YOU JUST DON'T LEARN, DO YOU?

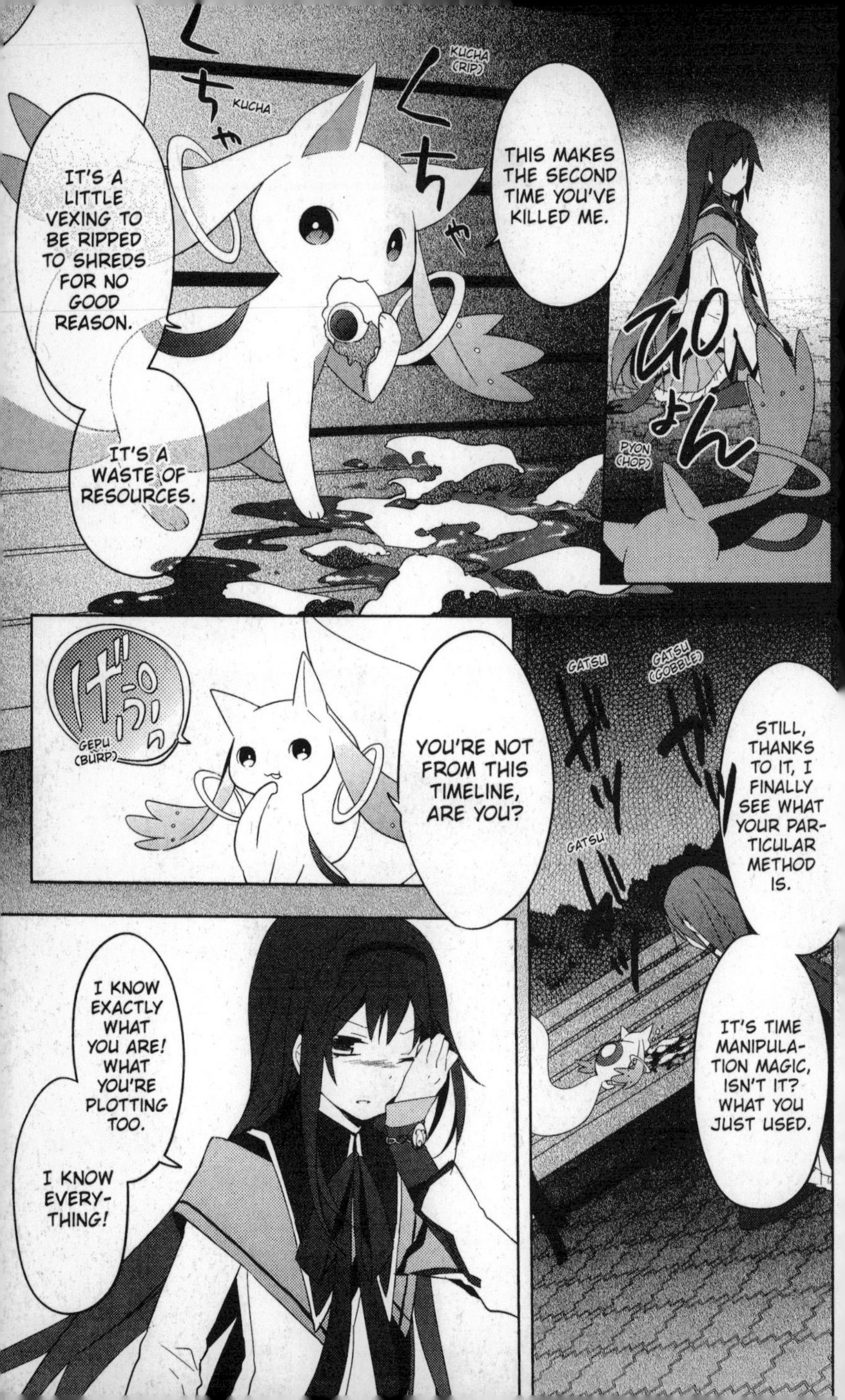
PYON (HOP)
THIS MAKES THE SECOND TIME YOU'VE KILLED ME.
KUCHA (RIP)
KUCHA
IT'S A LITTLE VEXING TO BE RIPPED TO SHREDS FOR NO GOOD REASON.
IT'S A WASTE OF RESOURCES.
GATSU (GOBBLE)
GATSU
GATSU
STILL, THANKS TO IT, I FINALLY SEE WHAT YOUR PAR-TICULAR METHOD IS.
IT'S TIME MANIPULA-TION MAGIC, ISN'T IT? WHAT YOU JUST USED.
YOU'RE NOT FROM THIS TIMELINE, ARE YOU?
GEPU (BURP)
I KNOW EXACTLY WHAT YOU ARE! WHAT YOU'RE PLOTTING TOO.
I KNOW EVERY-THING!

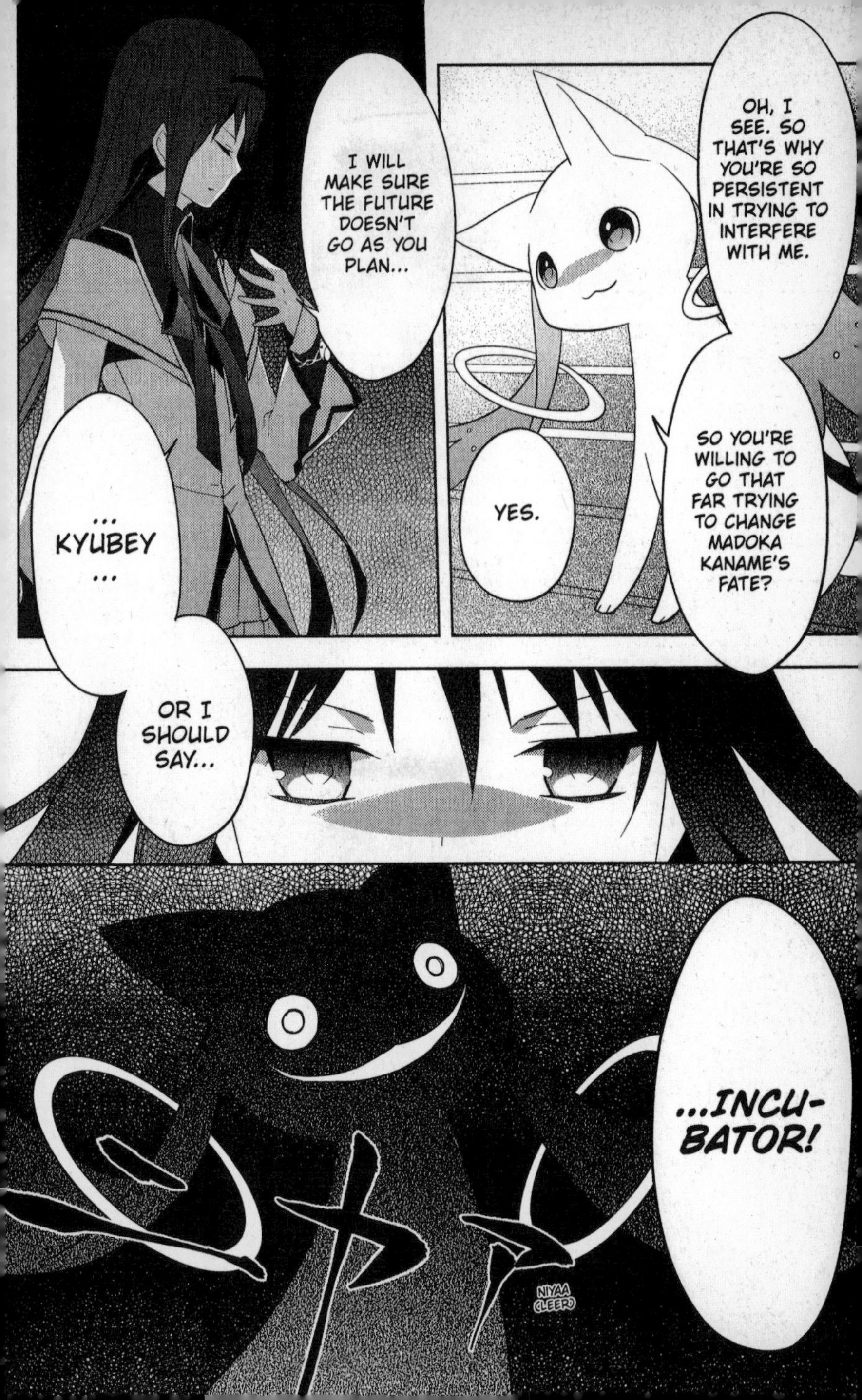
OH, I SEE. SO THAT'S WHY YOU'RE SO PERSISTENT IN TRYING TO INTERFERE WITH ME.
SO YOU'RE WILLING TO GO THAT FAR TRYING TO CHANGE MADOKA KANAME'S FATE?
YES.
I WILL MAKE SURE THE FUTURE DOESN'T GO AS YOU PLAN...
...KYUBEY...
OR I SHOULD SAY...
...INCUBATOR!
NIYAA (LEER)

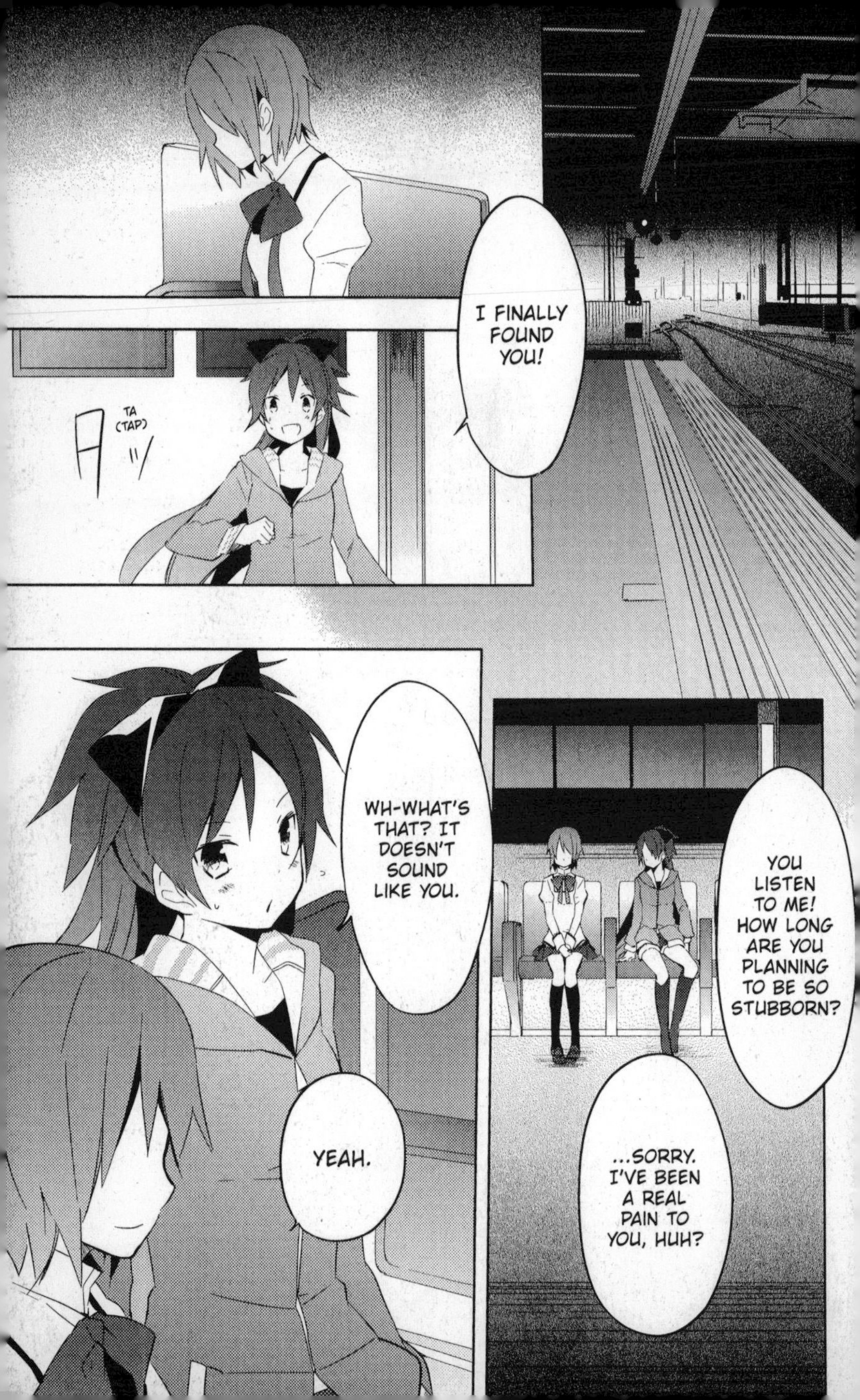
I FINALLY FOUND YOU!
TA (TAP)
YOU LISTEN TO ME! HOW LONG ARE YOU PLANNING TO BE SO STUBBORN?
...SORRY. I'VE BEEN A REAL PAIN TO YOU, HUH?
WH-WHAT'S THAT? IT DOESN'T SOUND LIKE YOU.
YEAH.

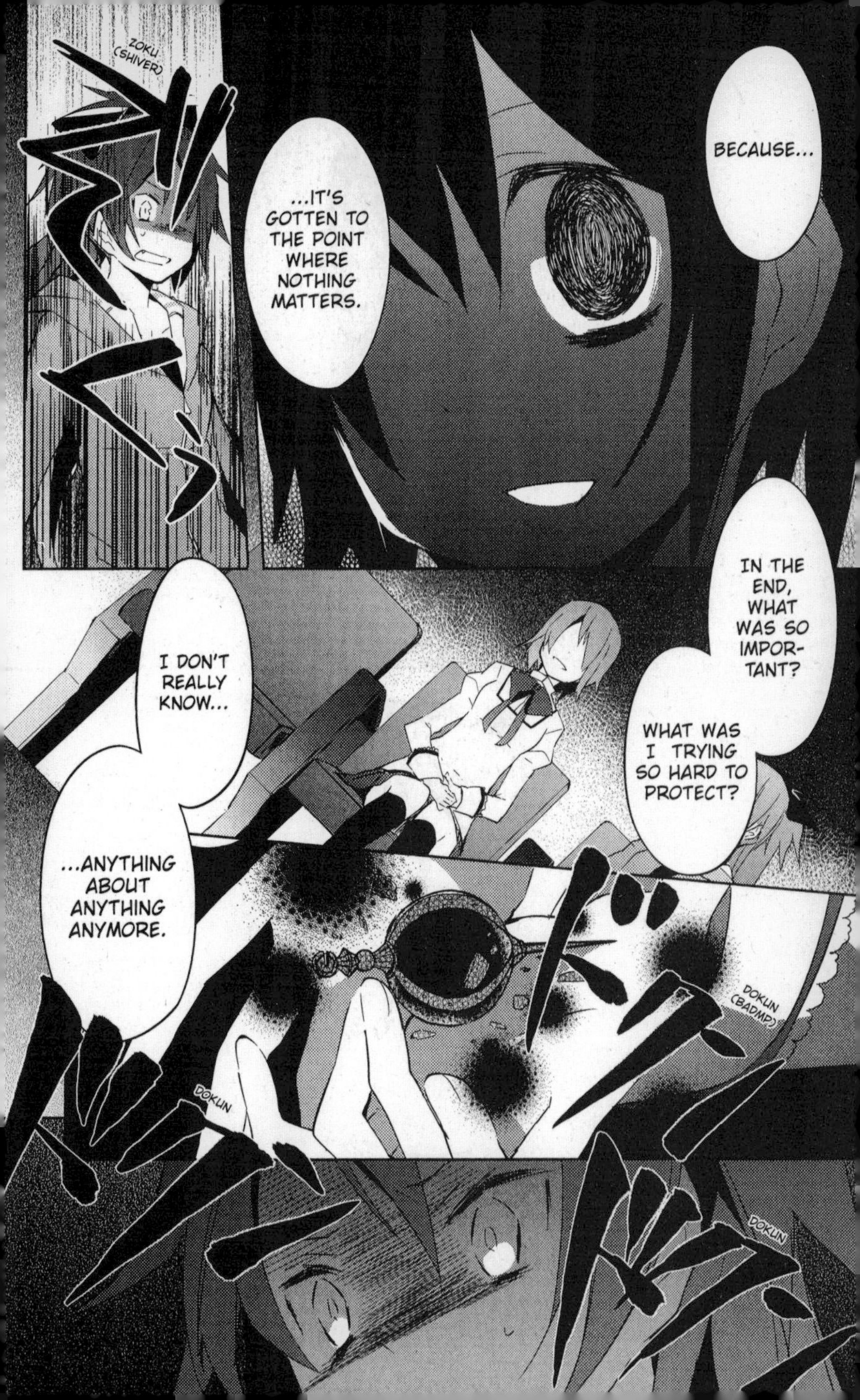
BECAUSE...
...IT'S GOTTEN TO THE POINT WHERE NOTHING MATTERS.
ZOKU (SHIVER)
IN THE END, WHAT WAS SO IMPORTANT?
WHAT WAS I TRYING SO HARD TO PROTECT?
I DON'T REALLY KNOW...
...ANYTHING ABOUT ANYTHING ANYMORE.
DOKUN (BADMP)
DOKUN
DOKUN

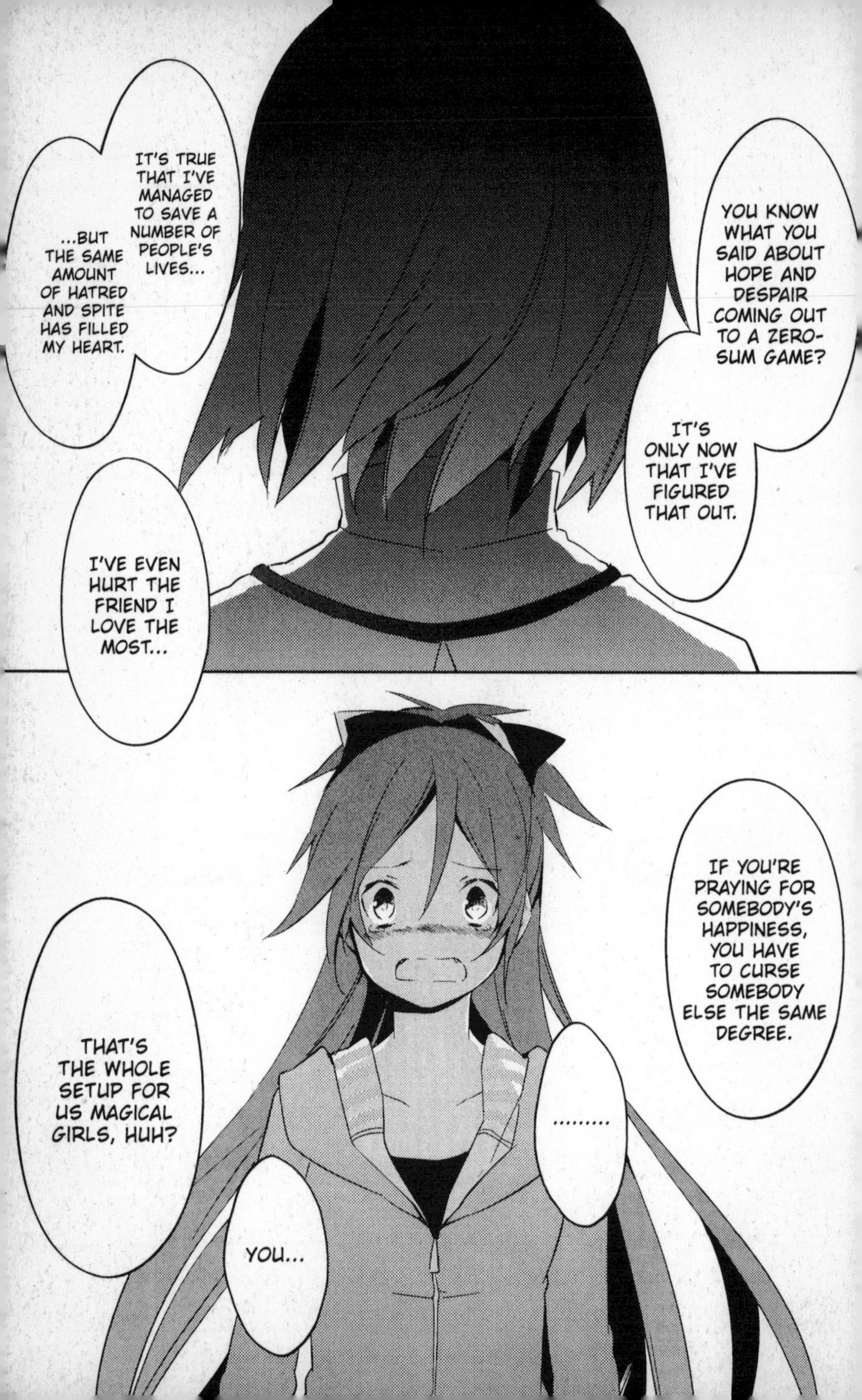
YOU KNOW WHAT YOU SAID ABOUT HOPE AND DESPAIR COMING OUT TO A ZERO-SUM GAME?
IT'S ONLY NOW THAT I'VE FIGURED THAT OUT.
IT'S TRUE THAT I'VE MANAGED TO SAVE A NUMBER OF PEOPLE'S LIVES...
...BUT THE SAME AMOUNT OF HATRED AND SPITE HAS FILLED MY HEART.
I'VE EVEN HURT THE FRIEND I LOVE THE MOST...
IF YOU'RE PRAYING FOR SOMEBODY'S HAPPINESS, YOU HAVE TO CURSE SOMEBODY ELSE THE SAME DEGREE.
THAT'S THE WHOLE SETUP FOR US MAGICAL GIRLS, HUH?
....
YOU...

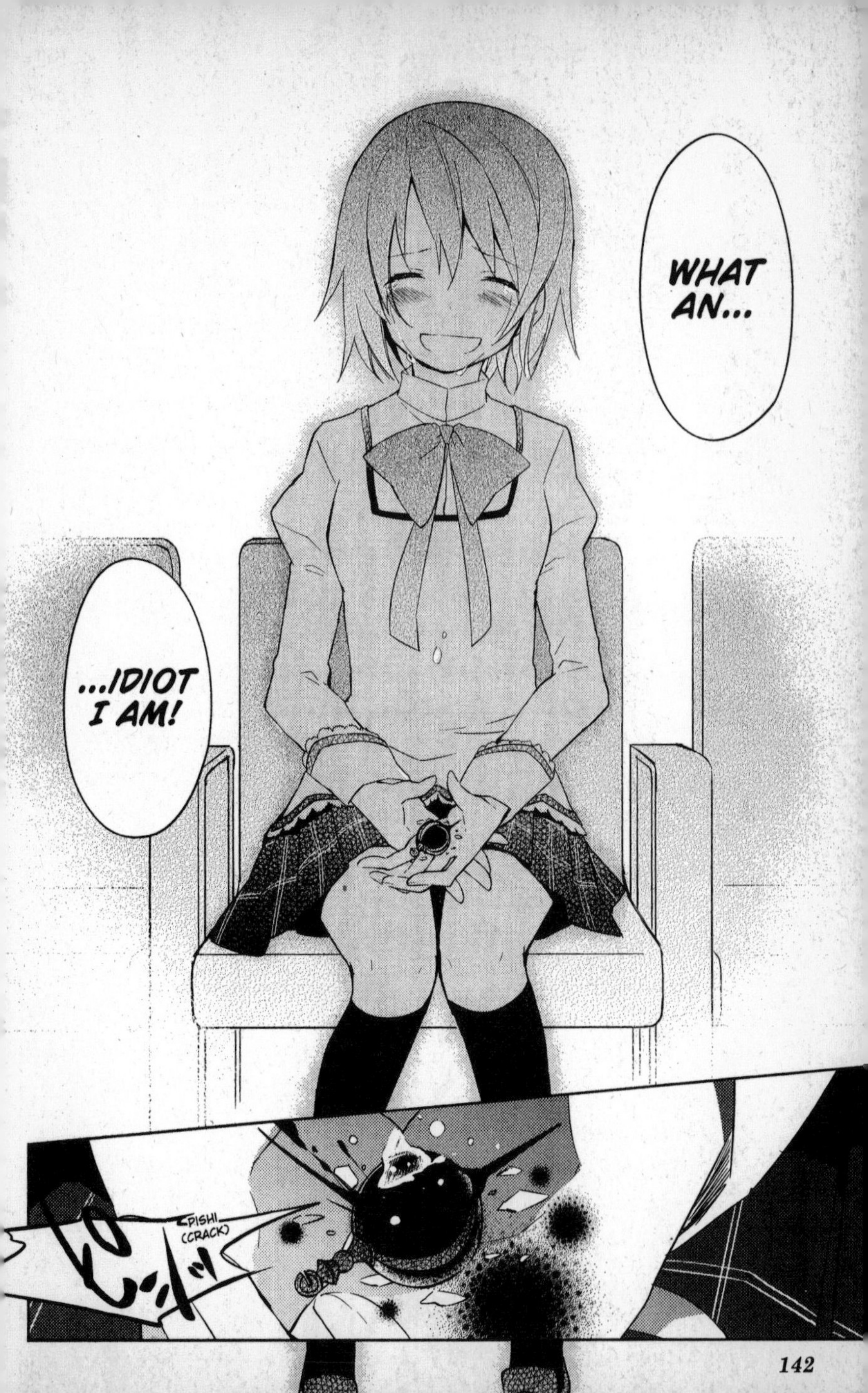
WHAT AN...
...IDIOT I AM!
PISHI (CRACK)

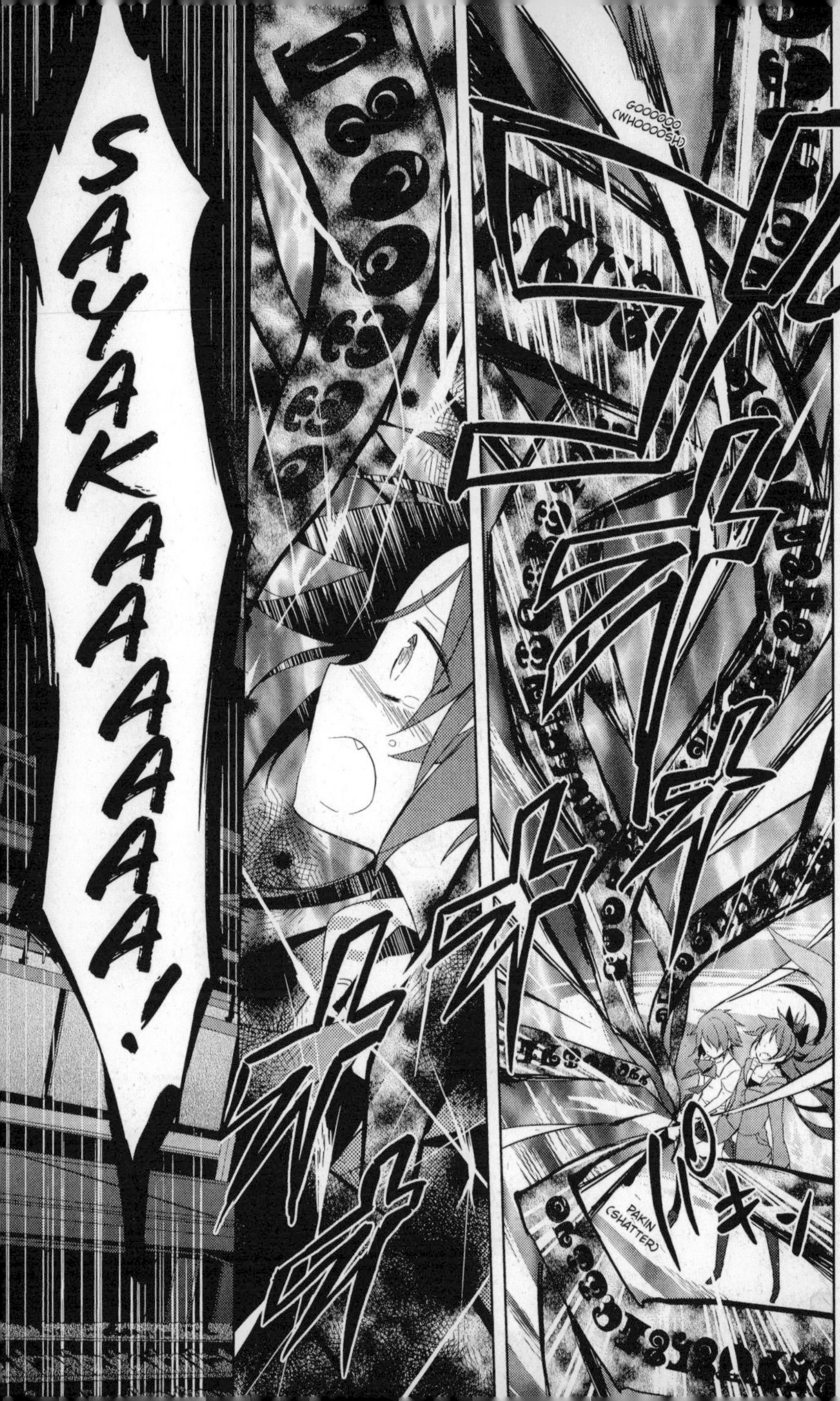
GOOOOOO
(WHOOOOOSH)
PAKIN
(SHATTER)
SAYAKAAAAAAA!

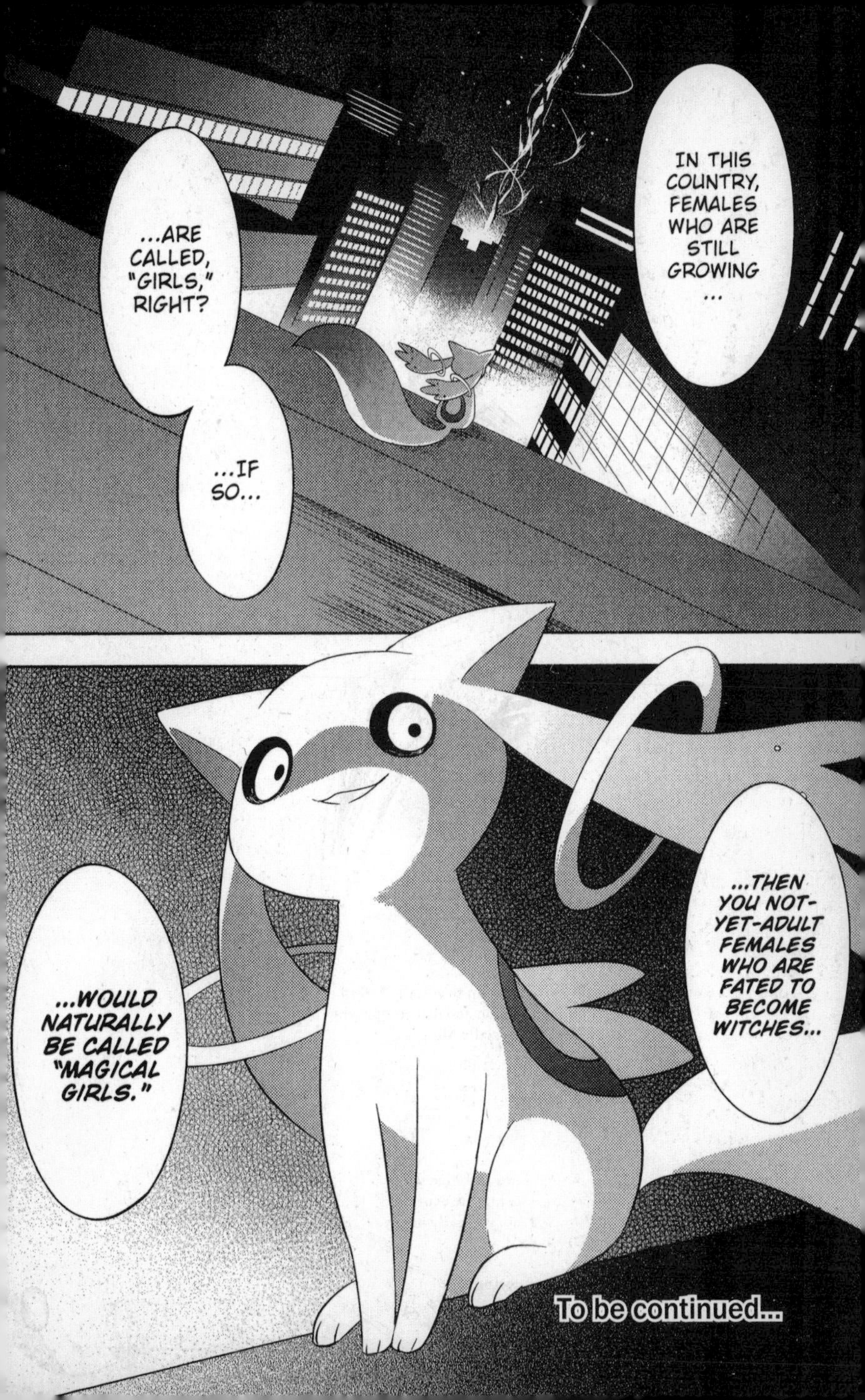
IN THIS COUNTRY, FEMALES WHO ARE STILL GROWING ...
...ARE CALLED, "GIRLS," RIGHT?
...IF SO...
...THEN YOU NOT-YET-ADULT FEMALES WHO ARE FATED TO BECOME WITCHES...
...WOULD NATURALLY BE CALLED "MAGICAL GIRLS."
To be continued...